:d
in Snares

Getting Started in Shares

Peter Temple

JOHN WILEY & SONS

Chichester • New York • Brisbane • Toronto • Singapore

Other Wiley Editorial Offices

John Wiley & Sons, Inc., 605 Third Avenue,
New York, NY 10158-0012, USA

Jacaranda Wiley Ltd, 33 Park Road, Milton,
Queensland 4064, Australia

John Wiley & Sons (Canada) Ltd, 22 Worcester Road,
Rexdale, Ontario M9W 1L1, Canada

John Wiley & Sons (Asia) Pte Ltd, 2 Clementi Loop #02-01,
Jin Xing Distripark, Singapore 129809

Library of Congress Cataloging-in-Publication Data

Temple, Peter.
    Getting started in shares / Peter Temple.
        p.   cm. — (Getting started in)
    Includes bibliographical references and index.
    ISBN 0-471-96669-X (pbk. : alk. paper)
    1. Stocks—Great Britain.   2. Stock exchanges—Great Britain.
    I. Title.   II. Series.
    HG5435.T46 1996
    332.63´22´0941—dc20   96-16208
                                              CIP

British Library Cataloguing in Publication Data

A catalogue record for this book is available from the British Library

ISBN 0-471-96669-X

Typeset in 11/13pt Palatino from the authors' disks by Dorwyn Ltd
Printed and bound in Great Britain by Biddles Ltd, Guildford
This book is printed on acid-free paper responsibly manufactured from sustainable forestation,
for which as least two trees are planted for each one used for paper production.

Contents

Introduction:
Learning the Rules
of the Game

This book is designed to help you become familiar with shares, how to investigate and assess their relative merits, and how to go about trading in the market.

The stock market—the collective name for the market where all types of shares and securities are traded—is a battle of wits. And you need to keep your wits about you to survive and do well.

Why is it a battle of wits? One reason is the market's sheer diversity.

There are buyers and sellers, short-term speculators and patient long-term investors. There are those who invest for income, and those who look to maximise their capital gains. There are professionals and amateurs of varying degrees of skill. There are domestic investors and those with an international perspective. All these individuals have different personalities, different goals, and a different view of risk.

57 VARIETIES

If the stock market were simply about trading a single uniform commodity—apples or oranges, wheat or deutschemarks, say—there would be plenty of excitement from the interplay of these different facets and objectives alone. But what makes the stock market fascinating is the rich variety of companies whose shares are listed. The Heinz slogan about '57 Varieties' applies in a big way in the stock market.

There are over 2700 listed companies in the UK and many more in other markets overseas.

All of these markets contain many different shares. There are shares in large companies, small companies, exciting high-tech companies, boring utilities running gas, electricity and transport, companies run by consummate professionals and others run by incompetents, rogues and charlatans, companies run by teams and companies run by a 'one-man band'.

There are shares in companies with lots of cash and companies with high borrowings. There are shares in companies that generate cash and companies that consume it. There are shares in companies that are sensitive to interest rates and those that aren't, and in companies whose fortunes are guided by the price of a single commodity, like gold, coal, oil or bananas.

Then there is the outside world of economics and politics and the cycles that shape it: of recession and boom; of high interest rates and low interest rates; and of devaluations, currency crises, elections, wars and all types of uncertainty.

And there is the psychology of how the crowd of individual investors that the market represents reacts to these various stimuli.

THE INVESTMENT GAME

If all this bores you, then investing in shares directly is not for you.

But there are few other human activities that combine the disciplines of sound analysis and diligent detective work, of astute timing with the delicious thrill of making money through backing the right horse or guessing right in a poker game.

The word 'game' is important.

The best definition of what makes stock market investment tick is actually contained in a dry economics textbook.

John Maynard Keynes wrote *The General Theory of Employment Interest and Money* in the early 1930s but Chapter 12, entitled 'The State of Long Term Expectation', is as relevant today as it was then.

Here is a flavour of it:

> The actual, private object of the most skilled investment today is 'to beat the gun' . . . to outwit the crowd, and to pass on the bad, or depreciating, half-crown to the other fellow . . . It is, so to speak, a game of Snap, of Old Maid, of Musical Chairs—a pastime in which he is victor who says 'Snap' neither too soon nor too late, who passes the Old Maid to his neighbour before the game is over, who secures a chair for himself before the music stops.

> These games can be played with zest and enjoyment, though all the players know that it is the Old Maid which is circulating, or that when the music stops some of the players may find themselves unseated.

> Or, to change the metaphor slightly, professional investment may be likened to those newspaper competitions in which the competitors have to pick out the six prettiest faces from a hundred photographs, the prize being awarded to the competitor whose choice most nearly corresponds to the average preferences of the competitors as a whole; so that each competitor has to pick, not those faces which he himself finds prettiest, but those which he thinks likeliest to catch the fancy of the other competitors, all of whom are looking at the problem from the same point of view.

In the paragraph above substitute the words 'most attractive' for prettiest, 'share' for face and 'investor' for competitor, and you begin to get the idea.

Keynes also says, 'The game of professional investment is intolerably boring and overexacting to anyone who is entirely exempt from the gambling instinct; whilst he who has it must pay to this propensity the appropriate toll'.

What gives these quotations some piquancy is the fact that not only was Keynes an outstanding economist but he was also the Bursar of Kings College, Cambridge, and managed its investment portfolio with considerable skill for many years.

So he was not just a theoretician. He played the game too. His example also shows that, provided the right techniques are practised, successful investment need not be unduly time-consuming. The Bursar of Kings managed the college portfolio with just a few minutes' attention at the beginning or end of each day.

Keynes was also famous for his distaste of long-term investment. To him is attributed the most famous of phrases on the subject: 'in the long run, we are all dead'. The General Theory also exhorts the reader to remember that long-term investment is inevitably more laborious and more risky than devoting one's study to 'guessing better than the crowd how the crowd will behave'. Investors are often castigated for short-termism, but not usually by companies whose shares are doing well, and invariably by people who have little active interest in investing themselves.

For the past 26 years I have made my living either working in or writing about the stock market. For much of that time I have been an investor myself. I am, of course, no Keynes. And even with 26 years' experience, I am only too well aware that it is still possible to be careless, to make silly mistakes, to buy the wrong share, or to sell the right one too early.

But nothing equals the feeling of having selected a share, seeing it rise steadily, doubling or trebling in value, and then selling it at the right price, neither too early nor too late, and pocketing the gain and beginning the process all over again.

THE OBJECTIVE

What I want to do in these pages is to give the average person with some money available to invest in shares the practical tools needed to begin investing successfully and some guidance on where and how to learn more about the market.

The aim, in short, is to cut through the jargon that many professional investors and stock market writers use and express these ideas in a simple, accessible and understandable form.

To understand markets we have to look at their history, the characters that people the market, and at the reasoning and emotions that in equal measure drive them. We need to investigate different types of shares and their characteristics, and to look at why it is important for everyone to appreciate what the stock market is and why it behaves as it does.

Later on in this book we will look also at the mental characteristics required to be a good share trader, and how an individual's financial circumstances dictate the type of investment activity he or she should pursue. Then there is the importance of setting realistic targets and having down-to-earth expectations. And there is the question of what the would-be investor might need to spend on the basic equipment to begin investing.

The object of all investment is to buy low and sell high. While bearing in mind what Keynes said about the activities of long-term professional investors, it is worth examining some of the techniques that experienced investors use to assess the worth of individual shares. This takes us into basic accounting concepts, and the importance of cash flow and balance sheet strength. It also takes us into learning how to calculate basic investment ratios and the importance to attach to them.

These ratios are not complicated but they are words that the average reader of the stock market pages of the daily or Sunday newspapers might meet on a regular basis: yield, price–earnings ratio, gearing, return on capital and so on.

As well as what the professionals term 'fundamentals', we also need to look at how studying the history of a share price can betray little details that might be important in timing purchases and sales. And there are also a variety of other investment techniques that help decision making.

Not having dealt in the stock market before, the first-timer will need the services of a stockbroker. How to go about choosing the right one is a subject in itself and we will look at this in some detail, as well as how to place an order with a broker and what happens, or should happen, afterwards.

Spreading risk is an important aspect of investment, and it is also worth looking at other types of securities and how these can fit into a coherent strategy designed to improve both income and capital gains. Different types of investment may be more appropriate at particular times in the market cycle, and we will look at how to assess this. Keeping score is important too. Measuring one's performance is an aspect of investment that is sometimes neglected by the private investor.

Most of the donkey-work that successful investing has always involved—keeping track of how much your shares are worth, and producing returns for the tax man—can now safely be computerised, and information and even dealing is available online through computer services accessed by modem.

We examine what these services offer, their advantages and their limitations. We also look at some of the more advanced share assessment techniques that the professionals use, and how the big changes that electronics and the changes in the way markets are organised will affect investors.

Finally, I will share with you some of my own experiences—both good and bad—as an active private investor over the past decade.

Above all, my aim is to get you started as an investor and dealing confidently with brokers and the other professional people with whom all investors have to interact, to get you assessing and investigating shares in the right way, timing purchases and sales correctly and building up good trading disciplines.

It is an easier process than it once was. The market is more accessible to the independent private investor, dealing costs have come down and information about investing is more readily available.

All will be well, provided that you learn to take the rough with the smooth and above all to remember that there is an indissoluble link between risk and reward. The investments that seem to offer high returns are the ones on which you can lose your shirt.

Genuine undervalued situations are rare, but they can be found, more often than not in places where few have chosen to look. Recognising those opportunities for what they are is part of the art of successful investing.

I hope that, having read this book, you will be able to find the occasional one.

CHAPTER 1

Investing in Shares: Fact, Fiction, Fear and Greed

All of us have been to a market. It might have been a local street market, a car boot sale, a Mediterranean fish market, a Middle Eastern souk or some other location where buyers and sellers got together.

The market for shares is not that different from any of these. At any Sunday morning car boot sale or antiques fair you can find run-of-the-mill items, overpriced rubbish and, just occasionally, an item whose true value has not been recognised.

Similarly, the UK share market (normally known as the stock market, or simply 'the market') contains shares that are worthy, but correctly priced, those that are of poor quality and over-priced, and those that are a bargain. Spotting the bargains is the objective of most investors.

What complicates matters is that there is a large number of different shares to choose from, and that over time each will move in and out of favour. A share that appears cheap now may look less attractive in a year's time. Either its price will have moved up, or else circumstances will have moved against it. Another that looked unexciting a year ago might suddenly see its prospects transformed.

Ultimately what governs the price of anything, and shares are no exception, is the interaction of supply and demand. But a point to bear in mind is that markets do not necessarily, or even often, act logically.

The history of the world's stock markets shows great waves of pessimism and optimism. Sharp turning points have not been uncommon, often marked by some dramatic event. The Wall Street Crash of 1929, the October 1987 crash, and the surge in the UK stock market that followed Britain's exit from the European Exchange Rate Mechanism in September 1992 are all examples of this phenomenon.

On a smaller scale, too, individual shares and different sections of the share market move in and out of favour. It happens for reasons that may have an element of logic but where the reasoning is often exaggerated. A good example from 1995 was the vogue for technology shares and, in particular, any share that had an involvement with the Internet.

When Netscape, a company that makes software for use by Internet surfers, floated in the USA in 1995, its price was driven up so far that the company, which had not at that time ever made a profit, was valued at some $3 bn.

The recent fashion for technology stocks is just one example. At different times in the past it has been privatised utilities, drug companies, biotechnology groups, public house operators and so on.

So, as Lord Keynes pointed out, the art of investment is not only to judge which shares look undervalued at any point in time, but also to anticipate and profit from the moods of the market and the dictates of fashion.

Selecting which competitors in the beauty contest are likely to catch the eye of the judges is the name of the game. Not only does one need a smattering of economics and accountancy to get to grips with the stock market, but also an understanding of crowd psychology.

Examining exactly what shares are and looking back at the history of 'the market' can help us understand all this better.

SHARES: WHAT THEY ARE AND HOW THEY WORK

We all think we know what a share is. You would not be reading this book if you did not have a view on that. But it is worth dwelling on the concept of shares and how share trading began in a little more detail.

At its simplest a **share** is a stake in a company. But its precise entitlements and legal status are what make it interesting.

The typical company might have creditors to pay and bank loans outstanding, as well as having shareholders. The point of shares is that they stand last in line for any pay-out if the company is wound up. But while creditors only get what they are owed and bankers only get their loan repaid, shareholders own what remains, in exact proportion to their individual shareholdings.

Let's look at an example to make this clear. Imagine a company called Universal Widgets. Universal Widgets has total assets of £100000 and has issued 30000 shares. It has unpaid bills (creditors) of £20000 and owes its bank £50000. What is left over, £30000, is owned by the shareholders. In the jargon this is known as shareholders' funds, or net assets.

Because Universal Widgets has 30000 shares outstanding, this means that each share has an underlying value of £1. A holder of 100 shares would be entitled to £100 if the company were wound up. But a holder of 200 shares would be entitled to £200, and so on. Each share represents an equal (or

share: a stake in a company, representing entitlement to the assets that remain after all creditors and lenders have been paid.

equity) stake in the business. For this reason shares are often known as equities.

Now let's take the example a stage further.

Suppose in the course of the year that Universal Widgets makes a profit, after paying off interest and taxes, of £20000. It can do one of two things with this profit. It can distribute some of it to share-holders in the form of dividends and keep the rest, or it can retain all of it. Either way, the money belongs to shareholders.

Say the company pays out a dividend of £6000 and keeps £14000 as **retained profits**. What happens? The shareholders receive a dividend of 20p per share (£6000 divided by 30000 shares).

Assuming there has been no change in bank borrowings or the amount owed to creditors the retained profit of £14000 increases shareholders' funds from £30000 to £44000. So the shareholders have done well. Not only have they had a 20p dividend for each share they hold, but the retained profits have increased the underlying value of their stake in the company from 100p per share to 147p (£44000 divided by 30000 shares).

The crucial point to understand, however, is that if the shares are freely traded in the market their price need have no precise relationship to the underlying value of the shareholders' net assets of the company. It is this fact that makes shares so interesting. In some cases shares do stand close to their **net asset value,** but many do not.

The precise relationship is governed by other factors: the company's prospects and the likelihood or otherwise of further profit increases in future; the level of dividend payments; whether or not the company has a high level of borrowings; whether its assets are an important factor in determining its profitability; and many other factors.

A good reason for this is that a company's most important assets—its brand names, perhaps, or

retained profits: profits after deducting all other prior charges, such as interest, tax and dividends.

net asset value: the underlying value of a company's capital and reserves worked out on a per share basis.

simply its staff and their relationships with customers—are often not included as assets in the balance sheet. 'People businesses', like advertising agencies or fund management companies, often generate profits disproportionately bigger than their conventional balance sheet assets might suggest was likely.

In addition, at any time the market may well be looking not at the most recent figures for a company's profits and underlying assets, but at how it expects them to change in the future. In other words, it is expectations that govern how share prices move.

Where does the psychology come in? Partly because if you buy the shares today, one reason you are doing so is on the expectation that profits will continue to rise and that therefore your shares will be worth more. But you may be doing so also for other reasons.

You could believe that the profits are not going to grow particularly rapidly but that the share price stands at a substantial discount to what a predator might think the company is worth. A friend may have told you that he has heard it is a takeover candidate.

Or you might buy them because you believe the market is going to rise and, if it does, then the shares will automatically go up in sympathy.

To illustrate the psychology of investment, look at the following stages of an investment:

- Stage One: Let's assume you invest £2000 in Universal Widgets and sit with the shares for a month or two. The price doesn't move much and you lose interest.
- Stage Two: Then one day you discover the shares have dropped 10% in a single day. The company has issued a warning to investors that its recent trading has been disappointing.

Your £2000 investment is now worth £1800. Do you sell and take the loss, or wait in the hope that the share price will eventually shrug off the bad news? You decide to sit tight.

- Stage Three: The next day the shares drop another 10%. In two days, your loss has grown to nearly £400!

Fear now replaces the original motive of greed that you felt when you bought the shares. You have lost nearly £400, but if you wait another day or two to sell, the shares could be worth even less. Better to get out now while you can.

- Stage Four: If you sell now you have crystallised the loss. What if the shares then recover?

All investors from time to time have to face the pain of losing money. But one of the points this example highlights, apart from perhaps explaining why markets swing around the way they do, is another very important aspect to equity investment: the concept of **limited liability**.

limited liability: the basis on which public companies are founded, that an investor cannot lose more than his original investment.

Limited liability means that an investor in a company's shares can lose no more than his or her original investment. An individual shareholder's liability, if the company is wound up, is limited to the size of the original investment—irrespective of how much its bankers and creditors might be owed.

On the plus side too, once you have bought your shares, there is theoretically no limit to how much they can rise: you will participate for as long as you hold the shares.

SHARES: THE HISTORY

The concepts of equity investment and limited liability go hand in hand and were originally designed to encourage investors to risk money in speculative ventures that might produce a big return, but equally could see a total loss.

The first public limited liability company to which investors subscribed for shares was The Muscovy Company, formed in 1553. The oldest company still trading is thought to be the Hudson's Bay Company, formed to trade with Canada and now domiciled there but still listed in London. Investors in other early companies, such as the South Sea Company, set up in the early 18th century, fared less well. The so-called South Sea Bubble, the product of widespread and rampant speculation, resulted in many fortunes being made and lost and in the idea of equity investment being set back for many decades thereafter.

It was in the 17th and 18th centuries that the idea of a market for trading in the shares of these limited-liability companies first took root.

Initially brokers met in coffee-houses in the City of London and traded shares face to face on the basis of the principle of 'my word is my bond'. One of these, Jonathans, became a subscription club and in 1773 changed its name to the Stock Exchange and subsequently developed a system of trading on a market floor, which lasted until the mid-1980s.

This system coalesced into a method of trading that relied on a dual structure. Stock*brokers* dealt with the public that wished to buy and sell shares and acted as their agents in the market. Stock*jobbers* acted as wholesalers, keeping a 'book' of shares in which they specialised and which they bought from and sold to the brokers, adjusting the price to reflect supply and demand.

The attraction of this system was that the jobbers were obligated to quote a price and buy and sell on demand, and therefore had to ensure that they had an adequate supply of stock, but not too much, to satisfy the demands of buyers and sellers.

As time has gone by many other stock ex-changes have adopted this essential principle, al-though some now adopt a different one. Aided by electronic systems, it is now possible to run a market based on the electronic matching of buying and selling orders at a particular price in what amounts to a continuous auction.

order-driven markets: a method of share trading by which buying and selling orders are automatically matched by computer.

These electronic **order-driven markets** have typ-ically developed in smaller financial centres but are now assuming greater prominence in markets like London, where order-matching—previously often done informally by a company's official stock-broker—is an essential component of that part of the market involved in trading shares in small companies.

Back in 1986, the stock market in the UK under-went a significant change. In response to pressure from competition authorities, the market abandoned many of its club-like practices and opened its doors to all and sundry. Many old-established brokers were taken over by foreign banks and others wishing to gain a presence in London, then, as now, seen as one of the major share trading centres in the world.

Another important change in October 1986 was that for the first time firms operating on the Stock Exchange could combine both jobbing (now known as market-making) and traditional, so-called 'agency', broking. At the same time, the market went from being centralised on a single trading floor to a system whereby market prices were posted on a central electronic bulletin board and, rather than taking place face to face, dealing was done over the telephone.

In effect the market migrated to large purpose-built dealing rooms and the cables that connected them, rather than being contained in a single physi-cal space.

There were those who bemoaned the passing of the market floor. But, unlike a market for produce or, say, antiques, for shares and indeed for other products like foreign currency there is no pressing need for a physical market.

This is because everyone can have confidence that the rights attached to buying a share are identical. Each share in a particular company has the same rights as every other one. In other words, the market is homogeneous. Although each company that issues shares may be different, unlike an antiques market there is no need physically to see or inspect a share to establish that it has the particular value the market says it has.

One of the interesting side effects of the new market has been the development of low-cost, so-called **execution-only** stockbrokers. Because there is no longer any need for a broker to be physically based in the City of London to trade shares, a number of brokers have set up in out-of-town locations to offer cut-price dealing services to private investors.

execution-only: _stockbroking that comprises only a dealing service, without any sort of advice._

By offering no advisory services and because of high throughput and sophisticated electronic trading systems, these brokers can offer independent investors a cheap yet worthwhile service that would not have been economic ten years ago. This has big implications for the way an individual investor can operate.

In the end, what makes a market function the way it does are the individual buyers and sellers who participate in it. Whether they deal frequently or only occasionally, what their attitudes and motives are, their financial requirements and their time horizons, all have an impact on the way shares move, and on what types of share they choose.

So, let's now have a look at some of the characters typically involved in the market.

ANIMALS IN THE MARKET JUNGLE . . .

Fred the Fund Manager

Fred is a fund manager. He works for a leading fund management group looking after the investments of a group of different pension funds. He is a 45-year old grammar-school boy who used to work for a stockbroker but got bored with the life and thought he would try life on the other side of the fence. But life for Fred is almost as cut-throat as the broking business.

The performance of his funds is measured on a quarter by quarter basis, and any dip in performance has to be explained to sceptical trustees who—since the Maxwell scandal—are very conscious of their responsibilities.

There are any number of competing fund managers who could do the job if Fred's performance falls away, so there is little point pursuing investment strategies that take a long time to come to fruition. The result is that Fred and his ilk are often accused of short-termism.

Mickey the Market-Maker

Mickey used to sell fruit and veg in Walthamstow market, but got into the City in the 1980s when all the big securities firms were recruiting traders. First he worked on the floor of the market, but now he spends his days sat in front of a bank of computer screens buying and selling shares from other market players and betting on their price movements to make his firm some money.

Mickey's actions can make the price of single share move up and down several percentage points in the course of a single day. Mickey is paid a big salary to do this, with bonuses on top, but the job doesn't have a lot of security. As he gets older, or starts losing his touch, or begins drinking too much, his duties will be taken over by someone younger and fresher.

Hugh Sloane-Portfolio

Hugh is a salesman for a blue blooded firm of stockbrokers. His job is to talk to Fred and people like him and get them to buy shares that his firm has acquired or to match a selling order from another of the firm's clients.

Not much up-top, but at least Hugh went to a good school and knows how to behave at the lunch table. Although Hugh and Fred have to talk to each other, their backgrounds are very different and they don't like each other. But Fred knows that Hugh's firm now and again can put some attractive new issues his way, so he doesn't complain too much and gives the broker an occasional order. Hugh meanwhile dreams of when his wife will inherit Daddy's money and they can retire from Clapham to life in the Country.

Marvin the Quant

Marvin is, of course, an American. He works for a firm of quantitative fund managers (known in the trade as 'quants'). Quants invest scientifically using the statistical properties of individual groups of shares and different markets to tune their investment strategy. Their deals are often large scale and managed by computers. Marvin looks forward to the day when computers can do all the work and he can go back to Harvard to finish his PhD in mathematics.

Aunt Agatha

Everyone knows Aunt Agatha. Widowed and of advancing years, shares are her little hobby. The modest capital she inherited when Bertie died is mainly invested to give her a steady income, but she keeps a little on one side to invest in interesting situations that her broker finds out about for her. She swaps tips with her cronies at the bridge club and then phones one of those nice young men at ShareLink to check them out. So far her little nest egg has not dwindled by too much, but she's still waiting to make a big killing.

Joe Soap

Joe works at the local detergent factory, but when his premium bond came up in the early 1980s he put some of the money into those new-fangled privatisation shares—and did rather well. He sold some of them straight away but kept a few and now has a modest little portfolio of water and electricity company shares, and some British Gas shares he forgot he owned.

If he knew more about the market he might invest more actively but there never seems to be the time—and anyway he can't stand those toffee-nosed brokers. Still, the management have just bought the soap factory from its old owners and reckon that they can float it on the stock market in a few years' time, in which case he might get some shares in that too.

Graham Average

Graham Average and his wife Deirdre live in a nice detached house in Surbiton. Graham works in Whitehall and Deirdre teaches at the local primary school. They have a comfortable lifestyle, their children have left home and a year or two back they inherited some money when Graham's father died. Some of the money has been put into a unit trust and some went to buy a new car, but Graham has always been interested in dabbling in the stock market and now wants to become more active to increase the size of his retirement nest egg.

. . . AND WHAT THEY DON'T HAVE IN COMMON

All of these people are connected to the stock market in some way, either professionally or because they have savings they wish to invest, or an existing portfolio of shares. But, as these simple examples show, they all have different motives.

Fred is assessed on a quarter by quarter basis, and on the basis of his performance against the market as a whole and against that of his competitors. It doesn't matter to him if the funds he is managing go down in value, provided that the market has gone down by more than that and his competitors haven't performed any better than he has.

Mickey is dealing on a very short-term basis, trying to make sufficient profit for his firm to justify his salary and bonus, and trying, above all, to avoid a big losing deal, which would mean instant dismissal.

Hugh Sloane-Portfolio may not get the sack (after all, he did go to the same school as his boss) but he does need to make sure that his clients keep dealing and he keeps booking commission for his firm. What he really needs is to avoid putting his clients into duff shares.

Marvin is looking for the package of shares that exactly matches the risk and return criteria he has fed into his computer model.

The amateur investors are more sensitive than the fund manager, broker or market-maker to an actual monetary loss. That an investment has gone down by less than the market is no cause for celebration; if they sell after a drop in price they have lost real money.

Aunt Agatha relies on her investments to produce income.

Joe Soap is vaguely suspicious about the market, but it has treated him well and he wants to find out more. But he is more likely to sell the shares he has than buy new ones.

Graham Average has money to invest and is looking for longer-term capital growth.

It is probably obvious from these descriptions that the stock market has horses for courses.

Different investors will invest in different ways over any given period of time.

Some will buy shares and hold them for long periods; others will trade shares more actively. Some will look more favourably on shares and other securities that return a decent income in the form of dividends or interest payments; others will be more interested in capital growth. Some will want to invest in big solid companies; others will want something with a little more spice.

And the actions of the professionals, for whatever reason, can either work for or against the interests of the private investor.

So what types of share are available for the investor to choose?

SHARE CHOICES FOR THE INVESTOR

For the purposes of this book we are assuming that the investor wants to buy plain, straightforward ordinary shares. But it is worth remembering that there are other types that can be considered. These may have their attractions in certain circumstances.

From the standpoint of ordinary shares, though, the following main categories stand out:

- Blue chips
- Growth shares
- Income shares
- Cyclical shares
- Smaller companies
- Penny shares
- Utilities
- Commodity shares
- Investment trusts

Let's just consider each of these categories separately for a moment and look at their characteristics.

Blue chips

So called because blue chips are supposed to be the most valuable in the casino, these are large, financially-solid companies that have been around for years and are widely held by both professional and private investors. They may be high street names like Tesco or Marks & Spencer, or more obscure industrial companies like BTR or Hanson. No investor is going to go radically wrong buying them, but equally their performance is unlikely to be racy. Typical examples: Sainsbury, Guinness.

Growth shares

Often more highly prized by investors, these are companies that have managed to produce consistent above-average growth in profits and dividends for several years, and look likely to continue to do so. The reason is usually good management methods or else a strong presence in a growing market. Ultimately companies like this can end up being blue chips. Typical examples: Rentokil, Carpetright.

Income shares

Income shares are companies whose share price action may be unexciting but which continue to pay out generous dividends and as a result yield very good returns to investors. Provided that companies like this have sound finances, the high dividend stream can continue for years. Companies of this type are conservatively managed, operating in mature industries that generate cash. Typical example: BAT Industries.

Cyclical shares

These are shares in companies whose fortunes are tied closely to the economic cycle. These companies normally show large swings in profitability and are valued accordingly by the market. Typical example: ICI.

Smaller company shares

Smaller companies can be the most exciting part of the market, since there is always the possibility of investing early on in a company that may become a growth stock or blue chip of tomorrow. Investment in smaller companies needs to pay particularly close attention to the quality of the company's management, and whether or not the company really has a unique selling point or a novel new product. In addition, smaller company shares often need to be given time to mature for their full share price potential to be realised. Although smaller company shares tend to perform better than their larger brethren in the long term, in down phases of the market they are liable to be poor investments. Typical examples: Surrey Free Inns, Antonov.

Penny shares

Penny shares are those priced at fractions of a pound, say 10p or less. They may be shares whose price reflects concern about their financial position, or simply companies that have gone out of favour with investors, or where profits are currently at a low level. Although there are big gains sometimes to be had in penny stocks, they require very careful investigation and can be risky. Typical examples: Dares Estates, Millwall Holdings.

Utilities

Utilities are a comparatively new investment category in the UK, dating from the wave of privatisations in the 1980s and early 1990s. They supply basic services like gas, water and electricity under an environment that is often heavily regulated. Many utilities are also income stocks but, as recent events have shown, they can have takeover spice too. The drawback, as also demonstrated recently, is that their regulated nature makes them subject to political pressure. Typical examples: British Gas, Severn Trent Water, London Electricity.

Commodity shares

These are investments in companies whose profits and therefore share price are dependent on the value of a particular commodity, such as gold or oil. Often in extractive industries like mining or oil exploration, or else in primary produce like wheat or other agricultural crops, the prices of commodity shares often move at variance with the rest of the stock market and tend to do best in the later stages of a stock market cycle when economic activity is strong. Typical examples: RTZ, Ashanti Gold.

Investment trusts

These are collective investments, set up with a fixed pool of money, in which investors can buy shares. There are many different types of investment trust, from those investing in a broad range of companies and markets around the world to those specialising in a particular sector or country. Their share prices tend to track the value of the underlying investment portfolio, sometimes with a discount, and they can be a useful investment for those with only a limited amount of money to invest, or as a means of investing in areas that might otherwise be too difficult or risky for an individual to contemplate, such as venture capital or emerging markets. Typical examples: 3i, Foreign & Colonial Emerging Markets.

Part of the art of investing is to pick from these different categories at different stages of the market so as to maximise either the income or capital gain required. This spectrum of categories of available shares also contains different categories of risk (and therefore potential reward), and these can be mixed and matched according to how cautious or adventurous an investment policy is being sought.

WHY THE STOCK MARKET MATTERS

It is possible that, having read thus far, you may have concluded that the investment scene is far too complicated to be interest to you. The stock market is remote and investment in shares can only ever be for the rich.

For most people this is a mistaken view.

Any individual with a life assurance policy or a pension entitlement has an indirect interest in the stock market and how it performs. Life assurance companies and pension fund managers take the savings of ordinary individuals and invest them on their behalf, in the stock market and in other investment classes.

Direct stock market investment by individuals is all about taking any surplus savings you may have and doing the same thing yourself.

Another thought-provoking aspect of this is to examine the willingness of successive generations in Britain to invest in property. Buying a house using borrowed money (a mortgage) is an investment decision.

It may be complicated by the fact that everyone needs somewhere to live and that therefore this geared-up investment in property can be justified on other grounds. But it is interesting to muse what might have happened if, instead of investing in property, the post-war generation had rented its housing and invested its income in the stock market instead. Property investment has its drawbacks, as the hundreds of thousands of people caught in a negative equity trap can attest.

Compare investing £100 000 in a broadly spread **portfolio** of shares, even at the very top of the market in 1987, with putting an equivalent amount into acquiring a semi in Surbiton at the peak of the property market in 1989. The share portfolio would be way ahead. And remember, too, that property is harder, more costly, and more stressful to buy and sell than a portfolio of blue chip shares.

portfolio: the collective name for an individual's holdings of shares in more than one company.

It is also the case that, partly as a result of the Thatcher era of privatisations, and partly because of changes to the structure of the City itself, the market has been getting more accessible to the man (and woman) in the street. Tax-efficient savings choices that take in direct equity investment are increasingly the norm. And information on shares and markets that was once solely the preserve of a privileged few is becoming more readily available at an economic price to those prepared to seek it out.

The next chapter looks at whether direct share investment is the right thing for you, what you can expect shares to do for you, what basic skills are needed to assess the relative merits of different companies, and how much the information that you need actually costs.

IN BRIEF

- The market in shares is little different from any other place where buyers and sellers get together.
- The share (or stock) market rarely behaves logically. It is subject to many whims and fashions.
- The value of shares derives from what is left over after bankers' and other creditors' bills have been paid. But shares offer the investor

limited liability. No investor can lose more than his or her original investment.

- Trading in shares demands a disciplined approach.
- Different individuals buy shares for different motives and have different time horizons.
- There are many different types of shares, not all of which will be suitable for or acceptable to different individual investors.
- Share investment should always be viewed in the light of an investor's other assets and financial commitments.
- The stock market is much more accessible than it once was to ordinary investors.

CHAPTER 2

Temperament and Tools

The stock market is not a place for the faint hearted.

As we found in the previous chapter, a characteristic of any stock market is its ability only to see life in stark terms.

Share prices often react sharply, either upwards or downwards, to the announcement of company results. This happens not because the figures are good or bad in an absolute sense but because they are better or worse than the outcome the market expected, however illogical or inaccurate that expectation may have been.

Shares can also move materially because of broking analysts' interpretation of the nuances of post-results meetings. The requirement is now placed on UK companies to disclose **price-sensitive information** as soon as possible. The consequent rarity of one-on-one analyst briefings, through which news might in the past have been informally leaked into the market, has tended to highlight surprises when they occur. It was thought that this rule would mean that violent gyrations in share prices would be lessened. In fact share prices have arguably become more volatile.

One of the other frustrations the average private investor may experience is that he or she may often be the last to get a particular piece of information.

price-sensitive information: information which, when made public, is likely to have a material impact on a company's share price.

By the time he or she does hear about it, the share price concerned may have moved. I believe that new technologies hold the key to solving this problem. More of that in later chapters.

A little while ago, the *Investors Chronicle* ran an article that outlined the various emotions to which investors could be prone, and how to guard against them. Some of the lessons it drew out bear reiteration.

One of the most important aspects of successful investing is that it often involves making decisions that run contrary to 'normal' human behaviour. The investor must learn to be dispassionate about the process of investing and the risks involved.

Thinking calmly and logically about the investment process can be difficult when significant sums of money are involved.

It is not unusual, for example, for large gains or losses to appear virtually overnight, or equally for an investment to sit neither gaining nor losing value for a long period before suddenly exploding into life.

Just as maddening, the market's reaction to long-awaited events can be subdued. There are any number of market maxims that detail how to react in such situations. 'Buy on the rumour: sell on the strike' is one often used about the oil exploration industry, for instance.

To put it more generally: in the stock market, as sometimes in life, it is 'better to travel hopefully than to arrive'. In other words, the market is all about anticipated events, and the reality—when it arrives—is often viewed as something of an anticlimax.

The important point is have clear and logical goals, a plan of action, patience and a willingness to take the rough with the smooth.

AVOIDING THE TRAPS

A look at some of the common traps that investors can fall into illustrates this best.

Trap 1. Averaging down

The scenario runs something like this. You invest a substantial amount of cash, perhaps a fifth of your portfolio, in a share. It falls 15% almost immediately. The temptation is to compound the error by buying more shares at the lower price. In fact, the correct course of action is to examine why the price has fallen and whether or not you made a mistake in buying the shares in the first place.

Either way, the optimum course of action is to cut your loss immediately. Doubling up in the hope that the shares will recover increases your exposure to a share that is already acting in a suspect manner.

The normal human emotion of pride, tinged with a little hope, in this instance suggests the wrong course of action.

Trap 2. Not running profits

As well as cutting your losses quickly, the next most basic lesson of stock market investment is to learn to 'run' your profits. In other words, don't sell purely because you have accumulated a good gain if there is no pressing reason to do so. The result could well be missing out on a much larger one. Like fine malt whisky, investments need time to mature and selling too early can mean missing out on vintage performance.

Keep your nerve and don't give way to the fear of losing an already handsome profit. But remember . . .

Trap 3. Not selling deteriorating performers

If a share has a good gain but the share price shows signs of flagging, it is prudent to sell before the paper profit already built up disappears entirely.

On occasion, investors feel that they should show loyalty to a particular investment that has served them well. This is absurd. In the book *The Money Game*—one of the best texts on investing ever written—the writer 'Adam Smith' (in reality a US fund manager masquerading under the pseudonym of the famous economist) coined an apt phrase to guard against this misplaced sentimentality. He said, to paraphrase slightly, 'always remember that a share doesn't know you own it'.

Loyalty or affection for a stock has no place in successful investment.

Trap 4. Not cultivating contrary thinking

There are times in investment when it is right to follow the crowd, but often it is those who buy when things looks blackest and sell when there is unbounded optimism who prove to be the really successful investors.

One of the best times to buy ordinary shares in recent years, for example, was in the turmoil that surrounded Britain's decision to leave the ERM in September 1992. On the other tack, in July 1987, a listed British company chartered Concorde for a week to fly a party of 90 analysts and journalists around its operations in the UK, Europe and North America. In hindsight, this proved to be a good signal of the top of that particular **market cycle**.

market cycle:
the collective name for the stock market's successive phases of 'bull' (rising) and 'bear' (falling) markets.

Don't follow the herd: better to follow your own instincts and researches. Remember that rampant corporate excess can be a good indicator that the market is overvalued.

Trap 5. Not diversifying risk

Later in this book we will look at the best way to build a sensible portfolio of shares. It is sometimes tempting, if a particular type of investment has worked well, to buy similar shares in the hope of repeating the trick. Comfort with the familiar is a basic human trait, but does not sit well with a rational investment strategy designed to minimise undue levels of risk.

To give an example, you may have made a good profit buying the shares of a small brewery, but the reasons for gain may be specific to that company: perhaps the impact of a change of management or some other factor. Buying the shares of other small breweries at the same time risks skewing your investment too much towards one industry. Then, if an adverse change does occur, all of your investments will deteriorate.

Employ some lateral thinking when choosing investments.

Trap 6. Clinging to the familiar

Few individuals like change or the unfamiliar. We might be more comfortable buying shares in Tesco or Sainsbury than we would buying the shares of an obscure small Midlands engineering company. But the chances of the price of a small, little-known company rising (under the right conditions) are far better than those in a well-known company that is well researched by City analysts.

One of the most successful US fund managers, Fidelity's Peter Lynch, positively revels in obscure companies. He describes his ideal investment as one that has not had a visit from an analyst for years, has an uninspiring name, has a business that is either obscure or downright disgusting, and is located in a nondescript town. He reasons that the more obscure and little-known a company's shares are, then the greater the share price potential when it is finally discovered.

Be brave and independent, but do your homework.

Let's just list the *positive qualities* that these examples show are needed:

- Absence of pride or any tendency to rely on forlorn hope.
- Patience and strong nerves.
- Absence of misplaced loyalty to inanimate objects (i.e. shares).
- Ability to go against the crowd and a mistrust of conventional wisdom.
- Independence of mind and thoroughness.

It is a rare investor who possesses all of these qualities. In my own case, as the examples in Chapter 10 will demonstrate, I am unemotional about the stocks I own, and a good, independent contrary thinker. I cut losses quickly. But the basic flaw in my investment strategy is a lack of patience and a tendency to lock away profits too early. Recognising one's own failings is the first step to correcting them, or at least trying to.

NO PAIN, NO GAIN

I suspect that a tendency to take profits too early is a fault to which many private investors are prone. It may reflect, in the case of those who come from relatively modest backgrounds, the fact that making money from investing in shares has not generally been the norm. Profits are therefore nailed before they get too big.

The perception that such money is unearned—and the feelings of guilt associated with it—can also cloud rational decision making.

In fact, most money made through investing in shares is hard earned, not least because the investor is putting his or her own capital at risk, and more often than not using up considerable mental energy researching investment opportunities and monitoring the performance of the shares chosen.

The important point about any investment strategy is to be realistic about what it can do for you: you must have clear and realistic goals and expectations.

To a degree, this becomes easier with experience, but it is a vital aspect to think about before investing. Many investors are paralysed by indecision precisely at the time when decisive action is required and a lost opportunity, or an actual cash loss, can be the result.

One important starting point is to set what might be called the 'pain barrier', often called a '**stop-loss**'. This is an amount beyond which a share will automatically be sold. In the case of my own investments, where I might normally deal in units of £4000–5000, I have set this barrier, not as a percentage, but at an absolute amount of £500. My only significant losses have occurred when I have ignored this rule in the hope that a share would recover—only to have to sell at a much bigger loss later.

stop-loss: a discipline by which shares are automatically sold if they fall by more than a certain absolute or percentage amount.

On the other side of the coin, I am reluctant to set a specific limit on when profits should be taken since this varies considerably with circumstances. A very rapid rise in a share for no apparent reason, giving a substantial profit, may be justification enough, especially if the share then begins to lose its momentum. Only experience can tell here.

The important point is to try to come to a realistic assessment of where you believe the share price could go over a specific period and what action you would take if this point is reached much sooner than you anticipate. How to assess the potential of a particular share will be covered in the next chapter.

Another crucial point is that although it is desirable to set some broad parameters for your trading, they should not be adhered to willy-nilly if circumstances change. If the outlook for a particular share suddenly improves (results prove better than expected; a takeover bid is in the offing; management changes have been announced) it may be wise to revisit your views about the likely share price potential. It pays to be flexible.

Finally, there is much to be gained—as your trading progresses—from studying both successes and failures to try to improve things next time round. If the mistakes of the past are studied, then it should be possible to avoid making them a second or maybe a third time.

With that in mind, let's have a look at a basic mental checklist that needs to be completed before we go on to the mechanics of picking and administering investments.

IS INVESTMENT IN SHARES THE RIGHT THING FOR YOU?

It is an old truism of stock market investment that the money you use should be money you can lose. In practice, of course, only an occasional investment may have to be totally written off, but most investors go through periods when they feel the pain of real losses as well as sometimes (hopefully) the euphoria of significant gains.

The real point here, though, is that investments often take time to bear fruit, and it is not helpful to be forced into selling prematurely because the cash is needed for other purposes.

The other sense in which this term is used is that cash earmarked for investment in shares should not be pre-empting funds that could be employed more efficiently elsewhere.

The budding investor should be satisfied that, for instance, he has sufficient cash to pay any outstanding debts, to take care of regular financial commitments, including a mortgage, insurance requirements, school fees for children, if appropriate, as well as general living expenses.

The requirement or desirability of investing in a pension scheme should also be assessed and priority also given to making an investment that way too. Most pension schemes represent a collective investment in the broad stock market, and since the investment can be accomplished in an attractive tax-efficient way, this avenue should be thoroughly explored before money is allocated elsewhere.

It is not unknown, for instance, for individuals to invest money themselves that could usefully be invested in the market indirectly through tax-exempt additional voluntary contributions to a pension scheme.

However, the last thing I want to do is dissuade an investor who wants to have the 'fun' of pitting his or her wits against the stock market from doing so.

The point is that part of the process of getting started as a share investor involves considering all of the available financial options and making a rational decision about the correct course of action to pursue.

It is not my job to specify a particular minimum level of available capital below which investment in shares should not be considered feasible. The advent of no-frills stockbroking has meant that dealing in shares can be accomplished by the man-in-the-street with the minimum of fuss and formality, and it is perfectly possible to start in a small way through investing a few thousand pounds, and gradually build up a portfolio of shares, and have some fun—perhaps investing in smaller companies, penny stocks, and new issues.

The ideal would be to have some 'drop dead' money—cash not earmarked for any particular purpose and not needed for the foreseeable future—amounting to perhaps £30000–35000. The reason for picking a figure in this area is that with a dealing unit of £5000, commission charges should be comparatively low, while a portfolio of five or six shares can be assembled, spreading risk.

But this is only a guide. And I am emphatically not here to advise the person with, say, a couple of thousand pounds to spare against investing in the market. Sadly, though, it is true that the bigger the amount you have to invest, the cheaper the process becomes.

AN INVESTOR'S CHECKLIST

With all this in mind, the following is a checklist of twenty questions you need to answer before proceeding further.

1. *Am I secure in my job or business and sure that I will not have any sudden requirements for cash to supplement my normal earnings?* If you can't answer 'yes' to this one, it may be necessary to set aside some cash to cover this eventuality.

2. *If in employment, do I have redundancy insurance to cover mortgage payments?* If no, see the answer above.

3. *Do I depend on my spouse/partner having a regular income, and how secure is he/she in his/her job? Could I weather the loss of this income without worrying unduly?* If not, make sure that there is some income-producing reserve set aside to cover this eventuality.

4. *Do I have sizable outstanding credit card bills or other debts that should take priority?* If so, as an expensive mode of borrowing, they should be paid off before any cash is earmarked for share investment.

5. *Have I sufficient capital/income to take care of regular items such as school fees over an extended period (and allowing for inflation)?* If not, cash should be earmarked for a savings vehicle to take care of this.

6. *Could I cover any unexpected private medical bills if necessary?* If not, consider private medical/permanent health insurance.

7. *Have I invested fully in a personal pension, that is up to the limits of my tax-free percentage of income?* If not, arguably this should have the first call on available income/capital.

8. *Am I likely to have the opportunity to invest in shares in the company I work for?* If so, you should consider whether you need to retain cash for this specific purpose.

9. *Am I expecting any major capital sums to come my way in the near future, e.g. from inheritances, maturing insurance policies etc.?* If so, tailor your investment strategy accordingly.

10. *Do I have a lump sum to invest now?* If yes, do not earmark all of it for shares. Consider investing some in fixed income investments and a proportion in other assets.

11. *Is my partner/spouse in agreement that it is desirable to invest money in shares?* If not, reconsider your decision.

12. *Is he/she aware of the risks involved in investing in the stock market?* If not, he or she should be acquainted with a realistic assessment of the risks.

13. *Having decided that a specific sum can be invested in the stock market, is it sufficiently large and is my tax position such for it to be worth while sheltering investment income or capital gains in some way?* If so, you may need to consider Personal Equity Plans or other tax-efficient investments.

14. *Assuming a specific sum is earmarked to invest in shares, am I primarily aiming to invest for income or capital growth?* Your choice of investment will be dictated by the answer.

15. *What tolerance of risk do I have?* It is important to determine this in advance and to recognise that higher than normal returns are only possible by investing in higher-risk securities where the possibility of some loss is greater. Your tolerance of risk may well depend on the size of the funds you are proposing to invest relative to any other assets you may have.

16. *Am I cool, calm and collected, or of a nervous, jumpy disposition?* If the latter, then the stock market is not the place for you.

17. *Do I have a broker through which I can deal in ordinary shares?* If not, think carefully and investigate a number before choosing one.

18. *If I do have an existing relationship with a broker, how do the firm's charges compare with others in the market, and is the service I am getting the one I require?* The answers to these questions will determine whether or not you might need to look elsewhere.

19. *Am I happy to have my investment held through the broking firm's nominee arrangements?* Settlement is simpler and dealing cheaper if you agree to this.

20. *Am I computer literate?* Computers are increasingly used by private clients to monitor their portfolios, access information and increasingly to deal through their broker. Being able to do all this greatly simplifies the administration of an investment portfolio.

From the answers to the above we can draw the 'identikit' investor profile of the person likely to be a successful in shares.

He or she is:

- Retired, in a secure job, or self-employed in a successful business.
- Has sufficient capital to cover contingencies such as sickness, redundancy, or the loss of a partner's or spouse's income.
- Has already fully provided for pension arrangements and other liabilities such as school fees.
- Is computer literate.
- Does not have an unduly onerous tax position.

- Is a calm and collected individual with a reasonable tolerance of risk.
- Has a spouse or partner who is happy with the decision to begin investing in shares.
- Is happy to trust a broker to handle some of the more mundane administrative tasks involved in share investment.

It is unlikely that every potential investor or reader will fit this identikit exactly. The most important aspect is, as we stated at the beginning of this chapter, that investment should only be conducted from a secure financial background. Investing in shares is not a way of getting rich overnight, and should not be undertaken with cash that might soon be needed for other purposes.

THE TOOLS

As well as not being for the faint hearted, investing in shares is not for the lazy either. The potential for success in any investment increases in proportion to the amount of time spent researching it. Keeping score, monitoring investments once they have been bought, is also an important part of making investment decisions.

At any point in time you may need to know when a particular share was acquired, what it cost, and what its current value and therefore your profit or loss is. Rather than wait for the evening or morning paper to arrive to find out how your shares are doing, you may wish to monitor them in the course of the trading day.

To evaluate shares properly, you will need to undertake research and be prepared to do 'number-crunching', and you may wish to see how the price of a particular share has performed in the recent past. You might want to obtain or subscribe to various publications in order to gain additional information and new ideas.

It is obvious just from this simple list that doing the job properly entails some costs. These costs can be broken down into a number of areas.

Newspapers and other regular publications

There are few successful investors who are not avid readers. To keep abreast of the market you need to read the *Financial Times* on a daily basis, and perhaps one other quality broadsheet. The *Daily Mail* is also particularly noted for its City coverage.

Sunday papers are often used as channels to leak information about corporate developments, new issues and the like into the market, and can be useful, although it is as well to avoid dealing on the basis of tips contained in them.

Magazines like the *Investors Chronicle* are a must; *The Economist* is a personal favourite of mine, although relatively few of its articles have a specific relevance to investment in shares.

You may also want to trawl for ideas in foreign publications, notably perhaps those relating to the US market. The European edition of the *Wall Street Journal* is readily available in the UK, as are publications like *Business Week, Investors Business Daily* and *Barrons*, a tabloid weekly of legendary influence in the US investment scene.

There is an important point to make about press coverage of the investment scene. Be certain to distinguish between information and opinion.

The value of a wide range of reading is that it broadens the exposure you get to information and ideas on investment. For example, profiles of companies in the *Investors Chronicle* often contain charts and salient accounting information.

You need not agree with or even pay attention to the magazine's view about a particular share to get value out of that article. The same applies to articles in other publications.

What might all this cost? For many years, I have both written about and practised the art of investment, using many of the publications mentioned. My monthly paper bill is currently in the region of £50–60. Magazine subscriptions come extra, although publications like the *Investors Chronicle, The Economist* and *Business Week* often do cut-price deals for a long-term subscription.

Newsletters

There are any number of newsletters published about the investment scene. They normally have a stock selection system or a particular speciality, recommend selected shares and contain periodic updates on their progress, as well as pontificating about events of the moment.

One problem about newsletters, apart from their cost (typically, £100 a year each), is the self-fulfilling nature of some of their recommendations. The fact that recommendations contained in newsletters are being mailed out to several thousand active investors each week or each month, often in smaller companies with a restricted liquidity in their shares, means it is not uncommon for newsletter recommendations to move a share price markedly.

Most newsletters operate either on the basis of a portfolio selection system—picking shares that fit certain predetermined criteria—or else have a particular specialisation. *Techninvest* is a good example of the latter, a specialist newsletter about high technology shares. It is highly thought of by a number of high-profile investors. The important thing is to find the newsletter that works for you, rather than to subscribe to a large number.

Books

Books on investment have enjoyed something of a renaissance in recent years with a number of popular titles being published for the first time and old ones revived. There are books that deal with every part of the investment scene; those written by or about successful practitioners in which they describe their experiences are perhaps the most valuable for the first-time investor.

I have already mentioned *The Money Game* by Adam Smith. Some other good ones are: two books written by Peter Lynch (*Beating the Street* and *One up on Wall Street*); *Market Wizards* and *The New Market Wizards* by Jack Schwager, a series of interviews with top share traders; and *The Alchemy of Finance* and *Soros on Soros* by George Soros.

It is a good discipline for the new investor in shares to read at least one good investment book a month. Visit any successful private investor, and you will see that more often than not their bookshelves are full of books about the art of investment.

However successful an investor you become, there is always room to learn more from the experience of others.

Reference material

Even the newest of newcomers to the investment scene will be aware that the big institutional investors—banks, insurance companies and pension funds—have a wealth of information at their disposal on which to base their investment decisions. Fortunately, when it comes to information, quantity does not necessarily equal quality. It is perfectly possible for the average investor to make an informed decision about picking out individual shares with the aid of just a modicum of reference material.

There are two indispensable aids to successful investing in shares. The first, the *Hambro Company Guide* (HCG), is a compendium of basic financial information on all listed companies, which also includes addresses, telephone and fax numbers, and a variety of other data. Armed with this publication, which costs approximately £105 per year for four quarterly issues, the investor is equipped to telephone or fax companies to obtain copies of annual reports and other background information.

The other guide that is well worth subscribing to, and which seasoned private investors swear by, is *The Estimate Directory* (TED). This contains regularly updated details of the forecasts made by City analysts for the vast majority of listed companies, as well as other information derived from this data and a simple share price chart of each company. An annual subscription to four quarterly issues costs around £130.

Other reference publications that some investors find useful include:

- REFs, a book of key accounts ratios for leading companies, and very useful for those looking for a short-cut to the financial number crunching that investigating shares in depth can entail.
- Various services detailing directors' dealings in their own company's shares, sometimes said to be a good indicator of the direction of a company's share price.
- McCarthy press cuttings on individual companies. Here, for an annual subscription and a modest supplementary per page cost, investors can get a transcript of all the relevant press comment on a particular company over a certain period.
- Extel 'cards' contain detailed information on individual companies, based on detailed analysis of a number of years' annual reports, as well as a considerable amount of other data. Investing institutions and brokers now by and large receive this service electronically via CD-ROM, but paper versions are available, the overall cost

falling as the number of cards ordered in any one year increases.

Although the cost of all this information may sound daunting, some of it represents the 'luxury' end of the market for those with cash to indulge their investing hobby. Those who want to keep the costs down can manage perfectly adequately with less.

Bear in mind also that a good local reference library may keep some of this information or have on-line access to some of the proprietary cuttings services such as FT Profile.

Software and data

Arguably the largest cost item for any serious private investor relates to getting hold of up-to-date information on share prices during the course of the trading day, and also getting information on prices and trading volume in a form capable of being downloaded into various types of **investment software**.

investment software: computer programs designed to facilitate the monitoring of shares, share prices and share dealings.

The business of computerised investing, what software packages are available, how to get hold of regular price data, as well as the Internet and World Wide Web and how they can help with access to relevant information, are all covered in later chapters of this book.

At this stage, therefore, I will confine these comments to price information, how it should be used and how much it costs.

Real-time (i.e. constantly updated) price displays are expensive and clearly unnecessary if the investor is out at work all day. Having said that, pager services, such as Sprintel's *Real Time Alert*, can provide near real-time updating of a limited range of share prices and other indicators for those on the move.

Market Eye: a well-known real-time share price display system used by active private investors.

Probably the most popular real-time service for private investors is ICV's **Market Eye** service, available through either a stand-alone terminal or a PC version. In both cases an initial investment in hardware is required and the company also then charges an annual service fee of around £1000 plus VAT for provision of the data. Exchange fees are levied on top.

The service contains all of the information an active private investor needs, including the ability to create customised pages of individual shares, news announcements made to the Stock Exchange by companies and various other services. These include a so-called 'limit-minder', which will beep if a particular share hits a limit pre-programmed into the machine. Data can also be downloaded from Market Eye into various commonly used investment software packages.

While all of this sounds sophisticated and exciting, and certainly will give the home-based private investor the feeling that he or she is involved in the market, my own experience has been that it can induce a feeling of pressure on the investor to deal rather more actively than might be wise.

The investment philosophy that I will put forward in this book emphasises the importance of selecting the correct shares and working out what they are worth, rather than looking at the money that can undoubtedly be made (and, of course, lost) by more active trading of shares.

With one or two exceptions, my best investment gains have come from careful share selection and from holding shares for relatively long periods of time—by which I mean periods of up to a year or more—rather than through shorter term trading. This has its place, but is probably best left to the professional.

In this context, the close monitoring of share price movements on a real-time basis through the trading day becomes something of a distraction. A weather eye can be kept on leading shares (the top

400 or so) through accessing the BBC2 and Channel 4 teletext pages. A modest investment in a dedicated TV set for this purpose will give a feel of how the market is moving throughout the day.

In these services, which are free, top shares are updated several times per day and the major market index is provided on a real-time basis. Channel 4's Teletext 2000 service updates share prices for the whole market on a once-daily basis. There is software available that can help to manipulate this data within the user's PC.

Where quality of data does become important is in its use in a computerised chart package. In my view it is worth using teletext for day-to-day share price information but spending a little more on share price information, and especially statistics on **trading volume**, that can be downloaded regularly and perused at leisure. Trading volume, particular in smaller companies, is often an interesting statistic to look at, for reasons that will be explained later. The various types of software package and different options for acquiring data will also be explored later in this book.

trading volume: the aggregate number of shares dealt in (either bought or sold) on any one trading day.

BASIC COSTS

It is important to be realistic about how much all of this will cost. So let's itemise the prices of some of the information sources and services outlined above:

	Annual cost
Newspapers: £60 per month	£720
Magazines and newsletters: say, four at £100 each	£400
Books: one per four weeks, say, £10 each	£130
Reference material: HCG and TED plus one other	£350
Software: mid-range package (one-off cost)	£200
Data: including intra-day and trading volume	£400

This adds up to a total of £2200, although some of these costs are one-offs and some, say for books, newspapers and magazines, may already be incurred anyway. If the extra cost of a real-time price display were to be added to this, then the total annual cost would exceed £3000 per annum.

I recognise that this is a rather off-putting figure. So let's look at how it is possible to do the job for less. Many investors do.

I view the *Financial Times* and the *Investors Chronicle* as essentials, as also (in my view) is the *Hambro Campany Guide*. On a yearly basis, these three items together cost about £400.

A basic software package can be had for under £100, and basic data can be downloaded from teletext for free using a teletext adaptor card (one-off cost under £200). For those with a modem and a direct Internet connection (roughly £15 per month), comprehensive price data can be downloaded from Electronic Share Information for £5 per month. Internet access also enables the City pages of *The Times*, the *Sunday Times* and the *Daily Telegraph* to be accessed free, so that City and investment commentary can be read without buying the papers. The Internet is also useful in its own right as an information source. Exactly how is explored later in this book.

The bottom line is that the **bare minimum** of annual spending is probably £400–650. It is, of course, possible to start in a smaller way. But the aspiring investor will find that he or she quickly comes up against shortages of either ideas or information required to make the right investment decisions in a prompt and efficient manner.

On the basis of the investment strategies and techniques described later in this book, I believe it is possible to envisage an annual return on capital invested over time in the region of 15–20%, including reinvesting dividends and other investment income.

Needless to say, this can in no way be guaranteed. What numbers like this mean is that with a portfolio of say £30000, the annual return might be £4000–5000, from which should be deducted the costs mentioned above. This would reduce the return somewhat, but still to a percentage in double figures.

In the light of inflation, at the time of writing in low single figures, this is still a good return. The real point, though, is that the bigger the portfolio the more may well be spent on information and other resources. But the cost will not go up in proportion. The individual with a limited amount of cash available to invest, say £2000 or less, must recognise that he or she is pursuing a hobby, with commensurate costs that may wipe out some of the gains that are made.

For the remainder of this book, however, we will presuppose that the reader is prepared to spend at the level indicated for the basic information costs, and that he or she is prepared to pursue a strategy of actively investigating investment opportunities thoroughly. In itself, of course, this involves an investment in time which should be costed out.

To paraphrase the remarks of Lord Keynes quoted in the Introduction, playing the game does involve an entry fee.

IN BRIEF

- Shares can be volatile, and investors are notoriously prone to bouts of fear and greed.
- Successful investors need to cultivate patience, strong nerves and the ability to think and act differently from the crowd.
- The first rule of successful trading: cut losses, and run profits.
- There is no minimum entry fee for investing in shares, but investing in shares makes more

sense if you can have worthwhile holdings in several different shares.

- Only invest money in shares that is not ear-marked for other purposes and after all other sensible financial commitments have been met. The money you use should be money you can lose.

- Successful investment involves buying information and using tools. These cost money. Allocate at least £400 a year for newspapers, newsletters and other reference material.

Checking Out the Numbers

City analysts have a habit of taking themselves too seriously. So they may feel that the title of this chapter devalues the job they are paid lots of money to do.

But it is worth getting away from the rather sterile debate among the professionals in the investment game about the merits or otherwise of so-called 'fundamental' analysis and 'technical' analysis. These tags are commonly referred to in the press. You may have wondered what they mean.

In both cases these names seek to imply solidity and thoroughness. But this supposed thoroughness is often not delivered. The difference between fundamental analysis and technical analysis is roughly as follows:

- *Fundamental analysis* starts from the underlying background to the company in whose shares you may be interested. It examines the industry it operates in, whether or not it has a competitive edge (say in terms of size, management, corporate strategy or innovation), and looks in detail at its past financial results over a period of years. It looks (usually in less convincing detail) at how they might shape up in the future.

That is the theory. In reality much such research is simply designed to maintain the broking firm's profile in the eyes of their clients and is at best superficial.

- *Technical analysis* says that looking at the fundamentals is irrelevant, since all of the information that is of any importance has already been reflected in the price of the shares. What matters more (technical analysts say) is the pattern of behaviour displayed by investors in the past—as reflected in the way the share price has moved as the forces of supply and demand have ebbed and flowed.

  To some degree this harks back to the quotation from Lord Keynes I used in the Introduction. The underlying merits of a share matter less than what everyone believes to be the case.

'Technicians', or 'chartists', as they are often known, therefore spend their time performing detailed analysis, both statistical and intuitive, of trends in share prices. The objective is to come to some conclusion about the best time to buy or sell particular shares. Fundamental analysts, of course, regard them as charlatans.

There is room for both of these approaches, and an investor ignores one or other at his or her peril. But do not worry. There is no need to go to the lengths City analysts claim to do to grasp the essence of what makes a company tick and whether its shares are good value or not. Taking a company's accounts and looking at some basic numbers is comparatively easy.

Being aware of the position of the share price and how it has fluctuated in the past is also a vital part of timing purchases and sales. At the very least it may stop you buying a share, picked for good fundamental reasons, at the wrong time. Conversely, sometimes charts can give such strong

buy signal: a strong indication from a price chart that will prompt the investor to research closely the 'fundamentals' of a company.

'buy' signals that they will prompt you to do further fundamental research on a share that you may not have considered before.

The fact that this chapter is the first of the two that deals with each of these aspects does not imply that I give any more importance to one approach or the other. The essential component of successful investment is information, and how you interpret it. And the more information you have, the better.

Everyday observations about well-known high street names are information (moreover, information that the average professional investor may not pay attention to), price movements are information, and the numbers contained in company accounts—and analysts' forecasts—are also information. All of this information can and should be used to come to a judgement about a share.

And while fundamental analysts will point out that charts often give incorrect or ambiguous signals, the same can equally be said of company accounts and other fundamental information. More of that later.

BASIC CONCEPTS

I hope every reader of this book will come away from reading it with at least a smattering of accounting knowledge. But I will keep it simple. There are two good reasons for this.

Firstly, the main reason is that it serves no purpose to get too embroiled in abstruse accounting topics. All you really need to know is that when you begin to find a set of accounts hard to understand, that is as good a reason as any for being wary.

Secondly, although I worked for 18 years as an investment analyst in the City, I have had no formal accounting training. My point in mentioning this is simple.

Understanding accounts can be learnt easily.

Interpreting company financial statements is comparatively straightforward, providing the reader has a sceptical turn of mind and some basic knowledge of the way businesses work. You do not need to be a qualified FCA to analyse a set of company accounts.

The basic starting point is a company's **annual report** and accounts. This is a document that the company is required by law to publish each year and to circulate to shareholders. It contains details of the company's operations over the previous year, and formal audited accounts.

The accounts contain a statement of profit and loss, a statement of the cash inflows and outflows experienced during the year—the revenue the company has received and how it has been spent—and the balance sheet, a statement of the company's assets and liabilities at its financial year-end. The numbers may be quite brief, with a lot of the detail consigned to notes at the back of the accounts.

I cannot stress enough the importance of reading these notes as part of the process of evaluating a company. Companies can and do hide embarrassing bits of detail in the notes, in the hope that they will get overlooked.

Getting hold of a company's report and accounts is usually comparatively easy. A telephone call to the company secretary's office, or even simply to the head office switchboard (the telephone number will be in one of the reference publications mentioned in Chapter 2) will usually ensure that a copy is sent out to you, even if you do not hold the shares. Very occasionally a letter may be needed.

If possible, try to get hold of more than one year's accounts. The further back you can go the better. Note also that reference books like the *Hambro Company Guide*, REFs, and *The Estimate Directory* sometimes provide details of the key ratios

annual report: a statutory document that any public company must produce each year, containing its audited accounts and certain other information.

we will talk about later in this chapter. These can be useful as an initial filter, but do not invest without first looking in more detail at the accounts. There is no substitute for crunching the numbers yourself.

UNDERSTANDING THE PROFIT AND LOSS ACCOUNT

We will now take each component of the annual report in turn, and look at them in brief to examine what they can tell us about a company.

Let's begin with our fictional company, Universal Widgets, to draw out some of the basic concepts.

Table 3.1 shows its profit and loss (or P&L) account. This is a pretty standard layout for a company P&L account, although the precise terminology may vary slightly from company to company.

Table 3.1   Universal Widgets: Profit & Loss Account (£m)

| | Year to December | |
	1995	1994
Turnover	125	100
Cost of sales	55	45
Gross profit	70	55
Operating expenses	20	15
Operating profit	50	40
Interest paid	10	10
Profit before tax	40	30
Taxation	13	10
Profit after tax	27	20
Minority interests	2	0
Attributable profit	25	20
Dividends	5	4
Retained profit	20	16
Earnings per share (p)	12.5	10.0
Dividend per share (p)	2.5	2.0
Shares in issues	200 m	200 m

For instance, turnover may become revenue or sales, interest paid may be cost of finance, and operating profit may be called trading profit. But the logical structure as laid out in the table will remain roughly the same.

There is one significant item missing, for which you will have to go to the notes, usually in the note relating to trading profit.

The missing item is **depreciation**.

This is the amount a company sets aside each year to replace a 'wasting' asset. Rather like depreciation on a car, the company's finance director will know that at some point in the future he will have to replace a piece of machinery or a fleet of vehicles. It is prudent for him, therefore, to deduct from profits each year, on an instalment basis, an amount that will add up to the expected cost of renewing these assets at the end of their life.

In fact, normally it is simply the original cost of the asset that is depreciated, with no account being taken of the fact that, due to inflation, the cost of replacing it may rise.

In the case of Universal Widgets we are going to assume that the depreciation this year is £5 m, included in the £20 m of operating expenses, and that it was £4 m in the previous year. The importance of this will become clear in due course.

Let's now have a look at some of the items in the table in more detail.

Turnover is simply sales revenue, normally stated net of VAT and any sales duties applicable. *Cost of sales* is the outside expense entailed in generating those sales, such as bought-in raw materials and the like. What is left is *gross profit*.

The essence of most companies is that they take these materials and process them in some way. In order to generate the sales in the first place it has been necessary to add some value to the raw materials. In order to do this there are internal costs—of

depreciation: *a notional amount set aside each year to cover the cost of replacing fixed assets.*

employing people, selling the finished production, administering the business, buying machinery, and so on.

These are known as *operating expenses*. After deducting these from gross profit, we arrive at operating profit. This is not the end of the expense. Most companies quite rightly finance part of their trading through borrowing to fund capital investment. Provided this is kept at prudent levels and done at reasonable cost, this is perfectly legitimate. But the cost of obtaining these borrowings must be deducted from profits via the *interest paid* item.

This leaves us with *profit before tax*. This figure is the basic unit that City analysts look at, although some complexities have been introduced here recently, which we will go into later.

Companies have to pay corporation *tax*, so that too must be deducted. *Minority interests*, that is to say the interests of outside shareholders in any subsidiaries that are partly-owned, must also be taken off (normally at the after tax profit level), and what is left is *attributable profit* for the ordinary shareholders in Universal Widgets.

Shareholders expect dividends. So in order to arrive at a figure for the cash available to reinvest in the business, these payments must be deducted to arrive at *retained profits*. This is the profit kept in the business to be ploughed back for the future.

So far so good. Well, not quite. The company has actually retained more than this. The figure for depreciation (£5 m in 1995) was only a notional book entry calculated by the finance director so, in cash terms, the company has retained £25 m, rather than the £20 m shown at the bottom of the table.

The *earnings per share* and *dividend per share* figures are simply the attributable profit and dividend figures divided by the total number of shares in issue, in this example 200 m.

KEY PROFIT RATIOS

Now let's look at some of the basic ratios that can be derived from these figures to give us clues about the company's performance.

First, *profit margins*. Like most other ratios, profit margins are a guide both to the efficiency of the business, and to the type of industry it operates in. Some service businesses, for instance, like advertising agencies or fund management firms, have limited bought-in costs but generate fee income on the back of their **intangible assets**—their client base and staff. Others, like supermarkets, operate on very tight margins but big turnover.

So what matters in all this is not so much the level of margin but its trend over time. An adverse trend, falling margins from one year to the next to the one after that, is disturbing and an explanation should be sought.

Margins are simply the ratio of a profit figure to sales. *Gross margin* is gross profit as a percentage of turnover, operating margin is operating profit as a percentage of turnover, and so on. Gross margin is a good measure to use in businesses like pub retailing, where there is a service element and a high level of bought-in products, but more normally operating margins are used.

The difference between *operating margins* and pre-tax margins is represented by interest. Higher or lower levels of borrowing manifest themselves in both the balance sheet and the profit statement. In the P&L account the way to measure this is to express pre-interest profit (in this example operating profit) as a multiple of the interest paid. In this case this ratio, known as *interest cover*, is 5 times, an acceptable level. The reason for being concerned about this measure is that an unduly low level of interest cover can leave profits vulnerable to an increase in interest rates.

intangible assets: non-physical assets (such as brand names, customer lists and staff) whose value to the business is hard to calculate.

Next, corporate tax. Current corporate tax rates are around 33%, but this is sometimes reduced by overseas profits arising in low-tax areas and by the tax deductions resulting from heavy past capital investment. If the *tax charge*, the percentage of pre-tax profits taken off in tax, is significantly outside the 30–33% range or has changed significantly in the past year, it is worth examining why.

PRICE–EARNINGS RATIOS AND DIVIDEND YIELDS

Finally in the P&L account there are earnings and dividends to consider. Although analysts look at headline pre-tax numbers, at the end of the day it is often the earnings figure that drives the share price. Shares are normally evaluated on the basis of the *price–earnings ratio* (PER), or **earnings multiple**. This is the earnings per share figure—usually the forecast for the immediate coming year—divided into the share price. In this example, let's assume that Universal Widgets' share price is 250p. This means that its historic price–earnings ratio, i.e. the ratio based on its latest reported annual earnings, is 20 times.

earnings multiple: the ratio of the share price to a company's earnings per share (also called price–earnings ratio).

This is relatively high, but not unduly so when we consider that these earnings have risen by 25%, from 10p to 12.5p in the past year, and therefore may well do so again. Let's assume that analysts, based on their long experience of looking at the company, believe that earnings per share will grow by another 25% this year, taking the per share figure up from 12.5p to 15.6p. If the company is to receive the same valuation in the market when these earnings are reported in a year's time, the share price must rise to 312p.

The problem is that earnings do not always grow as the market expects. Suppose for a moment, for the sake of argument, that Universal Widgets loses a valuable sales contract and that its earnings are likely to fall back to 10p rather than grow to the 15.6p the market first expected. What happens then?

First of all, you might expect that, if the 20 times PER were maintained, then the shares would fall to 200p. In fact, they may well fall by more than this, because the company's hitherto solid-looking pattern of growth has been tarnished. Companies which demonstrate that they are unreliable in this way normally stand on much lower multiples.

Say the multiple falls to 14 times. This means that although the slippage in earnings is only back to the prior year's level, the drop in the share price, from the original 250p to 140p (14 times the 10p earnings now expected), is 44%.

This works in reverse if shares on lower multiples produce better than expected results. The shares benefit not only from the better than expected rise in profits, but also from a rise in the PER. There is nothing automatic about this, but it is the way the market tends to react.

It is important to understand this point fully before moving on, as it is basic to the whole investment process. Looking back to the different categories of shares we itemised in the previous chapter, you can probably deduce that growth stocks will tend to have higher multiples than normal blue chips, because they will have higher growth rates. As they mature, their growth will slacken and they will become blue chips.

But income, in the form of dividends, is important too. In general, the onus is on shares to perform better than staider investments. Keeping the money in the bank or building society will normally yield lower returns than an investment in shares, because shares are more risky.

A higher return is required to compensate share investors for the extra risk that they may suffer a total or partial loss of their capital. Part of the return from a share is measured by its *dividend yield*.

In the UK dividends are paid to the investor after tax has been deducted, i.e. on a 'net' basis. The investor receives a tax credit for the amount of tax deducted at source. So the income return from a share is usually calculated on the basis of the gross dividend. With the basic rate at 20% the dividend payment is 'grossed up' by dividing the net payment by 0.8.

The yield is then calculated by expressing this annual gross 'income' as a percentage of the current share price. In the case of Universal Widgets, grossing up the 2.5p dividend payment by 0.8 means that the gross dividend is 3.125p. This amount represents 1.25% of the current 250p share price. The gross dividend yield is therefore 1.25%.

This may seem pretty puny when an investor could get maybe 4% with the money in the bank and perhaps 7.5% in a fixed interest stock. But the other component of any return that an equity investor might receive is the potential appreciation in the share price in any one year.

Let's go back to our earlier example and assume that profits grew as expected and the share price rose in line with them. The share price would have risen by 25% and adding in the 1.25% dividend yield on top would give a *total return* of 26.5%, a very healthy return indeed.

The ratio between earnings and dividends has a bearing on this too. The less a company pays out in dividends, the more it has to reinvest in the business. High growth companies tend to want (and indeed need) to retain more of their profits in order to fund their expected growth. Yields on growth companies therefore tend to be much lower than more sedate companies, but the opportunity for price appreciation is (in theory) that much greater.

The relationhip between earnings and dividends is known as *dividend cover* and is worked out by dividing dividends into earnings per share.

In this example, therefore, the dividend cover is 5 times (12.5p divided by 2.5p). A dividend cover of 2.5–3 times might be considered normal, one of 5 times high, and one of under 2 as low.

The risk of a low dividend cover is that if profits fall, the dividend may have to be reduced. Companies with low dividend covers tend to have higher yields to compensate for this risk. High yields and low cover normally also mean that the company's price earnings multiple is low, suggesting that the market also expects it not to produce much appreciation.

But while a proportion of income stocks may go on to cut their dividends, many do not, and their prices and share ratings recover, making them good investments. This is particularly the case if their income can be counted gross and reinvested, as for instance in a **personal equity plan**.

Reinvestment of gross dividend income has a powerful compounding effect on the shareholders' returns if it is done consistently over a comparatively long period. For example, a relatively modest 7% return compounded over ten years produces a gain of 97%, more or less doubling your money. Over 15 years the gain is 175%.

It is important to remember that the relationship between earnings, dividends and the share price is a dynamic one, and governed more by expectations of what may happen in the future than by past history. However, the presence of a good past record tends to underpin similar expectations for the future.

In fact, as accounting conventions have changed, the predictability of reported earnings has fallen, making them a less reliable guide to the underlying state of the business. Analysts now frequently adjust published profit figures to get them

PEP: *personal equity plan, a tax-efficient way of holding shares.*

onto a standardised and meaningful basis, stripping out items that are regarded as out of the ordinary. This can be confusing to the private investor.

In tandem with this, companies have been obliged to give a more explicit and transparent account of the way cash has flowed into and out of the business in any one year. It is to this next, very important, component of the annual report that we turn in the following section.

UNDERSTANDING CASH FLOW STATEMENTS

Our fictional company Universal Widgets' cash flow statement is shown in Table 3.2.

For brevity I have omitted some of the subtotals that normally crop up in corporate cash flow statements, but otherwise this table is more or less as it would appear in a normal set of accounts.

Table 3.2   Universal Widgets: Cash Flow Statement

	1995	*1994*
Net cash inflow from operating activities	46	48
Servicing of finance		
Interest	−10	−10
Dividends	−5	−4
Taxation	−12	−11
Investing activities		
Purchase of fixed assets	−30	−28
Sale of fixed assets	5	14
Purchase of investments	−6	−1
Sale of investments		
Net cash inflow/outflow before financing	−12	8
Financing		
(Increase)/decrease in borrowing	−9	4
Change in net cash	−3	4

The topmost figure is *cash flow from operations*. As its name suggests, this is the net amount of cash the company received from its operating activities in the course of the year. It is very important to remember that this is not the same as the operating profit struck in the P&L account. It will bear some relation to it but, as most small businessmen will recognise, making sales and booking profits are not the same as receiving the cash.

One difference between P&L account profit and operating cash flow is depreciation, which, as we mentioned before, is a notional charge that can be added back. This is to say, it does not represent an actual outflow of cash from the business.

There will be some other minor adjustments—it is normal, for instance, to take off any profit that arises from sales of fixed assets, since the revenue from the sales comes in elsewhere.

But the big factor is the *change in working capital*. Working capital is an accounting term, but in practice it means the total of stocks, and money owed to the company (debtors) minus money it owes to others (creditors). Sales and profits may rise, but money from extra sales is of no benefit to the company's cash reserves until it is collected.

Remember that we are not necessarily talking here about bad debts, but simply highlighting the point that profits recorded on the basis of invoices that have not yet been paid are not perhaps to be counted in the same way as cash that has actually been received.

Let's take our example of Universal Widgets. Its inflow of cash actually went down by £2 m between 1994 and 1995, despite the fact that operating profits went up from £40 m to £50 m. If we assume that depreciation didn't change much, what has happened to cause this?

One reason could be that although the company has been efficient at making sales, it may have done so by giving its customers extended credit terms. Or it may simply have been less efficient than before at collecting its debts. Similarly, its suppliers may have tightened their terms of trade and the company may have had to pay up faster for its raw materials.

This is not necessarily a remarkable state of affairs. But it is definitely a bad sign if the cash inflow from operations is radically different to operating profits. I have seen examples of companies reporting steady increases in profits but which, each year, reported much lower cash inflows, or even outflows. Needless to say, such situations cannot continue indefinitely.

Looking further down the table, we can see interest and dividends taken out. These may differ slightly from the P&L account figures because of difference in the timing of dividend and interest payments relative to when the company's financial year ends. For instance, companies normally declare two dividends a year, an interim and a final. The final dividend will be declared when the results are published (obviously this will be after the company's financial year-end) and paid a few weeks later—perhaps three months into the company's new financial year.

The dividend entry in the cash flow statement may well be a combination of the current year's interim payment and the previous year's final dividend.

Taxation is similarly paid in arrears and therefore may differ from the P&L account figure, which states the amount expected to be paid on the year's profit when the time comes to settle up with the taxman.

You can see by simple subtraction that after taking off interest, dividends and tax—all of which can be regarded as cast-iron obligations—Universal Widgets had £19 m left in 1995 but £23 m in 1994.

This is the cash available to reinvest in the business. In many companies this will simply be used for the *purchase of fixed assets,* either to replace existing plant and machinery that has worn out, or to put up a new factory. Offsetting this can be disposals of fixed assets, which bring in cash. Some fixed assets may no longer be needed and can be sold. Whether a profit is earned on the disposal is less relevant. What matters is the cash coming in.

Surplus cash flow may also be used to acquire *investments.* These can represent a variety of things. In Universal Widgets' case, it could be a small stake in Consolidated Flanges, a company with whom it has a long-standing relationship. Or it may be some other type of investment necessary to the smooth running of the business. It is here, under the heading *purchase of subsidiaries,* that an acquisition would be recorded.

After taking out the net amount of purchases and sales of fixed assets and investments, we are left (in this example) with a *cash outflow before financing* of £12 m in 1995 compared to an inflow of £8 m in the previous year.

Now contrast this with the P&L account in Table 3.1.

Profitwise, everything looks hunky-dory. The cash flow statement shows otherwise, illustrating the drawback of looking solely at earnings per share and profits to evaluate a company.

In this particular case, the cash deficit in 1995 had to be financed somehow, either by borrowing, or by the company dipping into its cash reserves. As it happened, it chose to do both—with cash falling by £3 m and borrowings rising by £9 m.

Before we look at the balance sheet, you may have noticed that it should be possible to arrive at a per share expression of cash flow and to compare this with the share price, as we did with earnings. There are differences of opinion about which figure to take, but provided a consistent figure is taken, it does not much matter about the precise definition.

The options are really to take cash flow before investing activities—that is, operating cash flow (the top figure) minus interest dividends and tax—or to take what is sometimes called *free cash flow*. This is the figure for cash flow before investing activities, minus the level of fixed asset purchases necessary to maintain the fabric of the business.

Since this latter amount is difficult to estimate, if opting for the free cash flow measure it is probably simpler just to take purchases less sales of fixed assets and knock this amount off cash flow before investing. Some figures for free cash flow exclude dividends. This is because it is not an unavoidable payment, like interest and tax, but is at the discretion of the management.

Either way, dividing whichever figure is chosen by the average number of shares in issue during the year will give a per share figure that can then be compared to the share price, and with the conventional earnings per share figures. Sharp divergences in the trend between the two need to be investigated further.

This is good point to look at the balance sheet, and the ratios that can be calculated simply from the figures contained within it.

UNDERSTANDING THE BALANCE SHEET

An accountant will always say that a balance sheet is simply a snapshot of a company's assets and liabilities at a particular point in time (the day the company's financial year ends).

It should surprise no one that a company's assets and liabilities—the money it is owed, the money it has to pay out, its borrowings and its cash reserves—all change from week to week and month to month, and that the timing of a company's year-end is sometimes dictated not only by tax

Table 3.3 Universal Widgets: Consolidated Balance Sheet

	As at 31st December	
	1995	1994
Fixed assets		
Tangible assets	250	220
Investments	10	10
	260	230
Current assets		
Stocks	25	20
Debtors	35	25
Cash	12	15
	72	60
Creditors		
Due within one year	40	45
Net current assets	32	15
Total assets less current liabilities	292	245
Creditors		
Due after more than one year	80	55
Provisions	10	10
Net assets	202	180
Capital and reserves		
Shares capital	10	10
Share premium account	52	52
Capital reserve	40	38
Profit & loss account	100	80
Equity shareholders' funds	202	180

considerations but also by which time of year will show its financial health at its most robust.

Table 3.3 shows Universal Widgets' balance sheet for 1994 and 1995.

There is another important feature of company balance sheets. This is that the difference between one year's and the next's is inextricably linked with the flows of cash into and out of the business.

We saw in the previous example that the company's cash flow from operations differed from its operating profit, because the latter took into account movements in working capital—notably leads and lags in the payment of invoices by customers and of bills owed to suppliers.

Similarly, the amount retained from profits each year goes over to the balance sheet as a credit and becomes part of the company's reserves.

However, before getting onto this subject, let's take the balance sheet item by item and look at what each item means.

The *consolidated balance sheet* is the one to look for in a set of company accounts, because that is the one that includes the company and all its subsidiaries. Accounts sometimes also include the parent company balance sheet. This can be ignored.

Looking at the table item by item, *tangible assets* are self-explanatory and are often represented by property and plant and machinery.

Intangible assets are sometimes included. These are often items that have a value, but one that is hard to measure. They can include contracts, mailing lists, brand names and the like.

In the current assets line we have *stocks*, which needs little further explanation, *debtors* (money owed to the company) and *cash*—again needing no explanation.

Creditors, money the company owes to others—bills for raw materials, duty to the government, perhaps a dividend to shareholders and so on—are typically not split up on the face of the balance sheet, but the detail given in a note. This is a touch inconvenient. The aim is to separate out short-term borrowings, trade creditors, and the rest.

Net current assets are simply current assets less current liabilities.

Total assets less current liabilities—sometimes called *net capital employed*—is another handy measure, the usefulness of which we will come to later. *Longer-term creditors* more often than not will be represented by borrowing and the detail again hidden in a note.

Provisions represent cash the company may feel it will have to pay out at some future date and against which it is setting something aside. The use of provisions, especially in the context of takeovers, can be controversial. This aside, though, many companies quite properly make provision to pay deferred tax—a tax liability likely to occur at some date in the future.

What is left over after all these deductions is termed *net assets*. In effect, they belong to the shareholders in the company and are therefore sometimes called *shareholders' funds*, or shareholders' equity. They are represented by the nominal value of the company's share capital, the share premium, which represents the value of shares issued at greater than the shares' original nominal value, and the company's **reserves**, including its accumulated retained profits.

There are a number of basic ratios that we will look at initially (some more complex ones will be looked at in Chapter 9).

KEY BALANCE SHEET RATIOS

The main ones I want to look at now are **gearing**, **return on capital** and current asset ratios.

Gearing is often used as a measure of the financial health, or rather financial risk, of a company. The normal definition is total borrowings minus cash expressed as a percentage of net assets. A typical gearing ratio might be in the 30–50% area. A figure of 60% may not cause too much lost sleep, especially if the business concerned is a stable cash producer, but gearing levels close to or in excess of 100% tend to be viewed with suspicion. This is

reserves: a notional balance sheet item represented by the company's assets and/or accumulated retained profits.

gearing: the percentage that total borrowings (minus cash) represent of a company's net assets.

return on capital: the percentage that pre-interest profits represent of capital employed (total assets minus current liabilities).

because more often than not they make the company concerned vulnerable to rises in interest rates.

Similarly, if interest rates are expected to fall, the shares of a more highly-geared company may rise disproportionately, because interest payments will fall and profits will rise, other things being equal. Balance sheet gearing is the counterpart to the interest cover in the P&L account. This is sometimes called income gearing.

Let's have a look at Universal Widgets' gearing figure. Assume for the moment that all of the figures for creditors, both within current liabilities and in longer term creditors, are represented by borrowing. The numerator of the fraction would be 40 + 80 − 12, the £12 m figure being the cash that is deducted before we divide the result by net assets. Hence gearing in this case is 108/202 or about 53%.

Another crucial measure of how well a company is doing is its *return on capital*. This shows the profits being generated by the business and compares them to the invested capital in the business. The convention is to take profit before interest and express this as a percentage of net capital employed; that is, total assets less current liabilities.

If this figure is less than the long-term cost of capital then there is clearly something wrong— because it is obvious that the company is not earning enough to sustain itself.

To calculate return on capital we need to go back to Table 3.1, the P&L account. Taking profit before interest as the top half of the fraction and dividing this by total assets less current liabilities gives a ratio of 50/292 or 17.1%. This would be regarded as satisfactory but not exceptional. Many companies manage to generate returns on capital in excess of 20% or even 30%, although the figure tends to be distorted by the timing of any revaluation of property assets and the like.

Profit before interest is taken as the numerator because net capital employed includes borrowings as part of capital, and therefore the interest attributable to it should not be deducted to arrive at the return.

The measure that excludes borrowings and interest is called *return on equity* and is defined as pre-tax profit divided by shareholders' funds and expressed as a percentage.

Purists take both of these calculations one stage further by calculating return on capital and return on equity, using as the bottom half of the fraction the average of two years' capital employed or shareholders' equity, reasoning that this better represents the capital that was in use during the year and which therefore generated the profit figures that are the top half of the fraction. It is hard to argue with the logic of this, but it makes the calculation somewhat cumbersome.

Last but not least, companies live or die by how quickly they get in their payments relative to paying their bills and by how much liquid resource they possess. One way to measure this is known as the *current ratio*. This is simply current assets divided by current liabilities. In the case of Universal Widgets the figure is 1.8 (72/40).

A more robust ratio to use is known as the *'acid test'* ratio. This is defined as current assets excluding stocks divided by current liabilities. This gives, in the case of our example, a ratio of 1.18 (47/40).

The reasoning behind this definition is that in extreme circumstances a company will find it easier to recover its other debtors than to realise the balance sheet value of its stock, which may only be in partly-finished goods.

If a company is viewed as being a forced seller of its stock, for example, it may have to discount it deeply to get any value for it, another reason for excluding it from this ratio, which measures the extent to which debtors and cash cover the money required to pay off short-term creditors.

Lastly, it is of course possible to express shareholders' funds as a value per share and compare this to the share price. This is known as book value or *net asset value (NAV) per share*. The shares in issue at the year-end are often used for this calculation. In this instance the book value is £202 m (net assets) divided by 200 m shares, or 101p per share.

HOW IS THE COMPANY PERFORMING?

As I mentioned above, there are a number of more sophisticated ratios that can be used, and we will cover these in Chapter 9. Nonetheless, the indicators described here will, when taken together and when viewed over a period of time so that a trend can be established, give a powerful sense of how a company is performing.

Are its margins rising or falling? Is it maintaining its rate of earnings growth? Is the trend in its cash flow at variance with the trend in profits? What level is gearing and has it been rising or falling over time? Is return on capital at a respectable level and has that been rising or falling over time? What does the 'current' part of the balance sheet look like and how has it been moving?

For those of a mind to do so, most of these calculations can be programmed into and saved in a simple spreadsheet that can be used over and over again. Boring though it may seem, I believe the relatively modest amount of time taken to extract the necessary numbers to calculate these ratios is time well spent for any investor. There is really no substitute for it.

Let's just recap and summarise the basic parameters needed to value a share:

- *Price–earnings ratio (share price divided by estimated future earnings):* Compare this with earnings growth and look for a PER significantly less than the expected rate of growth and that experienced in the recent past.

- *Yield (grossed up dividend expressed as a percentage of the share price):* Good growth stocks will almost certainly not have high yields. And of course yields rise and fall over time along with the general level of interest rates.

- *Total return:* What really matters in share investment is the likely price appreciation plus the return from the dividend. This is called total return. Estimate the appreciation by assuming that the company will stand on a similar PER to the current one in a year's time if profits come out as expected, and then add the implied percentage gain to the anticipated yield.

- *Cash flow:* Check that the company is not booking illusory profits by comparing cash flow from operations with operating profit. The figures need not be identical, but look for a divergence in trend.

- *Balance sheet:* Look at balance sheet ratios like gearing and current asset ratios in the context of the likely economic environment. High gearing may be an advantage if rates are likely to come down. If the environment is starting to get rocky, companies with liquid balance sheets will do best. Check that return on capital employed is a respectable figure.

UNIVERSAL WIDGETS: BUY OR SELL?

Let's look at how Universal Widgets stacks up on these criteria, assuming for the moment the price to be 250p.

Consider the facts:

- The shares have a historic PER of 20 times, but growth has been good and is expected to

PEG factor: *a share valuation yardstick that compares a company's price–earnings ratio to its expected earnings growth.*

continue at 25%. The PER/earnings growth ratio (sometimes called the **PEG factor**) is therefore less than one—a plus point.

- The yield is low, under 2%, but if the company maintains its growth path and the PER holds up, total return is going to be well in excess of 20%.
- However, cash flow is not healthy and is sharply diverging from the trend in profits. This could mean that the profits are being massaged. This is a black mark.
- Balance sheet ratios look healthy with gearing not unduly high. The current end of the balance sheet looks reasonably liquid.
- There is not, however, a lot of asset support for the share price. The price of 250p compares to the NAV per share of 101p.

Few shares that are worth buying have no minus points. The point is what weight you give to the pluses and minuses, respectively. But in the end you have to come to a decision one way or the other.

As I said earlier, you need not make this decision in isolation. It is equally important to look at the way the share price itself has been moving and what that can tell you about the possible future course of the shares. We will look at this aspect of investing in the next chapter.

IN BRIEF

- Analysing the fundamentals of company accounts is an important part of picking shares. Basic accounting knowledge can be picked up easily.
- Key measures of profitability are profit margins. These are the percentages the various levels of profit represent of sales turnover.

- Understanding cash flow concepts is central to investment. Cash flow can diverge significantly from profits and is almost always a more reliable indicator of a company's financial health.

- It is important for investors to understand the meaning of key balance sheet ratios like gearing, the acid test ratio, and return on capital.

- The importance of all financial ratios is less in their absolute level as in the trend they exhibit over a period of years.

- Valuing shares is best done by comparing price–earnings ratios with expected earnings growth, by comparing PE ratios and dividend yields with other similar companies, and by comparing the share price to the underlying value of the company's assets.

- The total return from an investment is measured by looking at its share price change plus its dividend yield. The income component of this equation can be significant and should not be ignored.

Analysing Price Movements: Timing your Trading

S hare price charts have an important role to play in alerting the astute investor to shares that look interesting and might warrant further research.

Conversely, interpreted properly, they can prevent an investor from making a badly-timed decision to buy or sell. Reasons that may look sound enough based solely on fundamental analysis can be overridden for a period until the charts look more auspicious.

Even though a share may look attractive, it could well be cheaper next week or next month, and using charts to get a feel for how the share price has moved in the past is a useful aid to better decision making.

There are those who believe that the charts are virtually all you need. For the moment we will disregard that view, although it does have some merit when trading particularly homogeneous products on a very short term basis.

For the purposes of this book, which is focused on investing in shares, I prefer to view technical analysis (charts) and fundamental analysis (number crunching and ratios) as two sides of the same coin—both equally important.

We covered the basics of fundamental analysis in the previous chapter. My aim is to do the same with technical, or chart, analysis in this chapter.

Just as there is a huge volume of written work on fundamental analysis, so the literature on chart analysis is equally voluminous. Price charts have been used for as long as there have been centralised markets for trading any commodity. Some techniques, such as candlestick charting (see later in this chapter), are known to date back as far as the 17th century.

What has sparked both professional and private investor interest in technical analysis is the ability offered by computers to chart share prices and their movements quickly and easily without fuss or repetitive manual labour. There are professional chartists who still like to keep a number of charts by hand, to 'get a flavour' for the way the markets are moving, but most individual investors are likely to find this approach unappealing.

We will look at what investment software packages do, and how they can help the investor, in Chapter 7. First it is necessary to have some understanding of the basics of technical analysis.

FIRST PRINCIPLES: UNDERSTANDING MARKET PSYCHOLOGY

As we saw in Chapter 2, one of the hardest aspects of investing is to discipline oneself not to fall prey to normal human emotions when buying and selling shares. Pride and hope have no place in investment decisions. Investing must be dispassionate.

For many, this is a hard skill to acquire. So, despite these strictures, the fact is that human emotions do play a part in the market. It is the quirks of human behaviour that can be observed in the way chart prices move.

The easiest way to explain this is by an example. Let's look at this in stages:

- Stage One: Let's say that you bought 1000 Universal Widgets shares at 100p. Imagine that the investment goes well and over the next few months the shares rise to 140p.
- Stage Two: Having made 40% on your money in a matter of weeks you might consider selling, but before you can, however, the market price starts falling back towards 100p, coming to rest at around 120p.

  No point selling now, you tell yourself. Wait until the shares go back up again.
- Stage Three: Let's say that the shares do just that. But as they approach 140p for the second time you have an interesting dilemma. When they reached this price before, some selling came in which depressed the price. Better get ready to sell if the shares hit 140p.

This intention to sell and the many similar ones made by other like-minded investors make the possibility that the shares will bounce back down from the 140p mark all the more likely. Almost, in fact, a self-fulfilling prophecy.

How other investors view the market can reinforce this too. Let's have a look at the situation from the standpoint of a different investor.

Imagine that he originally *bought* the shares at 140p a year or so back and had seen them fall back to as low as 100p in the meantime. He did not follow our earlier advice to cut losses quickly, but held on, hoping the shares would recover. But as they approach his initial buying price, the point where he can get out of the shares at no loss, the temptation to sell is overwhelming.

Imagine now that *you* successfully bought your Universal Widgets shares at 100p and sold them at 140p.

After selling at 140p the shares drifted down and again now stand at close to 100p. The temptation to buy again to try to repeat the exercise is also overwhelming, particularly if this cyclical pattern has been repeated more than once.

The very fact that several investors think this way and buy at around this price means that the shares will 'bounce' up once they hit 100p, perhaps triggering more buying interest from people who missed hitching a ride last time round. By the same token they may later bounce down from the 140p level for the reasons described earlier.

This mixture of the **herd instinct** and conditioned reflex can be very apparent on share price charts and buying and selling actions can clearly be timed to profit from them.

Some companies, generally the more mature blue chips, have share price charts that display pronounced cyclical patterns as the shares move in and out of favour with investors. The points at which investors collectively pause and think (and act) are known as **support and resistance levels**, for obvious reasons.

herd instinct: the tendency of investors all to act in a similar way at the same time, in response to an external stimulus.

support and resistance: price levels at which, based on past investor behaviour, buying or selling, respectively, is likely to intensify.

HOW SIMPLE TECHNICAL ANALYSIS WORKS IN PRACTICE

The operation of support and resistance levels is illustrated by the chart of Hanson plc shown in Figure 4.1.

Look at the period in the chart from mid-1994 onwards. After a steady (if laboured) upward trend the shares hit resistance at around the 250p mark and began falling. After a spell in the 225–240p area, the shares fell back further in late 1995, this period coinciding with the acquisition of Eastern Electricity, and worries over the group's gearing.

At around the 180–190p area the shares found support, a level that had previously proved

Figure 4.1   Hanson plc. © **Synergy Software**

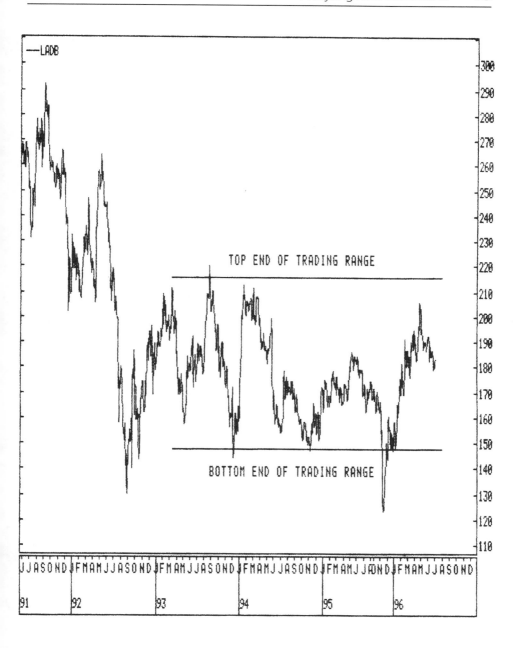

Figure 4.2   Ladbroke Group. © **Synergy Software**

sufficient—several times in the previous five years—to tempt investors into the shares. Investors saw the opportunity to make profitable trades buying at the support point. The hope was that the shares would go back up to nearer the point at which sellers had previously emerged. In fact this has not yet proved to be the case.

The objective of technical analysis is to assist in spotting the points at which profitable trades like this can be made. The decision need not be made irrespective of the fundamentals. Chart analysis can be used to time more precisely the purchase of a share that has already been identified as attractive on fundamental grounds.

reversal: a long-term change in the direction of a share price.

All technical analysis techniques are really geared to spotting turning points—sometimes called **reversals**—and making sure the investor makes the optimum decision when these occur. I mentioned earlier in this book the need for investors to have patience. Normally this means the patience to stick with a share until the idea behind a purchase bears fruit. But it can equally mean being patient enough to ensure that you do not hurry to buy a good share, but wait for the right price.

The method of using support and resistance does not work in all cases. The underlying fundamentals can change quickly and, if they alter in a major way, all bets are off.

Look at the chart of Ladbroke Group shown in Figure 4.2.

Many investors, myself included, have made money out of Ladbroke over an extended period, buying the shares at around the 150p mark and selling at around 200p. The shares reached 150p in late 1995 and the temptation might have been to buy.

profit-warning: a public statement from a company to inform investors that profits will be below earlier expectations.

Instead, the company issued a **profit warning** and the shares quickly fell to 125p. This might have marked the bottom of a new trading range, which would then have had its top end at around 150p, a new resistance point where all of the previous short-term buyers who were surprised by the fall would be looking to sell. At the time of writing the shares have broken back up through this level re-establishing the previous pattern.

There are a couple of lessons from both charts. The first is that trends and cyclical patterns are not necessarily reliable, and certainly do not hold good forever. When they do change, it is no good expecting necessarily that the old patterns will re-emerge. A fundamental reassessment has to be made, with the old assumptions cast aside and a new strategy formulated.

As the Ladbroke example shows, even when trading on the basis of cyclical price patterns, it pays to keep a weather eye on the underlying fundamentals. In Ladbroke's case the problem that caused share price weakness was National Lottery competition detracting from its core betting business. This is about as fundamental a change of scene as you can get, but equally an obvious point that the alert investor could easily have spotted.

Even in the case of an acknowledged growth stock that investors might feel should have a steadily rising price, it is important to remember that shares do not go up in a straight line. Often in instances like this they rise and fall successively, but each successive high point is higher than the previous one, and each low also higher than its predecessor.

Professional investors may even sell a share they like on fundamentals if they think the shares have got ahead of themselves, and buy back when they think they have lagged behind. For private investors, dealing costs normally make this a less fruitful exercise.

The process works in reverse too, with a share whose prospects appear to be deteriorating. The underlying trend may be down, but the pattern will be a zigzag rather than a straight line.

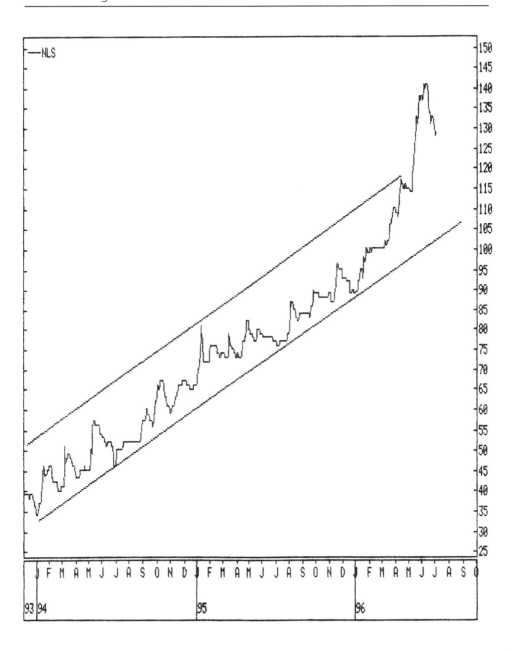

Figure 4.3 Northern Leisure. © **Synergy Software**

Figure 4.4   Enterprise Oil. © **Synergy Software**

trend channel:
the path formed
between two
parallel lines
joining successive
share price highs
and lows.

A good way of following a trend is by drawing one line through successive highs and another through successive lows. This should produce two roughly parallel lines, or a **trend channel**, delineating the boundaries of the pattern. It is important not to invent a pattern where none exists, but in many shares an established trend can be clearly marked out.

Look at the charts of Northern Leisure and Enterprise Oil since the end of 1993, respectively as good examples of an uptrend and a downtrend as you might expect to see (Figures 4.3 and 4.4). As an aside, it is possible to see that Enterprise bounced down off the earlier resistance level at around 500p. The breakout from the downtrend seen in early 1996 has been equally dramatic.

Northern Leisure has risen all the way from a low point of 6p to over 100p in a steady uptrend, with anyone selling on the way up (again, myself included, as I explain in Chapter 10) kicking themselves for their lack of patience and overzealousness in taking a profit.

All of these charts are simple line charts. They simply show the closing price of the shares on each successive day. But there are other types of chart format, which display different information. These are outlined in the next section. As we look at them, keep in mind the ideas of trends, trendlines, support and resistance.

DIFFERENT CHART TYPES

Line charts are a simple way of recording one piece of information: the progress of a share as measured by its closing price each day. But there are many other aspects of the way a share price moves that are useful to know too. For instance, it's good to have a record of the range of prices at which the share traded in the course of each day, and something which shows the volume of shares traded.

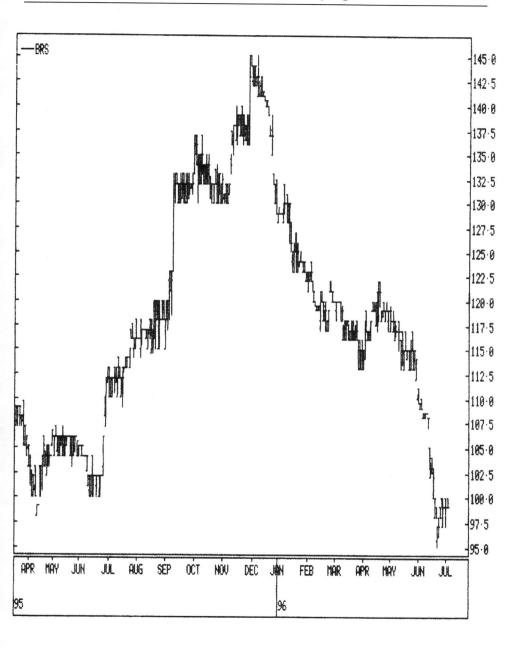

Figure 4.5   Burn Stewart Distillers. © **Synergy Software**

It is (or should be) intuitively obvious that if a significant move in a share is accompanied by a high level of trading activity, then that counts for more than if the same move occurred on next to no shares traded. If a lot of people are putting their money where their mouth is, it is usually worth paying attention.

US chart books often contain charts that display this information. They are known as bar charts. *Bar charts* show the daily high–low represented by a solid vertical line, with the closing price represented by a horizontal notch on the bar at the appropriate point. Volume is normally shown at the bottom of the page by a vertical bar. An example of this type of chart is shown in Figure 4.5 for the whisky company Burn Stewart Distillers.

A variation of the bar chart is the *candlestick chart*. This is constructed so as to give even more information. The candlestick is formed from two lines superimposed on each other. A thin line indicates the day's high–low range, while a thicker line shows the difference between the opening price and the closing price. If the shares have risen the candle is white; if the price has fallen, it is black (Figure 4.6).

Candlestick charts were first developed in Japan in the 17th century to plot the movement in the price of rice, and it is obvious from this brief description that they give more subtle degrees of information on movements in the price in the course of a single day than either of the preceding examples.

The other facet of candlesticks is that there are a large number of permutations of behaviour that can be illustrated by the charts, to many of which are ascribed a particular significance and (this being a Japanese invention) an evocative name.

More commonly used by professionals and amateurs alike is another different variation of chart, the *point and figure chart*. Point and figure

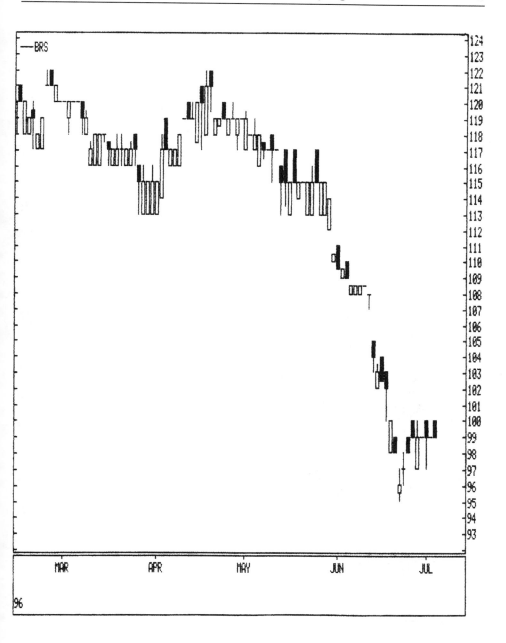

Figure 4.6   Burn Stewart Distillers. © Synergy Software

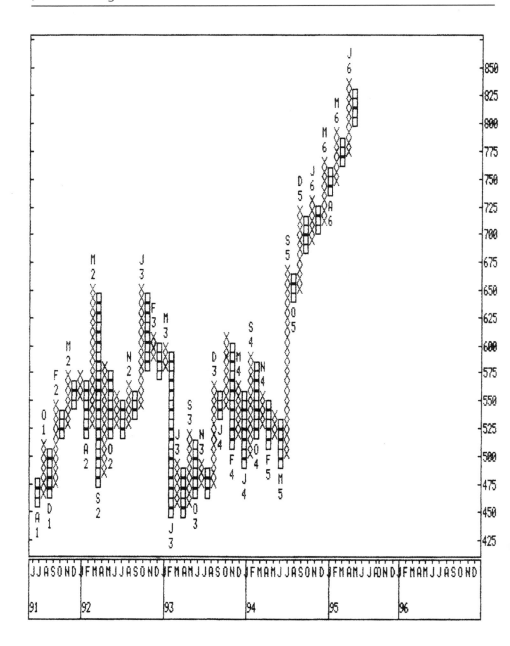

Figure 4.7   Bass plc. © **Synergy Software**

charts work on a different principle to the other charts described so far. They attempt to concentrate on the direction of a particular trend rather than the time it takes to reach fruition. They also have a method for filtering out insignificant movements in the price of a share.

This is best explained by a simple example.

A fragment of a point and figure chart for the drinks group Bass is shown in Figure 4.7.

The convention is that upward moves are presented by a column of crosses and downward moves by a column of zeros. The figures that crop up periodically in the chart—1, 2, 3, and so on—simply represent the start of a new month—January, February, March etc. The key to point and figure charts is that if a trend continues unbroken—i.e. the price moves up steadily, perhaps by different amounts each successive day with an occasional day with no change—irrespective of how long the process takes, the move is simply represented by a column of crosses (i.e. a single vertical line).

An important aspect of the point and figure chart is the size of price movement required to signify a change in direction and therefore a move to a new column. Clearly it is necessary to have a threshold below which a price movement is insufficiently large and can be ignored.

In 'heavyweight' shares—those with a price of, say, 500p and above—the threshold needs to be higher than if a share were priced at, say, 30p. In the latter case a ½p movement might be considered significant, while in the case of the £5 share, a move of anything less than 5p would be ignored. Hence, the legend on a point and figure chart will often say '5p reversal' or '½p reversal' to signify the size of change needed to alter the direction of the chart.

From this description of point and figure charts, you can see that they are likely to look somewhat different to normal line charts and bar charts, where each day has its own vertical column irrespective of how large or small the movement taking place. In a point and figure chart, upward or downward moves look more dramatic, especially if they continue over an extended period. Periods of indecision, with the shares gyrating up and down, produce broader patterns of noughts and crosses across the face of the chart.

It is in using point and figure charts that technical analysts often come in for criticism. There are any number of patterns that can be thrown up by such charts, and these are often given arcane names, producing a mystique that some feel gets in the way of rational interpretation. Hence 'double tops', 'head and shoulders tops', 'saucer bottoms', 'pennants', 'flags', 'wedges', 'triangles', and so on, are all supposedly detectable in point and figure charts, but equally on line charts too.

It is not so much the detection of the patterns on charts that is controversial, but the ascribing of predictive value to them, often to the exclusion of any fundamental analysis.

For example, to a head and shoulders top of the sort displayed in Figure 4.8 is ascribed predictive power as follows.

neckline: the level in a 'head and shoulders' share price formation which, if breached, may result in a substantial price movement.

The horizontal line is known as the **neckline**, with the shoulders and the head clearly visible above it. The theory is that if the share price breaks down through the neckline (and particularly if it subsequently rebounds and tries to break back up through it, but fails), then the downward move in the shares from there onwards will be numerically equivalent to the distance from the highest point on the chart down to the neckline.

In this example a decisive break down through 380p would be seen as a signal that the shares were headed for 280p, the neckline price minus the difference between the neckline and the high of 480p.

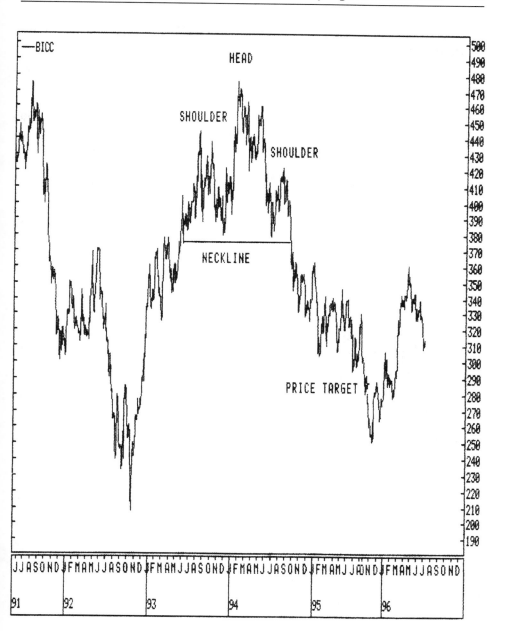

Figure 4.8   BICC plc. © **Synergy Software**

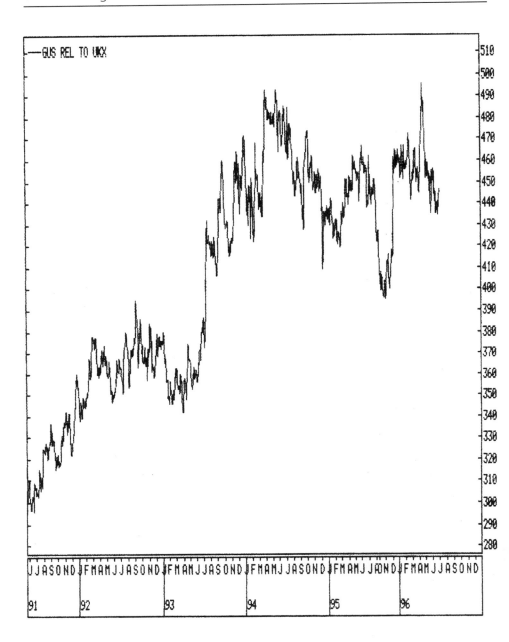

Figure 4.9   Price relative chart for GUS. © Synergy Software

It is also sometimes argued that the size of the downward move is related to the time period over which the top formed, in other words by the width of the formation as well as its depth. Others hold that this will govern the time it takes for the price target to be reached. In the case of BICC, the latter theory appears to have worked.

While it may be tempting to dismiss all of this as so much mumbo-jumbo, the fact is that rules like this often do work precisely because enough people in the market, professionals and amateurs alike, follow charts and react to their signals. This tends to make reality conform to the theory often enough for the true believers to retain their enthusiasm.

Lastly, many investors follow *price relative charts*. These show the price of a share relative to the movement in an index, normally either a market average or the index for the sector of which the share is a part. For instance, the price relative of Sainsbury might be calculated either with respect to the FT-SE100 or the FTA All Share Index, or else relative to the Food Retailing subsector index.

The price relative chart (as shown in Figure 4.9 for GUS) is calculated quite simply by dividing the one into the other, normally dividing the price of the shares by the value of the appropriate index on the same day. The interesting aspect of a chart like Figure 4.9, is that it gives a continuous guide as to how well or otherwise a share is performing relative to the chosen benchmark.

If the share price is rising faster than the index, or falling less slowly, the relative line will have a positive gradient; if the reverse is the case it will have a negative slope. Only if the shares are moving precisely in line with the benchmark will the line be horizontal. The most obvious use of a measurement like this is to spot when a share is moving out of (or back into) favour. This happens when the gradient of the line changes from positive to negative (or vice versa).

Care needs to be taken in making judgements on this score, though. What the private investor should be interested in is absolute performance.

Holding a share that outperforms because it goes down less than the market as a whole is a turn-off for most private investors. Positive relative strength is only really of interest to the investor if the general trend in shares is upward.

Before moving on from these different chart types to consider the various indicators that can be derived from share price data and the uses to which they can be put, it is worth making one general point.

In the USA, where charts are arguably more widely used by ordinary private investors than is the case in the UK, many chart books will juxtapose chart data with fundamentals such as bar charts of earnings per share and dividend payments. This re-inforces the view that neither 'fundamentals' nor the share price action should be viewed completely in isolation.

There is also the very sensible point that the more information that can be assembled, the better the decision is likely to be.

This is true even if charts alone are used. No investment decision should ever be made on the basis of a single chart or indicator in isolation. Different statistical indicators can be used for different purposes, but ultimately the best decision is likely to be made when several indicators flash a similar signal.

MOVING AVERAGES AND VARIATIONS ON THE THEME

It will probably surprise no one that share prices have always had a tendency to move around from day to day in a seemingly random fashion.

These day-to-day fluctuations, or 'chatter', in the price of shares is distracting to investors. They may alternately become encouraged on an up day, discouraged on a down day, and just end up puzzled.

One reason for the seeming randomness is that the market can exert a pull on a share price contrary to the way it might otherwise have moved. Produce some good news for a share in a day when the index falls 50 points, and the result may be a small fall in the share price. Conversely, bad news issued on a day when the market as a whole is strong might lead to no change in the price.

Large blocks of shares crossing the market on a particular day can distort the price, as can the positions that individual market-makers hold. The unwinding of large positions by market-makers often leads to sharp, and unpredictable, changes in the price of individual stocks.

In order to get a clear picture of how a share is moving, investors need to strip out these extraneous movements. One of the best ways to do this is via a *moving average*. The idea is that the share price each day for a period of days is taken and averaged.

Going back to Universal Widgets, let's say that the closing prices on ten successive days were as follows (in pence): 105, 106, 107, 107, 106, 100, 99, 103, 105 and 107. The average of these ten days is 104.5. Now let's say that on day 11 the price moved up to 110. The average of this price together with the preceding nine days is 105. It is possible to work this out by adding up all ten numbers and again dividing by ten. But the same effect is gained by taking the previous total and adding or subtracting the difference between the new day's price and the one 'dropping off' the other end of the sequence.

Now imagine this process being continued day after day for several months, with each day's price being added on, the tenth one back on the previous sequence being dropped off, and the result being averaged.

From the previous example it can be seen that despite fluctuations in the price, the change in the moving average from one day to the next is comparatively small. The raw price zigzags around the average. If the moving average line is viewed on its own it will represent a smoother picture of the underlying movement in the shares, with the day-to-day 'static' stripped out.

Moving averages can be calculated over a variety of time periods. The principle is that the shorter the average period, the closer will the moving average correspond to the underlying price. The longer the period, the smoother the trend.

For technical analysts and investors alike the significance of moving averages lies not in viewing them in isolation, but in watching both how they interact with the underlying price, and how two moving averages of the same share price but of different time periods interact with each other.

One use of this is to take the price and compare it with a long-term average, for instance the 200-day moving average. More typically, the method is to identify when a shorter-term moving average crosses a longer-term average when both are moving in the same direction.

Different pairs of time periods are traditionally used: the 20-day and 50-day averages are often compared, for instance, or the 30-day and 90-day. Better signals may be given in some stocks with different pairings of numbers.

'golden cross': the point at which a shorter-term moving average moves above a longer-term one, when both have recently resumed an upward trend.

The crossing points of moving averages are illustrated in the chart of BICC shown in Figure 4.10.

At the bottom of the chart it can be seen that the shorter average is moving up through the longer-term average and that both are themselves rising. This is normally construed as a very positive sign and is known in technical analysis circles as a **'golden cross'**.

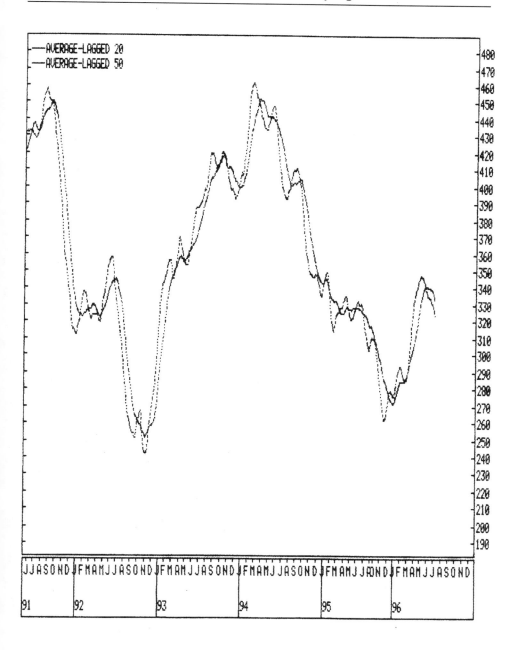

Figure 4.10   Crossing points of moving averages. © **Synergy Software**

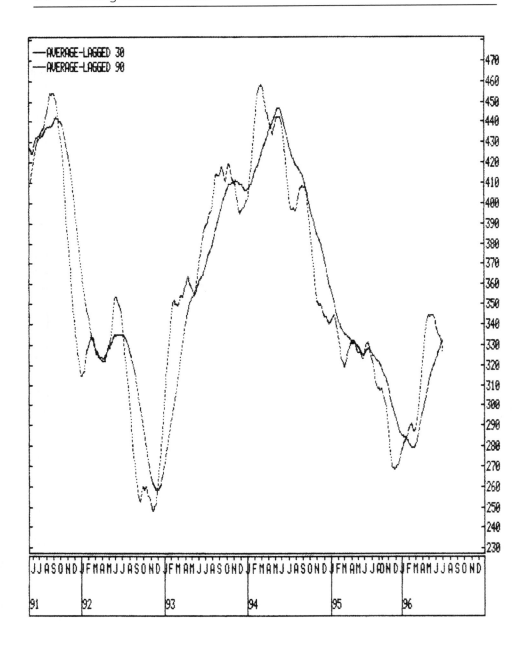

Figure 4.11   30- and 90-day pairing. © Synergy Software

The drawback of this approach is that if there is not much of a gap between the averages, in this case only 30 days, the lines tend to intertwine, and distinguishing which line is moving where is more difficult. A 30- and 90-day pairing on the same chart is illustrated in Figure 4.11.

As can be seen, the two lines can be distinguished more easily, but the drawback is that the signal of any turning point will be given that much later. The shorter-term pairing, on the other hand, may be quicker on the draw but will inevitably lead to an excessive number of trades that go nowhere and are quickly reversed, giving rise to excessive trading and higher dealing costs.

Observing moving averages, especially on shares that have displayed clear cyclical patterns in the past, can work well, but perhaps not by waiting until the signal is given. By then it may be too late, and the lion's share of the anticipated move may have occurred.

One way of getting some early warning that something may be afoot is to measure the gap between two moving averages. The *gap chart* for the 30- and 90-day moving averages of BICC is shown in Figure 4.12. Plotted on the same chart as the normal line chart, it would be seen to provide a somewhat earlier indication of turning points, with a possible buy or sell signal generated when the gap chart moves 30p apart and then changes direction.

It does not, however, give a sufficiently early warning to prevent trading taking place a little on the late side. Other indicators with more predictive power are required.

A variant of the gap indicator illustrated above is known as the moving average convergence and divergence indicator, or *MACD*. The principle is essentially the same but with the difference between the two averages drawn as a line chart, reduced to a

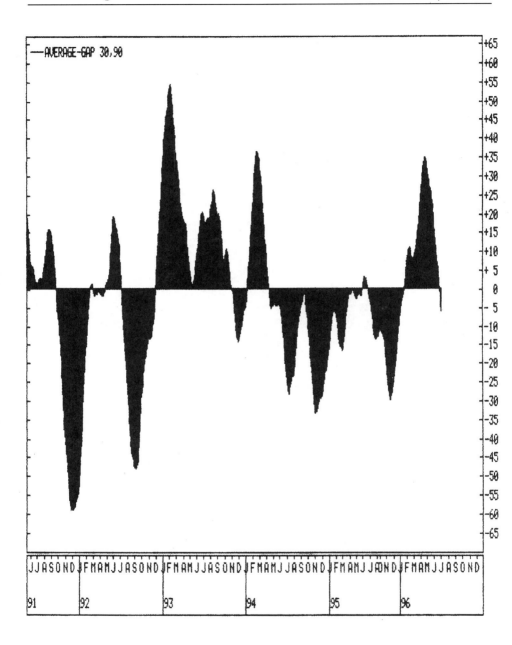

Figure 4.12   Gap chart for 30- and 90-day averages. © Synergy Software

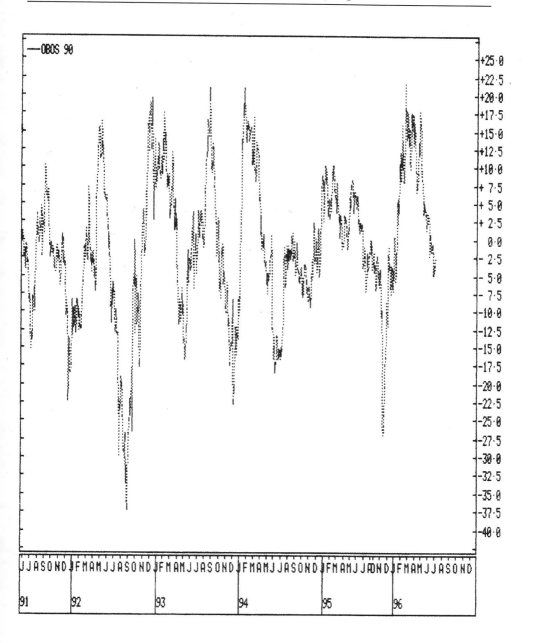

Figure 4.13   OBOS indicator for Ladbroke Group. © **Synergy Software**

trigger effect:
the use of
smoothing
techniques to
produce a line
which, when
intersecting with
the raw variable,
will give 'buy' and
'sell' indications.

base level of zero, and two differing time periods used to produced smoothed variations. Then, as with the moving averages themselves, the shorter-smoothed of the two will oscillate slightly more than the longer-smoothed, producing a **trigger effect**.

There are other ways of measuring momentum using moving averages. One of the simplest and most popular is the *overbought/oversold indicator* (OBOS). This measures the difference between the share price and a moving average. The particular type of moving average chosen is very important.

The idea is to strike a balance between a comparatively short-term average, which will produce a wildly fluctuating OBOS indicator, and a much longer-term average, which will move so slowly that the OBOS will simply tend to resemble the moves in the underlying share price.

Surprisingly often, individual share prices have a particular character. They will move either tightly or loosely around a medium-term moving average, with the price often swinging back once a particular maximum divergence is reached.

Look at Figure 4.13, which shows the OBOS indicator for Ladbroke Group, based on a 90-day moving average. As can be seen quite clearly from this chart, if the shares diverge by more than 15–20 points from the moving average, a reversal is normally likely. The reversal need not of course represent a marked change in the share price.

If, as was the case late in 1995, there is a sharp drop in the shares of Ladbroke and the shares stay at the new lower level, then gradually the reduction in the moving average (and therefore the narrowing in the gap between it and the share price) will eliminate the seemingly oversold indication on this chart. Where the OBOS indicator can work well is when it is looked at in conjunction with other indicators, including the current position of the price versus to past strong support and resistance points.

MOMENTUM AND HOW TO GAUGE IT

As most experienced market professionals will tell you, shares develop a momentum of their own. Spotting when upward or downward momentum is flagging is a good way of spotting the potential for a reversal in the share price, especially when used in conjunction with other indicators.

Those close to the market, traders who follow the prices of a small group of shares closely on a minute-by-minute and hour-by-hour basis, are the most likely to be attuned to changes in a share's momentum. But the phenomenon of share price momentum can be graphed.

The best analogy of momentum is a person bouncing up and down on a trampoline. The upward bounce will be quick in the early stages, slowing down rapidly as the maximum height is reached, and then reversing quickly as gravity takes hold. On hitting the trampoline on the way down, there will be a sharp drop in momentum back to zero and then an acceleration in upward momentum as the trampoline's springs do their work.

There are shares that are particularly prone to displaying these up and down movements, and there are also specialist (and expensive) software packages that can identify precisely how these cycles of momentum are formed and aim to profit from them by predicting their timing.

More common momentum indicators can be just as good, even though they may use less sophisticated mathematics. A simple *momentum* indicator will plot the moving change up or down in a share price over a period of days. A 21-day momentum chart, for instance, will aggregate the gains and subtract the losses seen in the share price over a 21-day period. The following day will drop the earliest change off and add in the new one. If the gain in the latest day outweighs the one made in the day now 'dropping off', the indicator will rise.

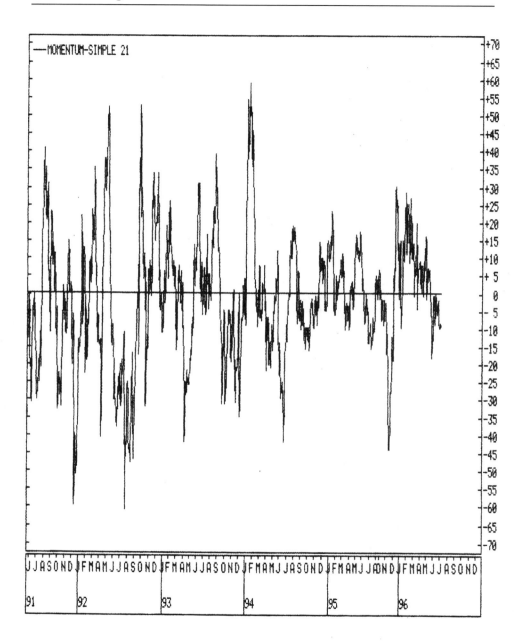

Figure 4.14 The 21-day momentum indicator for Ladbroke Group.
© **Synergy Software**

The 21-day momentum indicator for Ladbroke Group is shown in Figure 4.14.

An even simpler variant of this is the *Meisels indicator*. This indicator—named after its originator Ron Meisels, a Canadian stockbroker—simply adds up the number of 'up' days and takes away the number of 'down' days over a specified period, ignoring the size of the change that might have occurred in the price on any day. Taking, say, a ten-day moving period, the days when there are a net six plus or six minus days are comparatively rare. Out of ten days, for instance, this could only happen if there were eight up days and two down days, or vice versa.

When used in conjunction with other indicators, and support and resistance levels, the Meisels chart hitting plus or minus six can provide a good signal of a turning point.

A more sophisticated version of this is the *relative strength indicator* (RSI), sometimes called the rate of change (ROC) chart or the Welles–Wilder index, after its inventor.

This works on the same principle as the Meisels indicator, but aggregates the price changes over the period (normally 14 days). The index is then plotted as a percentage. If more than 70% of the aggregate change is upward, this is generally considered a sell signal. Conversely, a buy signal is generated if fewer than 30% of the last fourteen days' changes have been up (or 70% have been down). The signal is given when the indicator begins to reverse from this overbought or oversold territory.

The RSI oscillator is valued by technical analysts because, in a stock with pronounced cyclical tendencies, it tends to peak slightly ahead of the share price. No indicator works every time, but in conjunction with other measures, it can be a useful guide to timing trading decisions.

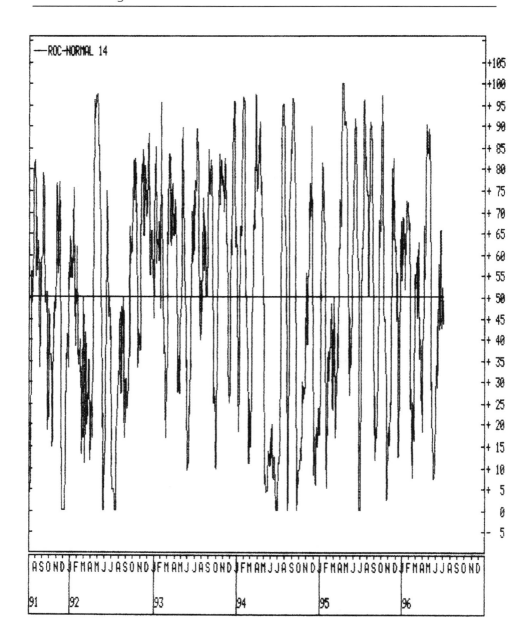

Figure 4.15 A typical RSI pattern. © Synergy Software

A typical RSI pattern is shown in Figure 4.15.

Another indicator that works well with share prices displaying strong cyclical tendencies is the *stochastic indicator*. Stochastics is a branch of statistical theory. But the idea behind it in this instance is comparatively easy to grasp. It measures the variation of a share price over time in relation to the high and low points for a particular period.

The explanation is as follows: at any one point in time, a share price will be sitting somewhere in a range of prices for, say, a 14-day period. The current price may be the highest point the shares have reached in the 14-day period, or it may be in the middle of the range of prices seen, or it may be the lowest point. The stochastic calculation simply expresses the difference between today's price and the lowest point for the period as a percentage of the difference between the high and low for the same period.

Let's take an example. Say that Universal Widgets' price over the past 14 days has ranged between 200p and 250p and the current price is 240p. The stochastic for this particular price is 80%. The price is 40p more than the low point for the period, 80% of the range of 50p over the period.

If on the following day the price moved up to 245p, the range would not change, and the stochastic measure would be 90% (45/50 times 100%). From this example it can be seen that when the price is at the high point for the chosen period the stochastic will be 100% and when it is at the low point, the stochastic will be zero. Fluctuations will be between these two limits.

Figure 4.16 illustrates a simple stochastic series.

As with moving averages, combinations of smoothed values can be used to produce a trigger effect to aid decision making. As also with moving averages, a valuable use of stochastics is to highlight divergence. If a share price moves up strongly

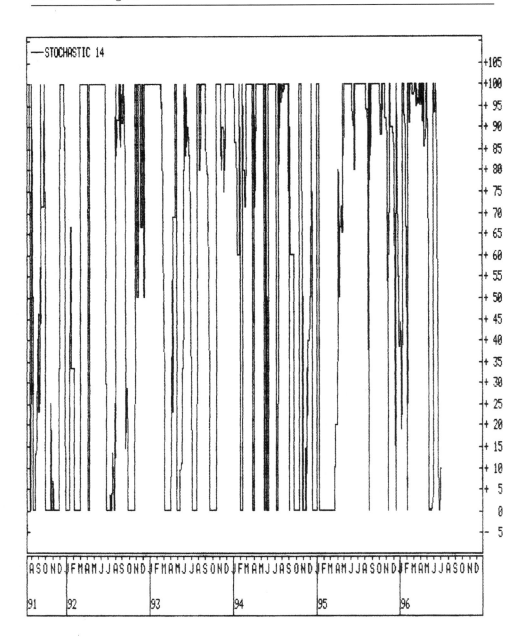

Figure 4.16 A simple stochastic series. © **Synergy Software**

but the stochastic fails to react, this may be seen as a sell signal, a sign that underlying momentum of the shares is contrary to that indicated by the share price movement. By the same token, a share price slump not accompanied by a significant move in the stochastic could be a sign that things are changing for the better.

CHARTS VERSUS FUNDAMENTALS

It should be obvious from the above that there is more to charting and technical analysis than meets the eye, and that the criticism that charts are simply concerned with the arcane identification of patterns on the random scratchings of the share price is ill informed.

Share prices can clearly be subjected to sophisticated statistical analysis and many traders can and do, with experience, make profitable trading decisions based on charts.

My own experience as an investor is that charts have worked well for me from time to time in certain phases of the market, and particularly when I have combined them with detailed fundamental analysis. Although trading solely on the basis of charts can and does work for some, one problem is the difficulty for the private investor at reasonable cost to get hold of real-time price information, and to be able to spare the time to sit watching a trading screen all day to spot profitable opportunities as they unfold.

Another factor is that many professional traders work on the tightest of margins and for the enthusiastic amateur the incidence of dealing costs and the difference between the bid and the offer price make frequent trading of this type a rather difficult way to make money.

Nonetheless it is clearly possible to use charts to make medium term trading decisions, and to use computer systems to take the donkey-work out of scanning the market for stocks that fit particular statistical patterns. With a normal 486 PC, scanning, say, 500 stocks to identify which displayed the symptoms of a 'golden cross' of 30- and 90-day moving averages takes a minute or two at most. Scanning the same list to find the stocks that were signalling oversold on other criteria, then looking at the stochastic and scanning that to find which stocks were standing at a low point takes the same length of time.

Scanning a combination of these indicators might yield only one or two stocks to investigate further. But as a filter it is an effective way of operating and will periodically highlight good investment opportunities.

We will look at the merits of different share price charting packages and how to download data for them in Chapter 7, as well as some more advanced technical indicators in Chapter 9.

But, assuming you have found a share to trade, the next chapter deals with how to go about selecting a broking firm through which to deal.

IN BRIEF

- Technical analysis, the study of share price movements, is an important part of timing the purchase and sale of shares that may have been picked out through fundamental analysis.
- Human psychology and conditioned reflexes play a part in the workings of technical analysis. These are often manifest in 'support' and 'resistance' levels at particular points in share price charts.
- Shares often move up and down in powerful trend channels. A break-out from a trend channel is considered a significant event, heralding a change in direction.

- There are many different types of price chart, often displaying subtly different variations of a basic pattern.
- Moving averages are a way of eliminating random short-term fluctuations from a price chart. The intersection of moving averages of differing length can be a significant indicator of changes in a share's direction.
- Momentum, the differences in speed with which a share is moving in a particular direction, are also used to time share purchases and sales.
- Using charts to time purchases and sales can be a frustrating business. It is particularly important not to use a single indicator as the guide, but to have it confirmed by several others.
- Using charts actively can induce over-trading. It is important to take into account dealing costs when working out the likely benefit of acting on a particular chart signal.

5 CHAPTER

The Mechanics of Dealing

For those who have never done it, dealing is part of the mystique of the stock market. Phoning up your broker, giving him the order to buy or sell your shares—what could be more exciting?

Nothing could be further from the truth.

The exciting part of investment is picking the right share, watching it rise, and selecting the right time to sell. The intricacies of how the deals are accomplished are mildly interesting but, once set up, are simply part of a routine that every investor becomes used to.

In short, it's what you buy (and sell) and when that's important.

The best way of looking at dealing is to use an analogy with the high street. There are many different types of shop: there are specialist boutiques, large expensive department stores, cut-price no-frills supermarkets, and many variations in between. There are shops where you are encouraged to seek advice and where the assistants are helpful and attentive—but where the merchandise is usually more expensive—and those where you might go because you know exactly what you want and a keen price is what you are looking for.

One of the factors that has traditionally put many people off the investment scene is the idea that share dealing is somehow the preserve of the rich, not something that ordinary people can indulge in.

The City bears its share of the blame for this. Certainly it was once the case that City brokers did not want to take on clients who were anything other than seriously wealthy. The idea of blue-blooded brokers having to deal with the man-in-the-street with his inconveniently-sized small lots of shares was anathema.

But times change. The opening up of the City to external competition, and the mass privatisations of the 1980s have brought many people into the share-owning arena for the first time, each with their own modest requirements for buying and selling shares.

The result has been some demystification of the City and its intricacies, and a lessening of the feelings of apprehension that many would-be investors used to get when contemplating buying and selling shares.

Another point is that the advent of the **Financial Services Act** has meant that brokers are now more tightly regulated than they once were. This does not stop share investments falling in value, of course. But it does mean that the investor is unlikely to be the victim of fraud or to lose money because his broker goes out of business for whatever reason. The client's relationship to the broker is enshrined in a legal agreement that defines the rights and obligations of each party.

Financial Services Act: the 1986 legislation that governs the conduct of City brokers, fund managers and personal investment advisers.

What this means is that the other more important aspects of choosing a broker—the level of service you feel you require; whether or not there are any specialist areas in which you might like to deal; settlement arrangements; whether or not you need advice—can rightly come uppermost in the decision-making process.

Let's therefore have a look at some of the issues involved in deciding between different types of broker, and some of the questions that need to be asked and answered.

AN HONEST BROKER . . .

If you read any 19th century novel, whether it be by Dickens, Trollop or some other author, the depiction of a stockbroker is usually of someone untrustworthy, devious and even dishonest.

This later gave way, typically in the 'Roaring 20s', to an image of tough and ruthless manipulators of markets, who sucked small investors into stocks at ever higher prices and then exited themselves just before the bubble burst. More recently, in the 1950s and 1960s stockbroking became identified with the epitome of suburban respectability, even to the point of lush suburban areas being known as 'stockbroker belt'.

More recently still, the image is of high-powered dealers paid 'telephone number' salaries and bonuses, and winning and losing millions (or even billions)—aided by sophisticated computer programs—as an increasingly volatile market moves up and down on a whim.

While all of these images contain some elements of fact, none is the whole story. There is no point denying that insider traders do exist now as in the past, that some stockbrokers even now have a less savoury reputation than others, and that—as the example of Nick Leeson demonstrated—for the high-fliers it can (and occasionally does) all go horribly wrong.

But just as there are accountants and solicitors whose work is less than satisfactory, and those who operate on the fringes of the law, they do not represent the vast majority of their professions. It is the same with stockbrokers. The vast majority of brokers, and perhaps especially those looking after private clients, are normal professional people dedicated to doing the best for their clients.

This is not to say that there have been no changes in the way the City has operated over the years. The advent of a greater degree of competition combined with the abandonment of the right to have fixed commissions in the mid-1980s, has led to a shake-out in the services provided by different broking firms. The end result has been specialisation by City houses. The broad division is along the lines of the clients they serve. Many broking firms, especially the larger ones, have opted only to service clients at the investing institutions and big companies.

The institutional investment and corporate finance business has often been combined with market-making and activities known as proprietary trading (where the firm risks its own capital trading in the markets).

Not only does structuring a firm like this involve high risks and high rewards, but overheads are also high, because the firm concerned requires the services of many hundreds of highly-paid professional staff and heavy investment in telecommunications, computer systems and other equipment.

At the other end of the scale is a large number of smaller firms, often based in the regions, sometimes with several branches, but with an office in London. These firms have typically chosen to specialise in dealing with private clients almost to the exclusion of other types of business.

Because firms of this nature normally fulfil a straightforward function to act as their clients' agent, they do not have the conflicts of interest that bedevil the larger **integrated securities houses**. For many of the latter firms, a private client business is viewed rather as an afterthought and certainly not integral to their business.

Private client brokers are not without their power in the market. Many have substantial

integrated securities houses: investment banks which combine stockbroking, market-making and corporate finance advisory activity, as well as trading on their own account.

numbers of clients and the collective funds of all these individuals can run into billions. Some private client brokers have also built niche corporate finance businesses, specialising in providing advice for the smaller companies that are also viewed by the big boys as too insignificant to bother with.

But the revolution in the City in the past few years has also brought other changes, including the creation of wholly new firms to service the private client market. These firms specialise in offering a highly efficient 'no frills' service and are often based in low-cost, out-of-town locations, maintaining efficient links to the market but able to offer discounted commission rates.

The growth of firms of this type has been facilitated by the fact that since the market 'went electronic' in 1986, there has been no need for brokers to be physically located in the City of London in order to be able to transact business.

As well as a number of distinct types of broking firm—large integrated houses not much interested in private clients; the private client specialist; and the large-scale no-frills dealing services—there are also a variety of different services open to the individual wanting to deal in shares.

These different types of service are outlined below.

. . . BUT WHICH SERVICE TO CHOOSE?

In the past broking services started from two assumptions. They are views that are still common, but now a little outdated. They are:

- that the broker is likely to know better than the client which shares are likely to go up and down;
- that everyone is likely to benefit if private client funds are managed collectively.

The belief behind both of these views is that the private individual is not really interested in the machinations of the stock market and would much rather delegate the job to a professional.

This has given rise to the assumption that the ideal and most economic structure for a private client broking firm is to have a relatively modest number of extremely wealthy clients (at the very least in the millionaire category) and for the broker to have absolute discretion as to how their funds are managed. This broker would probably only take on new clients by personal recommendation.

At the other end of the scale the newest category of broker is one who offers no advice, and is indeed precluded by regulatory statute from doing so, and simply transacts the deals as instructed by the client in the most efficient manner and as cheaply as possible. This broker would deal for anybody.

These represent the two extremes. In fact there is a range of permutations of style of service in between them. The range on offer is described briefly in the following paragraphs.

The *wholly discretionary* service means that the broker makes all the decisions for the client, acting on his or her behalf and only informing the client after the event. This has some advantages. The broker may be able to act quickly to take advantage of market opportunities and perhaps apply for exciting new issues on behalf of a group of clients, issues that an individual might be precluded from investing in directly.

For many investors the idea of surrendering total control is rather unnerving, and it is a moot point whether the performance of some brokers is any better than the investor might be able to achieve on his or her own with a little bit of effort.

One plus point for discretionary services of this type is that the broker is typically remunerated on the basis of an annual fee related to the total value of the portfolio. If the shares the broker selects do well, then this fee will rise. This provides a worthwhile incentive to get things right for the client and to a degree counters the concern that the account will be needlessly 'churned'.

The next tier of service is normally known as the *portfolio advice* approach. Here the broker is made aware of all aspects of the client's personal financial circumstances. Investment objectives will be set jointly and periodically reviewed. The broker may then be given limited discretion, or may offer advice to the client on how best to meet these objectives. In particular, there may be guidance on how best to invest in order to minimise any tax liabilities the client may have.

The charges for this type of service are normally a mixture of a fixed fee plus dealing commission, with supplementary charges sometimes made for services such as valuations and the preparation of tax statements for the Inland Revenue.

The stockbroking service that many investors will be most familiar with is the *dealing with advice* service. Here the broker earns most of his remuneration via dealing commission but will periodically inform the client when he has a particularly interesting investment idea, or a recommendation on a particular share.

Commission will be charged at a standard rate and the client will have a designated contact at that particular broker, with whom he or she can build up a relationship and who may be contacted from time to time for advice.

The point about this arrangement is that the relationship must be a two-way one. The client will wish to feel that he or she is getting a good service from the broker. And equally the broker will need to feel that the client is not wasting time and that orders result periodically from the service he gives. More frequent dealing on behalf of the client may be rewarded by the client getting a more thorough service from the broker, with the broker initiating calls disseminating information.

Basic research may be offered as part of the package. But the service will not as a matter of routine include any aspect of personal financial advice or tax minimisation. This service can be offered, but would be subject to extra charges.

The wholly new aspect to broking services introduced since the deregulation of the City in the mid-1980s is the idea of an *execution-only* broker. Here the client is offered simply a dealing service with no information or advice other than the quotation of a dealing price. On occasion, research may be offered on a cash or subscription basis, but the rationale of the execution-only broker is that the absence of any advice means that dealing charges can be kept to a minimum.

This type of service has proved very popular indeed with experienced investors who by and large pick their own shares, do their own research, and are prepared to accept the consequences of making their own decisions. It has also been extensively used by investors who have acquired small parcels of shares, perhaps as a result of privatisation issues, and simply need a broker occasionally when the time comes to sell a particular investment.

There are many brokers and share dealing operations advertising execution-only services, but not all of them offer truly discounted commissions. The choice is such that, if this is the route you choose to go, there is everything to be gained from shopping around and choosing the broker that offers the best combination of services at a price you are prepared to pay.

It is also worth remembering that while all the main high street banks now offer share dealing services, there is no obligation on anyone to deal through the broking service operated by their bank, although it may occasionally be convenient to do so.

A final and as yet fledgling category of service comes from those firms that offer *on-line dealing* via communications links, either through a private bulletin board system or over public networks such as the Internet and World Wide Web. These will be covered in more detail in a later chapter.

It is worth while stressing at this stage that on-line services are only as good as the dealing firm they are connected to, and that there is a considerable amount to be said for the personal contact represented by a telephone call to the broker. At the moment, services of this nature offer no significant savings in costs over existing telephone-based broking. They are unlikely to make much headway until they do.

Every broker's charging structure is different, but to give a rough idea, a wholly discretionary service might be charged out on the basis of an annual 3% fee related to portfolio value, a middling dealing with advice service might bear commission at 1.5% of the amount of money involved in a particular transaction, and an execution-only broking service would charge a flat rate commission on all transactions falling within a certain band, resulting in a commission charge of 0.7–1.0%. Some execution-only brokers operate low rates for frequent dealers and have an extra low rate for closing transactions (i.e. a sale following an earlier purchase) within a certain length of time.

THE 'JOB SPEC' FOR YOUR BROKER

The advent of much stricter regulatory controls on brokers, as well as the comprehensive training and examination regime that now exists for City personnel at all levels, means that while many people once chose brokers solely on the basis of personal friendship or word-of-mouth recommendations from trusted friends, this no longer applies.

Many brokers still do get new clients in this way. But, provided some elementary precautions are taken, it is perfectly possible to choose a broker almost at random and to pick one whose services are precisely right for you. Indeed, there are strong arguments in favour of not choosing a broker because of a personal relationship or as a result of the recommendation of a close friend. If things subsequently go wrong, personal animosity may be the result.

How does the individual investor, who may not have dealt in shares before, go about choosing a broker? A good starting point is a list of private client brokers produced by **APCIMS**. The list gives details of individual broking firms including phone numbers, addresses and brief descriptions of the type of service offered.

APCIMS: the Association of Private Client Investment Managers, a trade association for private client brokers (tel. 0171 247 7000).

From this list some initial selections can be made simply by answering for yourself a couple of elementary questions. The initial questions to ask are as follows:

- Question 1: Should I choose a small firm or a large one?

The answer to this is not straightforward. Large firms will normally have more robust finances and perhaps be better equipped to deal with all aspects of the service you may require. On the other hand, a smaller firm is better able to offer an individually tailored and more attentive service.

- Question 2: Should I choose a local firm or a London-based one?

This question really applies to investors who live outside London. My own preference here is to go for the local broker, provided you are satisfied that it can offer an equivalent range of services to a London-based broker, including the full range of dealing services and facilities to trade in a variety of different securities, not just straightforward equity shares. Many do.

Local firms have the advantage of being on the spot, so that any problems can be sorted out with a visit to the firm's office. They may also have a particular niche in researching the affairs of local companies, and have better information on these companies than some larger firms. Because of the electronic nature of the market, having access to the full range of prices and information on the wider market and its constituents does not present a problem for a **regional broker**.

regional broker: a small broker based in the regions but with, nonetheless, an electronic link to the market.

The next step is to whittle down the likely list to a handful that are hard to separate on most other criteria.

The way to do this is by specifying the types of services you would expect each firm on your 'shortlist' to be able to provide.

The following factors are particularly important (and the reasons are pretty obvious). If you have not decided in advance to go the execution-only route, the firm you choose should be able to offer:

nominee service: the service by which shares owned by an investor are registered in the broker's name, to ease administration.

- a full range of dealing services, including discretionary, portfolio advice, normal dealing with advice and execution-only
- commission rates competitive with the best in the market
- a dealing service in traded options
- a dealing service in overseas stocks
- a dealing service in fixed-interest stocks and convertibles
- an efficient **nominee service**
- approachable staff with a good telephone manner

- the ability to transact orders in the course of a single telephone call, or else at least an undertaking to phone back with a report within, say, 15 minutes
- the ability to provide portfolio valuations if requested
- the ability to provide managed or self-select PEPs on competitive terms if required

This 'job spec' for your broker raises a number of points that can be dealt with in turn.

WORKING OUT WHAT YOU NEED

In the first place, it is important that the investor has the opportunity to pass from one type of service to another without the inconvenience of having to change broker to do so. It may be, for instance, that an individual begins as a dealing-with-advice client of a broker and then, gaining confidence in the market, progresses to greater independence with a lower-cost execution-only service.

It goes without saying that commission rates should be competitive, although it is perhaps not always necessary to choose the broker offering the lowest commission rates.

When it comes to share dealing, as in most other aspects of life, you do get what you pay for. But equally it is important to weed out those firms offering an unreasonably expensive service. Some of these firms may pitch their commission charges high simply to discourage relatively small-scale investors, and it is as well to be alert to this.

Dealing service in areas other than straight UK equities should ideally be part of the package. It is certainly possible that at some stage the investor may want to deal in traded options, for instance (these will be discussed in brief in a later chapter), and the ability to do this without being forced to change brokers is important.

It is vital, for instance, for some types of option transaction, for the broker to be the same one through which one would deal in the ordinary shares of the same company. Not all brokers deal in options, so this is an important point to check.

Similarly, the investor may want the flexibility of being able to deal in the other markets if need be. These might include, for instance, buying American stocks or French shares. A broker should be able to offer a service that enables this to be done with the minimum of fuss, with details like safe custody, registration and currency all taken care of.

The ability to deal in non-equity share investments is offered by most UK brokers. There may be times, for instance, when the client needs to buy fixed-interest investments such as government stock, corporate bonds or convertible bonds.

Next on the list is that the broker should be able to offer an efficient nominee service. This is a mechanism by which the investor buys a particular share, but the purchase is registered in an account in the name of the broker's nominee company. This enables the broker to handle the administration of the stock concerned with much greater ease.

This has become an important issue in an era when settlement times are shrinking and do not permit the luxury of transfers being sent back and forth in the postal system when settlement deadlines still have to be met. The efficiency of brokers' nominee accounts varies and investors on occasion (and quite understandably) feel nervous that if the stock is not registered overtly in their name, they are laid open in some way to losing control of their shares or their money or both.

This is mistaken. There are strict codes of conduct governing the operation of nominee accounts, although it is worth while checking into the small print to satisfy oneself, particularly on the point that individual accounts are segregated within the nominee and not operated on a 'pooled' basis. It is also worth making doubly sure, as far as is possible, that the broker concerned is financially sound and has insurance backing to protect its own and the clients' interests in the event of any default. In the wake of the Maxwell scandal, this proviso is particularly important.

Above all, the operation of an efficient nominee should ease the administration burden for the client. The essential details to look for are:

- that the nominee account can be linked to a high interest bank account so that transfer of cash in and out of the nominee account can be made quickly and efficiently and that surplus cash is earning interest.
- that the account is designated in the client's name and not 'pooled'.
- that the shareholder receives normal documentation (i.e. annual reports) promptly from the nominee and can attend company AGMs without additional charges being levied.
- that the nominee account activity is conducted for a nominal fee and that details required for tax returns are provided promptly.

Charges related to nominee accounts are likely to be related to the number of stocks being looked after, but should not be more than, say, £10 or £15 per stock per year.

Nominee arrangements are fast becoming the norm in the City, particularly with the advent of electronic settlement, and the point will soon be reached where non-nominee arrangements are the exception rather than the rule, and settlement through these non-standard channels will either be unavailable or will cost more.

Although the efficiency of a nominee service is hard to gauge until it has been used for a while, an efficient nominee should work invisibly, with the client feeling he is still the shareholder and is in control of the nominee account, which the broker is administering on his behalf, rather than the other way round. This is not always the case.

Some brokers have for too long got away with bamboozling clients with jargon and with patronising them. An important test of a good broker is that their staff are approachable without being overly familiar, and that they are efficient, courteous and professional, putting the client at ease when he calls up, offering the appropriate level of advice unobtrusively, and dealing efficiently.

Dealing services also vary enormously in speed and efficiency. While it is acceptable to have to hang on to get through to a busy dealing desk at peak times in the market, inability to get hold of a dealer at any time is inexcusable. In most cases the dealer should be able to transact the deal while the client is holding on. This is especially true of execution-only brokers, many of which use automated computerised order-entry systems connected to major market-makers. In other cases, the broker should undertake to transact the order and report back by telephone within a matter of minutes if the client requests it.

order-takers: telesales staff employed by some brokers to act as intermediaries between clients and the dealers who execute their orders.

Some brokers operate through a system of telephone **order-takers**, who then collate orders and transfer them to the dealing desk some time later to be executed. The client does not get an immediate report back, and only discovers the dealing price when the contract note arrives in the post the following day. While many individuals accept service of this type as a fact of life, it is not necessary to settle for this, and the ability to report back that a deal has been done in a timely fashion should be perfectly compatible with, and indeed a particular feature of, an execution-only broking service.

portfolio valuation: service provided by a broker to bring the client up to date with the current value of his portfolio of shares.

Clients should also be able to order standard **portfolio valuations** if required, although these days it is easy enough to keep track of a portfolio of shares using a computer spreadsheet and a copy of the *Financial Times*. Certain information should be provided regularly as a matter of course. A statement of tax credits on dividends on shares held during a tax year should be provided promptly. An individual will require this to be able to complete his or her tax return. Small charges may be made for such services.

Lastly, it is important that the broker be able to offer the client the facility to invest in as tax-efficient manner as possible. In particular, most brokers offer the facility for the client to own shares through either a managed or self-select Personal Equity Plan run by the broker. Most brokers offer services of this type, but it is again as well to check that the charges made—which can vary considerably—are competitive.

HOW TO CHOOSE

The whole premise of this book is that it is perfectly possible for an individual to make his or her own decisions about investing on the basis of publicly available information and without excessive spending. In addition, it is worth bearing in mind that most private client brokers will only offer the discretionary and portfolio-advice style of service to individuals with substantial sums to invest. In this context the word 'substantial' means a minimum of £100000, and in some instances probably rather more than this.

What this means is that to all intents and purposes for the individual with, let's say, £20000–30000 to put into the market, the choice comes down to the dealing-with-advice or the straight 'execution-only' service. My own preference is for the execution-only type of service in virtually all respects.

However, it is perfectly normal for the first-timer to want to have some initial guidance on how to deal and on the ins and outs of the market. It is possible to some degree to get this from an execution-only trader, who may be able to help with factual questions. An execution-only broker is precluded by City regulations from offering any sort of advice, so do not ask an execution-only dealer for views on where the market is heading, or what he thinks about a particular company. He will not be allowed to help.

But, for most investors of an independent turn of mind (and an independent turn of mind is actually in my view a prerequisite for being a successful investor) execution-only dealing fits the bill perfectly.

There is one exception to this. This concerns dealing in traded options.

We will cover this aspect of the stock market in a little more detail later in the book. But at this stage let's just say that the newcomer to the options market will benefit from having a measure of advice for the first few trades, before switching to an execution-only service at a later date.

Paradoxically, option trading is one area of the market where doing one's own research is essential, but some preliminary hand-holding may be necessary. Even with a good idea, many investors buy the wrong type of option, lose money and are put off trading options for life because of it.

In the end, the reason for choosing one particular broking firm over another will be an entirely personal one.

The best way to go about it is to contact several, either by letter or telephone, and request further information. Most brokers have a brochure that they will send out to prospective clients.

Execution-only firms like Sharelink, Fidelity and City Deal are all approachable and down to earth. Consulting the pages of the *Financial Times* or the

Investors Chronicle should yield a satisfactory number of names and phone numbers. A standard letter sent to each one is probably the best approach and minimises the feelings of apprehension that someone new to the market may feel about telephoning a broker 'cold'.

My preference would be to ask for a face-to-face meeting before signing up. It is always good to get a visual feel for the nature of a particular operation: how friendly the staff are, how efficient and functional the offices (you do not want your commissions paying for unduly lavish offices) and how efficient the broker's systems.

Many brokers include with their brochures a questionnaire that will help the potential client decide what type of service he or she requires and help the broker to decide what type of service it will be economical to provide. It is important that you are not persuaded by the broker into signing up for a level of service with which you are not happy.

Once the final shortlist has been whittled down to one, and this fact communicated to the broker in question, the normal next step is to fill in a **client agreement form**.

This establishes client records for the broker, and will include such details as your address, telephone number, bank details and so on. It also represents a legal agreement between the broker and client, establishing the rights and obligations of both sides. The client agreement is required under City regulations and is designed to safeguard the interests of the client by establishing the ground rules of the relationship at the outset.

Among other things, it assures the broker that he will be paid for stock purchased by the investor, and vice versa. It will also be used to set up such details as a nominee account and, if necessary, a bank account linked to the dealing account.

client agreement form: *a form which establishes the contractual relationship between a broker and a new client.*

Once this form is completed and the paperwork has been processed, the client will be informed in writing and given an account number. If the account is an execution-only one, there will be no designated contact but the client will be given a telephone number, often a toll-free one, to call when he wishes to place an order.

The really important point about all this is that the process of dealing should not get in the way of investment decision making. The investor must be comfortable with the broker and confident that deals will be executed promptly and efficiently.

Calling your broker should become a routine matter that can be done with confidence. Making the right investment decision is the important part of the process. The physical act of dealing should be no more or no less complicated than ringing a theatre box office or an airline to book some tickets.

HOW TO DEAL . . . AND WHAT HAPPENS AFTERWARDS

Dealing in shares is essentially simple. Ring up the broker, give your account number to identify yourself, say you want to place an order. The dealer will ask what you want to do. Let's say you want to buy 1000 shares in Universal Widgets.

bid (offer) price: the price at which a market-maker will buy stock from (sell stock to) a broker. The offer is the price at which the client can buy shares and the bid the price at which he can sell.

Enquire what the price is in Universal Widgets. The dealer will check the price on his market price display screen. Say you know that the price is around 200p. The dealer will quote the price back to you as two figures. The lower price, known as the **bid price**, is the price at which you would be able to sell; the upper, or **offer price**, is the price at which you can buy.

The difference between the two is the spread, representing the 'turn' the market-maker keeps for making a continuous market in the shares. The dealer comes back on the line and says '198–202'. You ask the dealer to buy 1000 shares.

The dealer will ask if you want to place a limit on the price at which you want to deal, in case the price has moved in the few seconds that have elapsed since the price was checked. Placing limits is not, in my view, a particularly good idea unless the share price is gyrating wildly. You have made the decision to buy and your objective is to buy the shares in the market at the best price available at that time. Wanting to set a dealing limit may be a sign that you are less than wholly convinced that the decision is the right one.

You can simply say 'buy (or sell) at best', and the dealer will execute the order for you there and then. You can either hold on while the order is done, or ask the dealer to ring you back with a report on the price at which he has dealt. Before transacting the order the dealer should always read it back to you for confirmation: 'Buy 1000 Universal Widgets at best'. The report will simply come back: 'Bought 1000 Universal Widgets at 202p'.

What should happen next is that in the following morning's post a contract note will arrive stating the time of the deal, the number of shares involved, the price, commission and any other charges and the net cost to you of a 'buy' order, or the proceeds of a 'sell' order.

Assuming that your broking account is linked to a bank account, your account will simply be debited with the amount stated five days from the date of the deal. Sale proceeds will be credited in the same way. The broker, assuming you have an account with the nominee, will hold the share certificates on your behalf, sending you statements of your nominee account holdings from time to time. All that remains to be done after that is to keep track of the price via teletext or a newspaper every day to see how your shares are doing.

CREST: the computerised settlement systems for UK equities introduced in July 1996.

Settlement for share purchases currently works on a rolling basis with deals done one day being settled five business days later. An electronic settlement system known as **CREST** has been launched (from July 1996), which will progressively remove most of the paper flows related to share settlement.

This means that it will become more important for private clients to have nominee arrangements with their brokers. Contract notes will still be issued and these, together with the periodic statements of holdings that will be issued to clients as part of the CREST system, represent all the proof the client will need to demonstrate that electronic records are correct. Share certificates will eventually become a thing of the past.

It is planned thereafter to take share settlement down to trade date plus three days (T+3). Alternative arrangements will be available for those who wish to settle on different terms and who wish to remain outside the paperless system, but those options are likely to be relatively costly.

Although many private clients, especially the more elderly, are not keen on nominee arrangements or the idea of 'paperless' settlement, the system is likely to prevail and those new to the investment game are unlikely to give it a second thought.

So far we have looked at how the market works, what personal skills and physical tools the investor needs to be able to make investment decisions, and at how to appraise shares using both fundamental analysis and share price charts. We have also, in this chapter, looked at how to choose a broker and the mechanics of buying and selling shares, and at how these deals are settled.

It is time now to look at how to build up a sensible portfolio of shares and measure its performance. This is covered in the next chapter.

IN BRIEF

- The mechanics of dealing are mundane and should be put in perspective. The important aspect of investment is how you select a share and how long you keep it, rather than how you buy and sell.
- There are several different types of broking service. The more the broker holds your hand, the more he will charge.
- The premise behind this book is that the reader will be capable of making his or her own investment decisions and therefore can opt for a low-cost, execution-only service.
- Charges vary and it is worth while shopping around. Beware of hidden extras.
- It is essential that investors pick a broker that has a well-organised, properly protected nominee service. This simplifies the administration of share transactions considerably.
- Choose your broking firm carefully, if possible through a personal visit.

Designing your Portfolio

I made the point in an earlier chapter that the amount the average investor should have available to invest in the stock market is governed by the need to have a spread of investments to limit risk. In this chapter we are going to look at the reasons why this is important, and how to go about building up the right mixture of shares.

Although ordinary shares may seem the most important and eye-catching part of the investments you may have, they are likely to be only a part of your overall assets.

For instance, just as we might look at a company and examine whether it has liquid assets or not, or how much borrowing it has relative to its assets, so the individual investor needs to construct a personal balance sheet to determine what type of investment strategy is most appropriate.

YOUR PERSONAL BALANCE SHEET

Let's take a couple of examples to make this clearer.

Fictional Investor Number One

Like our earlier example of Graham Average he might, say, be a 50-year-old married professional person. Perhaps he works as a self-employed consultant. His children are grown-up and no longer a drain on his income.

He lives in a house that is worth £250000 on which, because it was bought many years previously, the mortgage is only £50000. He recently inherited a property worth £75000. From the sale of his stake in an earlier business venture he has capital of £50000. His income from consulting and his wife's earnings comfortably cover all of his outgoings. He is contributing to a personal pension. This is invested in a unit-linked vehicle and has a value of £200000.

What investment strategy should this person pursue? To determine the rght course of action we need to work out what net assets he has already.

These can be listed as follows:

- equity in the main property of £200000
- equity in the inherited property of £75000
- free capital of £50000
- £200000 invested in a pension fund
- Last, but not least, no immediate requirement for investment income

What do these figure tell us? One fact is that the **free capital** that might be available for share investment represents quite a small proportion of the overall total. This individual's total assets are in excess of £500000, but only £50000 of that is actually available in cash.

Another important fact is that the pension scheme assets are likely to be conservatively invested. Although individual circumstances differ, there is by and large a duty on pension fund managers to invest conservatively. Moreover, in the wake of the Maxwell situation, this requirement on fund managers is being tightened up, especially for managers in well-established corporate pension schemes that have a lot of pensioners.

free capital: the amount an investor has available to invest after all other commitments and contingencies have been provided for.

It is likely, therefore, that the pension portion of the assets will be invested in a mixture of leading blue chips on the one hand, and government stock or safe fixed-interest investments on the other.

One might question whether keeping the inherited property is a sound investment decision. It may be being rented out to give an overall return of say 8%, but the individual needs to be conscious that in an era of low inflation, its value may not rise and its total return may therefore be inferior to other forms of investment. So whether or not to keep this property is an investment decision in itself.

The conclusion from this brief résumé is that this individual could profitably invest in smaller growth companies. The stable, though arguably unexciting, return from property and the fact that the pension fund assets are also invested conservatively, combined with the absence of any requirement for income leads to this decision.

Fictional Investor Number Two

Like our earlier example of Aunt Agatha, she is a widow who has a modest pension, just enough to live on, but somewhat less than she was accustomed to before her husband died. Let's look at her assets:

- the pension brings in an income of £500 per month
- she owns her own home, a modest house worth £100 000
- her husband's life assurance brought her a capital sum of £200 000
- there is an obvious requirement for investment income

It can be seen quite clearly here that the circumstances are entirely different. It is important to this investor that capital is preserved, but also that it generates income, whereas our self-employed professional has plenty of income and assets already locked away in conservative investments.

So, given the relatively low return from property, it would be sensible for this individual perhaps to move to a smaller property, and release some capital for further investment. Her investment decisions may also be influenced by whether or not the pension is likely to rise with inflation. If not, some route must be found to produce an inflation-proofed investment income while attempting to preserve capital.

What both investors have to come to terms with is that there is a link between the return that an investment generates and the risk involved. The higher the return offered or perceived, the likelihood is that the risk of some loss of capital will be higher. As the disclaimers on most forms of investment say: 'the value can go down as well as up'.

Another point is that there is a link between liquidity and return. **Liquidity** is the ease with which an investment can be turned into cash without penalty. The best illustration of this is the difference between the interest earned in a so-called high interest bank cheque account, and that earned on, say, a building society deposit that requires three months' notice. When I last checked, for example, the former offered annual gross interest of 1.7% and the latter 6.5%. The difference represents the price of instant liquidity.

liquidity: the ease with which investments can be bought and sold.

Also, remember that investments such as property are notoriously illiquid. They may offer a seemingly high income return but they have to be sold through a cumbersome and time-consuming process. Neither can they be part-sold. Either you sell all the property, or you don't sell. No way has yet been found to sell half and keep half, as share investors sometimes do to protect a gain.

Lack of liquidity in a share is unlikely to trouble most modest private investors. But smaller company shares are harder to buy and sell in quantity than those in leading companies, for obvious reasons. This is often manifested in greater volatility and in a wide spread between the bid and offer prices quoted for the shares, which can affect the profits or losses investors make.

INVESTMENT CHOICES AND MARKET TIMING

Although this book started from the premise that investment in shares should only be conducted with money surplus to immediate requirements, it can be seen that in reality the process isn't really as simple as that.

Decisions need to be made at the outset about the following:

- How important share investments are likely to be in the context of an individual's total assets, including equity in property and accumulated pension contributions.
- Whether or not investments are required to produce income while preserving capital.
- Whether or not investments are required to be relatively liquid in order to be available to meet unforeseen events.

Let's assume for a moment, though, that you are in the position of our first individual. Reasonably well set-up, you have decided in principle to invest your surplus £50000 in small companies in the hope of making better-than-average returns.

What is the next step? Well, one advantage that private investors have is that they don't need always to be 'in the market'. The professionals have to invest come what may, because they have regular and substantial flows of cash that must be allocated to some form of investment. The investor, pondering what to do with some surplus capital, faces no such pressures.

So the first point is to make sure that the timing is right for investing in shares. Bear in mind at this point that the stock market normally anticipates (or, as the professionals say, '**discounts**') events that are likely to happen in the future. The economy may be booming, but if the market—that is, the aggregate of all investors, both professional and private—comes to believe that boom is soon likely to turn to bust, then the market will begin to fall.

'discounting': the process by which the market anticipates events and adjusts the price of a share accordingly.

Market timing is a subject in itself, and being too cautious is a recipe for missing out on substantial potential gains. But there are certain good indicators of different phases of the market that should be kept in mind.

It is as well to be aware, for example, that:

- Sustained increases in interest rates are generally bad for markets; the prospect of steady interest rate reductions are bullish.
- Periods of great popular interest in stocks and shares, and especially speculative ones, generally presage a downturn.
- When interest rates are high, the economy stationary and some topic other than the stock market is dominating the conversation, it is usually a good time to buy shares.

Let's short-circuit this process and say that our investor has decided that the time is right and that he wishes to get involved in the shares of smaller speculative companies. Although each of the companies in which he chooses to invest may be risky individually, it is possible to structure things so that the risks inherent in each one are offset, or at least reduced, overall by the spread of investments chosen.

This sounds obvious. In other words buy shares in, say, six different companies and risk is automatically reduced. Right?

Wrong.

It is vitally important to make sure that the constituents of the portfolio are as diverse as possible. Why? Because if that isn't the case, the adverse factors that affect one will affect the rest.

Say, for instance, you believe that a particular drug company has developed a cure for cancer. You believe the share price will go sky-high on the news.

Now think about it a little more. It could be good to hold the shares, but it might be risky if at the same time you held other drug companies.

Why? Well, although the other shares might move higher in sympathy, they could be developing competing products that would suffer if their competitor proved to have the magic cure. Equally, if the drug proves not be effective, or has unfortunate side effects or provokes the authorities to regulate the entire drug market, all of the shares in that sector will suffer.

The best strategy in these circumstances is therefore to pick the best share in each of a number of different sectors, rather than to go all-out for one particular area. In other words, as the statisticians would say, avoid having two shares whose businesses are closely correlated.

This has to be tempered by the fact that different groups of sectors do move in sympathy at different phases in the market's cycle. For instance, those sensitive to interest rates tend to move first, followed by consumer goods, manufacturing and finally— late in the cycle—commodity-based companies. But this formula does not work in every cycle, or at every point in every cycle, and companies within sectors can of course buck the overall trend.

While we noted earlier that good investments tend to have in common the fact that they offer 'something new', the nature of that special ingredient can differ in the case of different shares, and mixing different types of unique selling point in different shares may also help to lower risk.

For example, let's say you have four shares. One is a drug company with a new wonder drug; the second is a down-at-heel manufacturing company with a dynamic new chief executive; a third is a pub company benefiting from structural changes in its own industry; and the fourth is a bus company benefiting from privatisation. We have something new in all cases: innovation, management change, structural change and legislative change.

All are legitimate reasons for investing, and all of the companies are in different industries; most importantly, none of the potentially adverse factors for one is likely to affect the others.

SMALLER COMPANIES AND PORTFOLIO RISK

There are other aspects to portfolio diversification.

One is that buying a single category of share can increase risk, and rewards. For example, smaller companies' shares tend both to rise and fall faster than the market as a whole. Smaller companies generally outperform over time, but tend to do particularly well in the later stages of bull markets, and perform badly in bear markets. Simply buying smaller companies alone can increase risk.

This is not to say that the risks are not worth running.

Having a disparate portfolio when investing in smaller companies is only prudent, because greater concentration can be disastrous. But also, having spread the portfolio, making a conscious decision to invest in smaller companies because, for instance, you feel the market is likely to be buoyant and that smaller companies have been left behind, is a legitimate tactic.

It should be recognised, however, that this tactic involves a greater degree of risk than, say, mixing some small company investments with those in the shares of bigger, more solid organisations.

There are some other important aspects to portfolio diversification and risk control.

One is to make sure at the outset that each investment is of a standard size. In other words, you should have a standard **dealing 'unit'**. If you have £40 000 to invest and want to invest it in a maximum of eight companies, make sure each investment is roughly £5000.

This simplifies making decisions, particularly if investments fail to perform, since the decision making process is not complicated by the fact that different portfolio constituents are of markedly different size. Those with £5000 to invest might use units of £1000.

Equally, it is important to have a pain barrier, or 'stop-loss', a point beyond which an investment is automatically sold without a second thought. In my own investment decisions I have tended recently to work with £5000 dealing units and more often than not to sell if any investment lost more than £500. If you have made the decision to buy correctly, then a 10% fall in the price should not happen.

Table 6.1 shows stop-loss levels for shares of different prices. It is important to bear in mind, however, the influence of dealing costs and the **bid–offer spread** in the stop-loss process.

For instance, using a 10% stop-loss, the overall effect of cutting a loss on a £5000 investment with the shares priced at 50–54 would be in the region of 20% after allowing for the spread and dealing costs. Dealing costs are a comparatively minor part of this equation. There is really no way round this problem.

On the other hand, if an investment rises sharply in value, it is also important to keep an

dealing unit:
the normal amount of money an investor will allocate to invest in any one share.

bid–offer spread: the gap between the current buying price and the (lower) selling price for the same share. A factor when working out the effective cost of trading a share.

Table 6.1 Impact of Bid–Offer Spread and Dealing Costs on Stop-Loss Position

These are the prices at which you can deal (illustrative):

Spread on:	50p stock is	250p stock is	500p stock is	Dealing costs (Fidelity Active Trader)			
				Purchase	Sale	Stamp Duty	Total
Dealing unit	48–50	247–50	495–500	£	£	£	£
Stop-loss middle price is	45	225	450				
But allowing for spread . . .							
£5000 . . . sell at . . .	44	223	447	50	15	25	90
so loss is . . .	£600	£540	£530				
£3500 . . . sell at . . .	44	223	447	20	15	18	53
so loss is . . .	£420	£378	£313				
£1000 . . . sell at . . .	44	223	447	15	15	5	35
so loss is . . .	£120	£108	£106				

So total loss on a 'stop' set 10% below original offer price is:

Loss	Stock type	50p stock	250p stock	500p stock	Adding dealing costs of:
Dealing unit					
£5000	Absolute	£690	£630	£620	£90
	%	13.8	12.6	12.4	
£3500	Absolute	£473	£431	£366	£53
	%	13.5	12.3	10.5	
£1000	Absolute	£155	£143	£141	£35
	%	15.5	14.3	14.1	

eye on the balance of the portfolio. This is a good problem to have, of course, but thought should be given to making sure that there is a strategy in place, if a share becomes a heavy portfolio constituent because it has risen rapidly, that covers how and when to sell if its performance starts to falter.

OTHER WAYS TO DIVERSIFY

So far we have looked at the idea of diversifying risk solely from the standpoint of investing in ordinary shares. The rationale of this book is to examine all aspects of investing in shares, and other titles in the 'Getting Started . . .' series cover other forms of investment. But it is impossible to discuss the concept of portfolio diversification without at least mentioning the role that other types of investment can play in adjusting the risk in a portfolio to more acceptable levels.

When making a statement like this the implicit assumption is that the risk should be reduced, but it is possible to use alternative forms of listed investment to increase the risk profile, and therefore the potential return, on (say) a portfolio of unexciting blue chips.

We will therefore touch in brief below on various different types of investment alternatives to ordinary shares and their role in increasing or reducing portfolio risk.

Let's start from the assumption that the investor has £50 000 to invest in total, and currently has £30 000 invested in a mixture of large blue chip companies and more speculative smaller companies. If this sounds too grand a figure, it could just as easily be divided by ten, and the same principles would apply. We will outline the diversification strategy that could be pursued and its impact on portfolio risk and income.

Strategy One: Keep the Balance of £20 000 in a Bank Deposit

This strategy has the advantage of retaining liquidity in order to increase investment in other areas at short notice if the need arises. Interest rates on bank deposits are, however, lower than virtually all other forms of fixed-interest investment. And simply leaving cash in a bank deposit has no dynamic impact on portfolio risk.

Strategy Two: Invest the Balance of £20 000 in Government Securities

Government securities, or '**gilts**', are fixed-interest stocks issued and guaranteed by the British Government. They return a fixed income, with interest normally paid twice-yearly. Stock is available in both a fixed term and undated form, and in a variety of maturities, as well as in strictly fixed interest and in a form where interest payments are fixed to the RPI, so guaranteeing to preserve the investor's capital.

The yield on a government security, and indeed on any fixed-interest investment, can be calculated in two common ways. One is known as the running yield, which is simply the annual gross income expressed as a percentage of the price of the security.

The other is known as the **redemption yield**, or yield to maturity, which takes into account both the running yield and any capital gain or loss that might result if the security is held all the way to maturity. If a stock is bought at below its face value and held to maturity, when it is repaid at par the redemption yield will be higher than the running yield (vice versa if it is acquired when the price is above par).

Using gilts as a complement to a portfolio of equities has a number of implications. Equities (and for that matter fixed-interest investments) are both

gilts: fixed income securities guaranteed by the British Government.

redemption yield: the notional yield on a fixed-income security were it to be held until maturity, comprising the annual percentage income to be received as well as the capital gain or loss that will accrue from the current price to the redemption price.

Table 6.2 Impact of Differing Returns on Gilts versus Equities

Portfolio type	Amount (£)	Features/assumptions	Capital gain	Income	Total return over two years	
					Absolute	%
Shares	25 000	7% compound pa gain; 3% yield	3623	1553	5176	20.7
Gilts	25 000	12% gain over 2 years; 6% p.a. yield	3409	3400	6809	27.2
Combined	50 000	As above	7032	4053	11 085	22.2

at risk if interest rates rise. Higher interest rates choke off economic activity and lower the relative attractiveness of the normally lowish yields on ordinary shares. And, since the income on gilts is normally fixed, if interest rates rise and bond yields rise in sympathy, the effect is for gilt-edge security prices to fall. (See Table 6.2.)

However, astute choice of maturity date can limit the risk. Let's say, hypothetically, you are happy with your share portfolio and have significant gains on it. You do not wish to sell and realise the gains, but you want to limit the overall risk that interest rates might rise over the next two years.

Buying a government stock that stands below par but that matures in two years' time will guarantee an eventual capital gain that will offset at least some of the fall in equity values in the meantime if rates rise, while in all probability giving extra income at least equivalent to that on the equity portfolio.

Let's look at an example. At the time of writing the Treasury 6% stock of 1999 stands at 98, i.e. 2 points below par. The stock has a running yield of 6.12% (being 6/98), but the redemption yield, including the two-point appreciation in the run-up to maturity, is 6.6%.

It can probably be seen that, in its most extreme form, buying gilts simply equates to keeping cash on deposit. But a wise choice of stock, maturity date and the position of the price in relation to the par value (normally stated as £100% in the case of gilts) can produce a much more creative solution to the risk problem.

It is also worth noting that the yields on certain gilts can reveal a number of other facets of the market and the economy. There is an historic relationship, for instance, between the benchmark 20-year gilt yield and the yield on equities. In the years before equities grew in popularity, yields

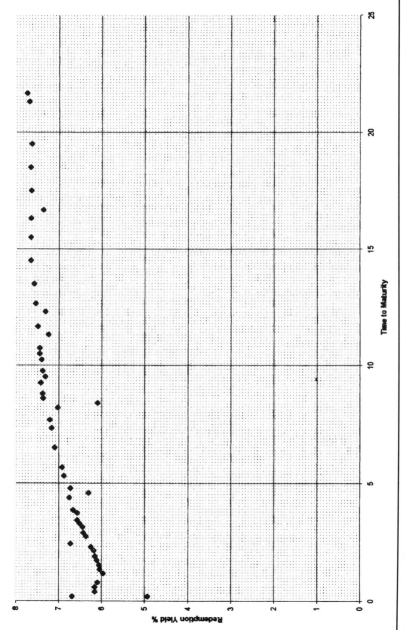

Figure 6.1 Yield Curve—Gilts (December 1995)

on ordinary shares were higher than those on gilts, and this disparity was known as the **yield gap**.

Now, it is more common for equity yields to be below gilt yields, and this relationship is known as the reverse yield gap. Its position at any one time can tell us a lot about the relative over- or under-valuation of equities relative to gilts, and therefore whether to skew one's investment strategy towards one or the other. Another good guide is the shape of the yield curve. This shows the redemption yields on gilt-edge stocks ranked by maturity date. At present it looks like the curve shown in Figure 6.1.

The normal situation is for the yield curve to slope much as it appears in the chart. Investors normally demand higher yields for stocks that have longer to go to maturity, because they are at risk to price fluctuations in the meantime for longer. If the curve is too steep, this probably indicates that short-term interest rates are unsustainably low and can only rise, despressing the market in shares. Conversely, an inverted yield curve, where short-dated yields are higher than longer-dated ones, may mean that short rates can only come down, or that the long end of the gilt market is vulnerable to price falls.

By the same token, the yield on undated gilt-edge stocks (currently 7.8%) is normally reckoned to be a proxy for what is known as the risk-free rate of return. Government stocks are believed to be as near riskless as it is possible to get, and therefore the yield on Consols or War loan, uncluttered by calculations on their position at maturity, is viewed as the purest of benchmarks. The current yield gap between 2.5% Consols and the FTA All Share Index is 3.89%. The risk-free yield is roughly double the yield on the equity market.

In fact, the real risk in holding gilt-edge stock is that inflation erodes the investor's capital. To offer investors protection in this respect, the Government

yield gap: the relationship between the price of long-term government securities and the average dividend yield on ordinary shares.

has issued index-linked stocks, where the interest payment is connected to movements in the RPI.

This means that the difference in yield between an index-linked stock and a fixed-interest stock of similar maturity will be a guide to the market's view of the likely future trend in inflation. For instance, at the time of writing the yield on the 4.625% index-linked stock maturing in 1998 is 4.11%, and the average redemption yield on the conventional gilts maturing in 1998 around 6.4%, implying that the market believes inflation between now and mid-1998 will run at around 2.3%.

Strategy Three: Invest the Balance of £20000 in an Index-Tracking Fund

As most interested observers of the investment scene will probably be aware, there has been an upsurge of interest in recent years in index-tracking funds. These are collective investment vehicles, managing large aggregated pools of money on behalf of many small investors. They deliberately invest in such a way as to track either the FT-SE 100 Index, or the FT All Share Index, or some other benchmark.

Vehicles of this sort represent a useful tool for investors who are uncomfortable with the level of risk they perceive to be inherent in their portfolio and wish to change it with the minimum of fuss.

Crucial to choosing the right amount to invest in funds of this type is a concept known as the 'beta factor'. This is a statistical measurement, based on the past performance of a portfolio, that attempts to isolate that part of the performance of an individual stock or portfolio that is simply reflecting the impact of a move in the market, and the part that is specific to the stock or portfolio concerned.

beta factor: a measure of the sensitivity of a particular share price to a given percentage movement in the market.

Put simply, the beta factor measures the likely movement in the stock for a given percentage movement in the market. If, for instance, the beta factor on a company is 1.1, this means that a 10% upward move in the market would be likely to see an 11% upward move in the price of the stock (10% × 1.1). Similarly, if a stock had a beta of 0.95, a 10% rise in the market would produce only a 9.5% rise in the price of the stock.

Organisations such as the London Business School produce tables of the beta factors for quoted companies, and indeed they can sometimes be derived in certain technical analysis packages. Simple observation of the movement in a particular share price may give one a good handle on whether it has a high or a low beta.

Smaller companies, more highly geared companies, and those involved in high-tech or capital-intensive industries will tend to have higher betas than those companies that are regarded as large, safe and boring, those that operate in industries normally regarded as stable, and businesses that generate cash.

So, for instance, brewers, food manufacturing companies and broad-based industrial companies have lower betas, other things being equal, than small electronics companies, biotechnology companies and mining stocks.

It is worth taking a little time to understand the nature of the portfolio of shares you have invested in and, having done this, to decide whether or not you are comfortable with the level of volatility it possesses. (See Table 6.3.)

The point about investing part of the portfolio in an index fund is that, by definition, the index fund's beta will be exactly 1.0, i.e. the fund's value will rise and fall exactly in line with the market. Hence, investing in an index fund is a way of raising (in the case of a beta below one) or lowering (in the case of a beta above one) the overall volatility of a portfolio.

Table 6.3   Impact of Index Tracking Investment on Volatility Portfolio

Portfolio	Amount invested	Beta	Effect of 10% gain in market	Effect of 15% fall in market
Shares	25 000	1.2	3000	−4500
Index tracker	25 000	1	2500	−3750
Combined	50 000	1.1	5500	−8250
Change in shares alone (%)			12.00%	−18.00%
Change in combined (%)			11.00%	−16.50%

Strategy Four: Invest the Balance of £20 000 in a Unit or Investment Trust

The preceding strategy alluded to the fact that there are many investment choices, one of the most popular being collective investment vehicles such as unit trusts. These are open-ended pools of money, which grow or contract as investors either buy or redeem units. Their value reflects the underlying portfolio.

closed-end fund: a collective investment with a fixed number of shares in issue and a strictly limited pool of money to invest.

Investment trusts, by contrast, are 'closed-end' funds, managing a fixed pool of money but whose shares are listed on the Stock Exchange. Investment trust shares often stand at a discount to the underlying value of their assets, for a variety of reasons.

My own preference is for investment trusts because of the discount factor and because of the reasonable degree of prior knowledge one has about the contents of the portfolio and the management style of the trust. That said, the unit trust industry is by far the most popular with ordinary investors.

In the context of our hypothetical portfolio adjustment exercise, there are two possible uses for unit/investment trusts. One is as a way of getting 'instant diversification'. If, for instance, an investor had only (say) £3000 to invest, the realistic alternative might be to buy two separate holdings in completely disparate companies. This would still have substantial risk. If one of the companies were to hit hard times, for example, the collapse in the share price would have a disastrous effect on the performance of the portfolio.

An alternative would be to put the whole £3000 in a long-established broadly based investment trust or unit trust. The possibility of buying shares in such an investment trust at a discount is an added attraction to an investor, who also now has the stimulus of owning shares and being able to follow the price on a daily basis.

In the case of an investor with a holding of more volatile smaller company shares, investing in a broadly based UK trust would again have the effect of diversifying the portfolio and lowering its volatility relative to changes in the market.

Investment trusts and other collective investments have another use, however. They can be used as a relatively safe means of investing in territory that might otherwise be considered unduly risky, or where the complexities of dealing and settlement effectively put them out of bounds for the private investor.

So, our hypothetical investor might, for instance, be perfectly happy that the existing portfolio he has gives a good spread of exposure to the UK stock market, and happy too that the level of risk and volatility of the portfolio is absolutely right for his needs.

But he also feels that (say) Latin America and Eastern Europe are likely to be the boom areas of the investment business over the next ten years and wishes to invest some of his remaining funds in these areas. It is impractical (and excessively risky) to even attempt to invest individually in these areas, but there are a number of specialist investment trusts that invest in these areas, and in which ordinary private investors can buy shares. Before doing so, however, it is essential to check out the performance of the trust, the record of the managers or fund management group that is sponsoring it, and the nature of the investment portfolio.

The process of doing this is rather similar to the process one might go through in checking out the credentials of a particular company. At the very minimum, an annual report or prospectus should be obtained to have a look at some of the detail prior to investing. It is, however, again worth remembering the axiom about risk and return.

Emerging markets, to take this example, may seemingly offer high returns, and by proxy so will the collective investments through which it is possible to invest in them. But the corollary is that the risk is also higher. It is therefore essential that an investment of this type is only contemplated when the risk in the rest of the portfolio is not particularly high. If it is, then some other form of risk reduction strategy (either buying gilts or index-tracking funds) should be considered alongside the emerging market investment.

One last word on investment trusts: investment trust shares often stand at a discount to the underlying value of their portfolio, and statistics on this are published daily in the *Financial Times*, but discount levels vary considerably, widening if the market is in a prolonged 'down' phase and narrowing

Table 6.4   'Double-Whammy' Effect of Variations in Investment Trust Discounts

	Starting Value	*Market +10%*	*Market +20%*	*Market –10%*	*Market –20%*
Net asset value	100p	110p	120p	90p	80p
Discount (say)	20%	15%	10%	25%	30%
Price of trust	80p	93.5p	108p	67.5p	56p
Gain/loss (%)		17	35	–16	–30

as it improves. Buying investment trusts when the market is depressed can give the investor a profitably and relatively risk-free 'double-whammy': the NAV of the trust will rise, say, in line with market, but superior performance will be generated by a narrowing in the discount.

This is illustrated in Table 6.4.

Strategy Five: Enhancing Returns through Tax-Efficient Investing

In recent years there has been considerable growth in the use of tax-efficient savings vehicles, notably Personal Equity Plans. Each tax year up to £6000 can be invested in a general PEP and a further £3000 in one linked to a single company. Husbands and wives have separate allowances so a married couple in theory could invest up to £18 000 a year in these vehicles. Investment in PEPs is not tax-deductible but gains on the shares held in a PEP are free of capital gains tax, while dividends are free of income tax.

There are drawbacks, however. Firstly, if you opt for a managed PEP, say one linked to a unit trust or investment trust, there may be significant initial and ongoing yearly charges which deplete some of the benefits.

Even in self-select PEPs, which do tend to be less costly in this respect, there are charges for dealing. The advantage of a PEP, however, is that it enables the investor to reinvest dividend income tax free. If the shares concerned are held for a long time the compounding effect of this can be substantial.

There are pluses and minuses to PEPs as a means of portfolio diversification. The first is that their value depends on the individual concerned being a taxpayer. Higher rate taxpayers fare best in the PEP environment, for obvious reasons. It is also generally considered unwise to let tax considerations drive investment decisions, and the long-term nature of PEPs rather argues against much of what this book has been about, namely selecting good undervalued shares, holding them until their potential has been recognised and then selling them.

It is possible to do this within a PEP but PEP funds must always be more or less fully invested. There is no sitting on the sidelines if you expect the market to fall. Having said that, the possibility now exists of including bonds within a PEP portfolio, and this makes some sensible form of diversification possible. The ongoing level of charges (typically 1% of portfolio value per year) tends to have a dissipating effect on performance, and the investor should check this out carefully before committing to a PEP.

One big disadvantage is that if funds are withdrawn from a PEP before five years are up, tax becomes payable and this has an inhibiting effect if funds are required to meet unexpected contingencies. In other words, the higher return available on a PEP over and above similar non-PEPed investments, essentially reflecting the impact of the tax relief less the charges made, has to be traded off against the reduced liquidity implied by the fact that there are penalties for early withdrawal.

Another tax wrinkle to bear in mind is that gains on conventional investments can be rolled over and gains tax deferred by reinvesting the funds in unlisted investments, such as securities quoted on the new Alternative Investment Market (AIM). Tax becomes payable once such investments are sold, but as a way of postponing the incidence of a tax bill, AIM stocks have their uses.

They are, however, significantly riskier and less liquid than normal shares, and readers should bear in mind the general advice to make investment selections objectively without taking too much notice of the tax status of particular categories of investment.

Better to select a good stock that rises in value and pay gains tax, than select a poor one that has tax-exempt status but falls in value.

Strategy Six: Enhancing Returns through Using Traded Options

As we outlined in a previous section, it is perfectly possible for an investor to be concerned that the profile of his or her portfolio is not risky enough. In other words, he or she may feel that the market looks set for a rise but his or her own shares are too safe and therefore offer too little prospect of a good return. It might be, for instance, that the investor has pursued a conservative investment strategy in a period when the market has been drifting but now feels that an upswing is in prospect and therefore that the current rather conservative holdings need spicing up a little.

While it is of course possible to do this via selling the existing holdings and buying new, more speculative ones, this strategy incurs dealing costs, may attract capital gains tax, and will also mean that the investor has the bid–offer spread to overcome before the new investments begin showing a true profit.

The traded options market can be used in a variety of ways to counteract this problem and open up the possibility of enhanced returns.

Trading in options is a huge subject, and readers interested in pursuing this topic further are urged to read up on the subject in more detail before beginning to trade. A book on trading in options written by Brian Millard is to be published by John Wiley and Sons, while my own book, *Traded Options: A Private Investors' Guide*, gives a comprehensive introduction to the subject, complete with worked examples.

In brief, however, options can be used in a number of ways. Buying a **call option** (that is to say, an

call (put) option: a contract that gives the holder the right but not the obligation to buy (sell) a parcel of shares at a fixed price for a specific period of time.

Table 6.5   Impact of Options on a Conservative Portfolio

				Value after:			
Portfolio constituent			Starting value (£)	Market +10% over 3 months	Market +20% over 6 months	Market −10% over 3 months	Market −20% over 6 months
Amount	Type	Beta					
£4000	Blue chips	0.9	4000	4360	4720	3640	3280
£1000	XYZ 160 call option (6 months to expiry)	n/a	1000	1720	2400	120	0
	Underlying stock price		180	200	220	160	140
	Price of option		25	43	60	3	0
	Combined portfolio value		5000	6086	7120	3760	3280
	Portfolio gain/loss (%)			22	42	−25	−34

option to buy shares at a specific price for a specified period of time in the future) involves the investor in a limited outlay but, if he is correct in his judgement about the market and a particular share, then using an option is a relatively inexpensive way of backing this judgement without disturbing an existing portfolio. (See Table 6.5.)

The investor will retain greater flexibility if he buys a call option that is in-the-money; that is to say, where the exercise price of the call option is below the current market price—so that the option already possesses some intrinsic value.

In addition, an option with a long time to expiry will be more expensive, but also offers more time for the buyer's judgement to be proved correct.

If the judgement is wrong, in terms of direction, timing or both, the investor stands in theory (and in practice) to lose the entire amount spent on the option, but this is the limit to the loss. It is worth remembering, however, that the value of the option when purchased by the investor is likely to include some so-called time value; that is to say, the price of the option will be greater than its intrinsic value.

This time value clearly becomes worth less and less the nearer the option gets to its expiry date. At expiry, the value of the option will simply equate to its intrinsic value, if any.

An example of the way gearing works on options is shown in Table 6.5. It can be seen that the geared nature of options work means that the overall beta factor of a portfolio will be increased materially through the purchase of, say, a call option.

Options can also be used in other ways. For instance as an investor you may have decided to take a profit (or cut a loss) on a particular share, but you still wish to retain some protection in case the share rises after the transaction has been completed.

Buying a call option also achieves this objective.

Option contracts are denominated in lots of 1000 shares, so selling say 5000 shares but at the same time buying five contracts in a call option with an exercise price close to the price at which you sold gives you protection if the price rises after you sell.

Because options are commonly used in this way as insurance, the price of an option is often known as its 'premium'. In the same way, buying a put option (an option to sell shares at a specified price for a particular length of time in the future) at the same time as buying the underlying stock buys insurance against the price falling after the underlying stock has been purchased. If this happens, the value of the put option will increase as the value of the stock falls.

Lastly, if it is anticipated that the value of particular stocks and the market as a whole will fluctuate within a narrow range for a lengthy period of time, the investor can 'write' (i.e. sell) a call option against an underlying holding. The advantage of this is that the writer of an option keeps the premium paid by the buyer of the option, but may not have the option exercised against him if the price of the underlying share fails to move sufficiently during the life of the option.

The worst that can happen is that the share price will move in the buyer's favour and be exercised, requiring the writer to honour the option contract at the exercise price. This means, in effect, that the writer of the call option will sell the stock at the exercise price of the option plus the option premium.

For example, let's assume that you hold 3000 Hanson shares. The price is 180. You do not believe that the price will move significantly for the next three months. You therefore write three Hanson 180p call options for a price of 12p. It will only be worthwhile for the holder of the option to exercise it if the price of Hanson moves above 192p in the next three months. If it does not, the 12p premium that you as the writer of the option have received represents additional portfolio income. If the price moves up to 200p and the holder of the option exercises the option then all is not lost. You still keep the option premium, meaning that you in effect sell the stock at 192p, participating in most of the rise, and come out with capital intact.

These strategies, buying call options to increase portfolio 'gearing', buying calls or puts as an insurance policy or hedge against a transaction in the underlying shares, and 'covered call writing' are the simplest of all option strategies, but should be considered by investors looking to adjust the risk–return profile of their portfolio.

It is also worth noting that as well as options on individual stocks, it is possible to buy options on the FT-SE 100 index. This is a way of gaining exposure to overall changes in the market, and may be appropriate in certain circumstances.

You may decide, for instance, that the market is headed lower. You sell your entire portfolio and buy short- or medium-dated gilt-edge stock standing below par, but you wish to insure against your judgement on the equity market being wrong. You therefore earmark a small proportion of the cash realised to buy a 'footsie' call option, with a strike price close to the index point at which you sold your holdings.

This will then provide the necessary insurance for the period of the option. Note that index options of this type come in two forms, American-style exercise and European-style exercise. American-style options permit exercise at any time up to expiry. Individual equity options are of this type too. European-style options only permit exercise on the expiry day itself, and therefore have a lower premium, because the writer of the option is not exposed to the risk of exercise in the meantime.

Lastly on this subject, it is worth noting that not all brokers offer a facility to deal in options. Not all of those that do offer an option trading facility permit private investors to write options. Indeed, uncovered writing of call options (i.e. where the investor does not hold the underlying stock to match the option transaction) is known as 'naked writing' and should be avoided at all costs, since it exposes the investor to unlimited risk of loss.

Before contemplating any option trades, readers are strongly urged to study the subject fully and if possible to attend some of the many trading courses organised by LIFFE for private investors.

MEASURING YOUR GAINS AND LOSSES

The alert reader should have deduced by now that the important point about all investment activity is the assessment of risk and reward, and of choosing a level of risk that is comfortable and appropriate to the individual's financial circumstances and liquidity needs. The strategy adopted depends on the amount available to invest and whether income is or is not a requirement.

Those with sufficient funds to enable eight or ten shares to be acquired with £3000–5000 invested in each might well stick entirely to picking out individual equities using the techniques described elsewhere in this book.

Those of more modest means might contemplate investing part of their capital in some individual equities and the remainder in a broad-based investment trust or index-tracking fund. Those with a more modest amount to invest but with a taste for a greater degree of risk might invest part of their capital in an index-tracking fund and give effect to views on individual shares by buying call or put options (depending on their view).

Those requiring income may invest part of their portfolio in gilts and part in high-yielding equities, supplementing this when it is felt appropriate by covered call writing to further enhance portfolio income. Those pursuing simple 'buy and hold' strategies should consider doing so through the various tax-efficient vehicles available.

Investors have to try at all times to assess whether they believe the market is likely to rise or fall and whether they are happy with the risk this poses to their portfolio, that it will either fall in value or get left behind in a rise.

It is important for investors to try to measure as accurately as possible what level of risk their portfolio possesses, and how it will act under certain market conditions, but also try to discriminate between temporary short-term market movements, which may be largely ignored, and major trends and changes in direction.

There is also a balance to be struck between over-active trading, which will only enrich your broker, and total inactivity, which will lead to profitable opportunities being missed. It is also necessary for strict trading disciplines—running profits but cutting losses and operating a stop-loss system—to be maintained at all times. This is particularly the case if option trades are being undertaken as part of portfolio strategy, since the limited time factor weighs heavily on the option buyer.

It is also good practice to measure the performance of your portfolio at regular intervals against a benchmark like the FT-SE 100 or FTA All Share index, to assess how your trading is going. Chapter 10 contains the results of an analysis of my own dealing over nearly a decade of private investing.

Analysing your performance in this way may provoke questions as to the right strategy to follow. The necessary parameters can easily be programmed into a proprietary spreadsheet package, or simply kept up to date with pencil and paper. In my view the investor should know the overall value of his portfolio and the profit or loss on each of its constituents on a daily basis.

A questioning approach is always appropriate, and in particular perhaps in analysing why particular trades did not pay off, and working out what distinguishes successes from failures.

Measuring portfolio gains and losses, highlighting new opportunities through searching a database of share prices, and being aware of price movements and the opportunities they throw up are all tasks that are aided considerably by using various types of investment software and computer-based services. What each of these products and services does and how they can help the investor will be considered in the next two chapters.

IN BRIEF

- The concept of spreading risk is a vitally important part of investing.
- The degree to which investment in shares should be diversified is determined by the individual's own personal 'balance sheet'.
- Markets move in broad cycles, and share investment should only be contemplated once one has understood fully the current position of the market cycle.
- It is important to avoid investing in shares whose business activities are similar.
- There are a number of ways of diversifying risk and enhancing returns. These include: gilt-edge stock, index-tracking funds, and unit and investment trusts.
- Investing tax-efficiently can be important in raising investment returns, but it is important not to let the tax break drive the investment decision.

- Traded options can be used in different ways to enhance portfolio income and to increase returns while at the same time increasing risk by a defined amount. Investors should read widely on this subject before using these techniques.
- It is a good discipline to measure your investment performance and to analyse your share trades to get pointers to improve results in the future.

Computer-Aided Investment

This chapter and the next concentrate on how computers can be used to simplify and automate some of the routine tasks of investing. They also look at how the phenomenon of the Internet and other electronic media can be used to obtain that all-important investing 'edge'.

Before less technophile readers get put off by this, I must stress that using computers is by no means the be-all and end-all of investment activity.

Being thorough and exercising judgement have always been the most important aspects of succcessful investing.

But using computers to accomplish some of the more routine tasks is important, because it frees up the investor to concentrate on the more creative part of the process: hunting out companies that are undervalued.

Another important consideration is that the professionals operate using sophisticated computer systems. The Barings debacle demonstrates that this is not necessarily a guarantee of success, particularly if the information generated by them is not promptly or correctly acted on. But if the private investor wishes to compete on as level a playing field as possible, then access to timely information and the means to analyse it are important.

Lastly, the interest generated by articles in popular publications like the *Investors Chronicle* and the *Financial Times* on the subject of investment software, information sources and other similar topics makes it very clear that many private investors also see this as an important part of the discipline of investment.

Successful independent investing is all about being thorough in research, meticulous in accounting and measurement of performance, and painstaking in the identification and monitoring of trading opportunities. It is, or should be, hard work. Those who have read this far almost certainly possess the characteristics needed to succeed.

What computers do is to make these tasks a little easier.

I believe that many budding investors have in the past been put off acquiring investment software by brokers who have a vested interest— in the form of discretionary commissions, and fees earned for valuations and capital gains tax (CGT) calculations—in making sure that their clients stayed less computer literate than they were.

Increasingly, investors are beginning to take the initiative in this area. Brokers who ignore the trend towards computerised investing may risk a gradual erosion in their client base to their more technologically-aware competitors.

Equally, there are many misconceptions about investment software. One, fostered in part by the software and hardware suppliers themselves, is that vast computing power is required to make an investment software package work effectively. Another is that these packages are priced outside the reach of those with a relatively low budget. Nothing could be further from the truth.

So, let's begin by exploring some of the functions that investment software can perform, before moving on to look at different types of software packages and data-gathering systems, and what they can and cannot do.

WHY USE INVESTMENT SOFTWARE?

In this chapter I am starting from the assumption that all readers will have some understanding of the way the tax system works, and of elementary bookkeeping. Some of these issues, insofar as they relate to investing in shares, were covered in earlier chapters.

Self-employed for over eight years, I operate a number of different methods of keeping track of my cash, investments and business finances. Employed individuals and retirees may have a somewhat different perspective.

While I have to keep close tabs on my liquidity and on who owes me money, those who have a salary or pension guaranteed to come in on a particular day each month may focus more closely on analysing their personal spending, and keeping track of the outgoings. There are packages— Microsoft Money and Intuit Quicken, for example— which take this approach to the *n*th degree. In these programs regular spending and investing can be monitored, and the packages can be used to slot figures easily and quickly into tax returns.

With income tax self-assessment looming in the UK, using software like this will become increasingly important in the future. It may even create investment opportunities in the shares of companies involved in producing software and other aids to ease this process.

In my own case, for business purposes I have used a mixture of both manual and computerised bookkeeping for some years, with the Sage

Table 7.1   Finance Summary

Stock	Amount	Cost	Price	Value	Gain/Loss	% value
Agricultural Agencies	10000	5165	0.65	6500	1335	38.96
Digital Properties	10000	4050	0.49	4900	850	28.69
Universal Widgets	2000	5206	2.84	5680	474	33.26
SE total		14421		17080	2659	100.00
						% total
SE total				17080		35.50
Money market account				600		1.25
Current account				−160		−0.33
Business account				4500		9.35
Reserve account				1275		2.65
Building society				13500		28.06
Debtors				11321		23.53
Total				48116		100.00
Tax due 1 July 1996	Income	2500		3450		
	NI	950				
VAT and other creditors				1844		
Short-term net assets				42822		

computer package I use producing figures that my accountant can easily translate into a tax return and a set of business accounts.

The result has been that for day-to-day monitoring of my investments and business and personal liquidity I have used a simple Excel spreadsheet, which looks something like the one shown in Table 7.1 (the numbers and stocks are fictitious):

As you can see, this has the big advantage of simplicity. I can see at a glance what my investments are worth at any one time (I rarely have more than five or six), how much profit they have made or lost, what percentage each represents of the total, and how the Stock Exchange-related portion relates to my cash resources, and my business debtors and creditors.

The important aspect of this is that ensuring adequate liquidity at all times is a vital part of investment discipline. I am occasionally caught out, but have never been forced to sell shares in order to meet pressing bills, a state of affairs that should be avoided at all costs.

It is also worth remembering that, provided the individual has a PC equipped with Excel and some means of downloading prices in **ASCII** format, so that they can be easily imported into a spreadsheet, then the graphing facility in Excel will produce charts on demand. Similar facilities are, of course, available within other spreadsheet programs.

ASCII: standard format through which data collected in one computer system can be translated for use in another.

However, investment software is usually taken to mean something more than this. Investment poses special accounting problems that are difficult (though arguably not impossible) for the lay user to write into a spreadsheet. The main differences are in the incidence of dividends, scrip issues, rights issues, capital gains tax, indexation and so on.

Equally, the charts normally used in helping to make investment decisions are frequently more complex, as the earlier chapter on the subject indicated, than simple moving averages. Some of the most useful indicators employ complex statistical formulae.

This is actually one reason why many investment software packages are (or were originally) written for the DOS, rather than the Windows, format. Most of the DOS packages are reasonably user-friendly but, in investment software, there is a clear trade-off between functionality on the one hand and the familiar Windows ease of use on the other. Windows packages are available, and in increasing quantity, but the ultra-sophisticated packages are often DOS-based or, if available in Windows, will generally be slower to complete the more complex tasks.

As we saw earlier, in Chapter 3, the advent of computerised chart packages has speeded up the calculation of these complex indicators and, equally importantly, has enabled huge databases to be scanned quickly for key indicators in a matter of minutes. This is no substitute for proper judgement, but systems like this can throw up anomalies that merit further research.

The following outline of how investment software programs work is based mainly on software produced by Synergy Software, mainly because this is the system with which I am most familiar and which I use personally. However, other packages will be alluded to later in this chapter. No recommendation of any particular package is intended or should be inferred.

The suitability of different packages will vary from investor to investor, depending both on the budget available and on the amount of time the investor has at his or her disposal to pursue investment activities, and on the complexity or otherwise of the individual's tax position.

At the end of this chapter we survey briefly the main investment software packages available and their prices and functionality. From this it can be seen that packages can be purchased to suit all pockets, ranging from some priced at well under £100 to those retailing at over £1000.

USING INVESTMENT SOFTWARE
ACCOUNTING FUNCTIONS

Most investment software packages come with two basic components: one is a module that allows the user to perform various accounting functions and store data relating to transactions; the other is a chart drawing function, of varying complexity depending on the nature of the package.

Actually, there are some software packages (those produced by Updata, for example) that do not have a portfolio management **module**, but that have been deliberately designed to be compatible with a proprietary cash management package such as—in Updata's case—Intuit Quicken.

module: a segment of an investment software program with a specific function, such as managing transaction data or drawing share price charts.

There are a number of important functions that are normally written into a standard investment software package that are not present in some of the more basic personal finance programs or else, if they are present, are less easy to configure. It would, however, scarcely be worth shifting from a sophisticated package like Quicken, which has an extensive module for tracking investments, simply to gain a little extra flexibility in a specialist package. The advantages of one over the other may not be that significant.

The complexity normally arises because there are inevitably a number of calculations that need to be performed that are peculiar to the investment process. These can be listed as follows:

- Recording transaction prices and the incidence of dividends.
- Calculating figures for return on investment that include both income and capital gains.
- Accounting for scrip issues, scrip dividends, takeovers, rights issues and stock consolidations.
- The maintaining of a running cash account, including realised capital gains and dividend income.
- The working-out and formal presentation of indexed capital gains tax calculations.
- If appropriate, the storage of a certain amount of fundamental data, including earnings per share, dividend and net asset value figures, dividend dates, directors' dealings, the timing of results announcements, and other factors.

Table 7.2 Stockmarket Deals, 1996/97

BOUGHT					SOLD				Gain/Loss	Dividend Income	Other Income
Amount	Price (p)	Value	Date	Stock	Amount	Price	Value	Date			
				Starting capital			28000	6.4.96			
500	319	1619	3.7.96	Central					–1619		
500	307	1558	21.8.96	Central	1000	267	2657	13.11.96	1099		
1000	118	1198	3.7.96	Idaho	1000	145	1443	5.3.97	245		
1000	213	2162	3.7.96	Biltmore					–2162		
1000	235	2385	21.8.96	Biltmore	2666	257	6786	2.9.97	4401		
1000	129.5	1314	3.7.96	Scrumpy					–1314		
1500	111.5	1697	7.8.96	Scrumpy	2500	123	3045	27.10.97	1348		
1000	170	1725	21.7.96	Harrow	5333	188	9950	2.9.97	8225		
1000	184	1868	24.7.96	Chester	1000	195	1941	4.8.96	73		
2000	116	2355	24.7.96	Stilton	2344	393	9138	2.9.97	6783		
5000	27.5	1395	7.8.96	Premier	5500	55	2996	27.10	1601		
2500	93.5	2373	21.8.96	Mountain	2500	143.5	3519	20.7.97	1146		
7500	18.5	1401	7.11.96	Colony					–1401		
7500	19.5	1476	5.3.97	Colony	15000	101	15059	2.9.97	13583	1402	572
1000	287	2898	13.11.96	Belter	1000	333	3298	2.9.97	400		
1000	546	5592	20.7.97	Hastings	1000	405	4011	27.10.97	–1581		
Total inv.	33016				Total realised		91843		58827	1402	572
Total CG	58827				Net divs./other inc.		1974		Net int./CG		
					Total return (%)		217.15				

Table 7.3 CGT Indexation Allowances, December. Source: Inland Revenue

Year	Jan	Feb	Mar	Apr	May	Jun	Jul	Aug	Sep	Oct	Nov	Dec
1995	1.032	1.026	1.022	1.011	1.007	1.006	1.011	1.005	1.001	1.006	1.006	–
1994	1.067	1.061	1.058	1.045	1.041	1.041	1.047	1.041	1.039	1.038	1.037	1.032
1993	1.093	1.086	1.082	1.072	1.068	1.069	1.071	1.067	1.062	1.063	1.064	1.062
1992	1.111	1.106	1.102	1.086	1.082	1.082	1.086	1.085	1.081	1.077	1.079	1.083
1991	1.157	1.151	1.147	1.132	1.129	1.124	1.126	1.124	1.120	1.115	1.111	1.111
1990	1.261	1.254	1.241	1.205	1.194	1.189	1.188	1.176	1.166	1.157	1.159	1.160
1989	1.358	1.348	1.342	1.318	1.310	1.306	1.305	1.301	1.292	1.283	1.272	1.269
1988	1.459	1.453	1.448	1.424	1.419	1.414	1.412	1.397	1.390	1.376	1.370	1.366
1987	1.507	1.501	1.498	1.480	1.479	1.479	1.480	1.476	1.472	1.465	1.457	1.459
1986	1.566	1.560	1.558	1.543	1.540	1.541	1.545	1.541	1.533	1.531	1.518	1.513
1985	1.652	1.639	1.624	1.590	1.583	1.579	1.582	1.578	1.579	1.577	1.571	1.569
1984	1.735	1.728	1.723	1.700	1.694	1.689	1.691	1.676	1.672	1.662	1.657	1.658
1983	1.824	1.816	1.813	1.788	1.781	1.776	1.776	1.759	1.751	1.745	1.739	1.734
1982	–	–	1.897	1.860	1.846	1.841	1.841	1.840	1.841	1.832	1.823	1.826

The table shows capital gains tax indexation allowances for assets sold in December 1995. Multiply the original cost of the asset by the figure for the month in which you bought it. Subtract the result from the proceeds of your sale: the balance will be your taxable gain. It is not possible to use indexation to create, or increase, a loss. Suppose you bought shares for £6000 in November 1985 and sold them in December 1995 for £13 000. Multiplying the original cost by the November 1985 figure of 1.571 gives a total of £9426. Subtracting that from £13 000 gives a capital gain of £3574, which is within the CGT allowance of £6000. If selling shares bought before April 6 1982, you should use the March 1982 figure. The RPI in December 1995 was 150.7.

I have a confession to make, however. I have never tended to spend too much time recording details of transactions in an investment software package, preferring instead to use a simple spreadsheet in which I enter completed transactions, the dates of purchase and sale, and the gain or loss, with a cumulative total at the bottom of each phase of trading. Scrip dividends, rights issues and other similar stock events can usually be incorporated simply by adding in an extra notional amount of stock purchased.

An example of how my system works is shown in Table 7.2.

The other details required, for example to calculate total return on investment, come out in the wash. Because I operate through a broker nominee account and a high-interest money market account, all of the necessary details on dividend and interest income are given to me at the end of every tax year, while my accountant works out the capital gains tax liability (if one exists).

For those without a tame accountant, the CGT calculation facility is a useful adjunct to most packages. It does, however, necessitate the user keeping the **indexation tables** up to date, entering the details into the appropriate section of the software on a regular basis. The figures required are published frequently in the national and weekend press and in investment magazines.

Examples of CGT indexation factors are shown in Table 7.3.

Most investment software packages also allow for the grouping of shares, within the portfolio management module, into separate portfolios so that in theory (for example) separate husband and wife portfolios could be kept up to date, as well as those perhaps of other relatives. Shares held in PEPs could be accounted for separately too. Some brokers and financial advisers use versions of packages like this for keeping their client records up to date and

indexation table: a table of values showing indexation factors to be used when calculating capital gains tax liabilities.

generating reports such as valuation statements and the like.

Common to most software packages is the creation of individual records for each share that is dealt in. The details include the timing of purchases and sales, when dividends come in, and any other corporate events.

Details entered in these datafiles can then also be sorted and displayed in different ways, for instance as a chronological sequence of purchases, sales, dividend income, scrip dividends and so on, eventually reconciling to the amount of cash available for investment.

Since the system is linked to the price files created elsewhere in the package for graph drawing purposes, it is obviously possible for the latest prices to be automatically included in the portfolio management segment for valuation purposes.

This means that the investor can see at a glance how much he or she has made or lost in the market over a particular period of time, and how much his or her portfolio is worth.

Reports can normally be designed either in standard formats or in formats defined by the user. As well as the normal report formats, some packages allow the user to include information such as average buying price, price–earnings ratio and total return, as well as including dealing costs, the individual shares' sector classifications, market capitalisation and so on.

Because a long time-series of price information is available, other parameters capable of being displayed include the price change over a variety of historic time periods—daily, weekly, monthly, quarterly, yearly, or between any two specified dates for either a specific portfolio, group of portfolios or set number of shares.

As already noted, calculating capital gains tax is also an important function of this part of the

Table 7.4

290196	
Client: 1	
Daterange Selected ALL	
CGT Report for Br.Land	
120694 sale of 5000 shares at consideration	19950.00
020492 purchase of 5000 shares added to post 82 pool at cost	9552.50
Indexation factor from 020492 to 120694 = .043	
Indexation on cost of 9552.5	410.76
Indexed post 82 pool comprises 5000 at consideration	9963.26
Unindexed post 82 pool comprises 5000 at consideration	9552.50
120694 sale of 5000 shares offset from post 82 pool-consideration	19950.00
Number of shares offset = 5000 with sale proceeds of	19950.00
Cost of shares sold	9963.26
Profit on sale	9986.74
CGT profit	9986.74
Total CGT liability for 120694 sale =	9986.74
Aggregate CGT liability for Br.Land =	9986.74

software. Most investment software will be able to take account of indexation, to account for shares purchased before the CGT base date of 1982, and to print out summaries of capital gains tax liabilities on either an actual transaction basis or on a 'what if'—i.e. the notional calculation if a given holding of shares were to be sold at the current price. The reports are normally standardised to contain enough detail to satisfy the Inland Revenue.

An example of such a report is shown in Table 7.4.

I have refrained from making specific recommendations on particular packages at this point, but a summary of the characteristics of a number of software packages is given at the end of this chapter. Potential software users are advised to obtain literature and, if possible, a demo disk for the package of their choice before buying.

USING INVESTMENT SOFTWARE CHARTING FUNCTIONS

Chapters 4 and 9 cover in some detail how to use a variety of different chart types and indicators, ranging from the simple to the complex.

Software packages differ greatly in the sophistication with which they approach this subject, with the more expensive packages providing a much greater range of chart indicators. It is normal, however, for even low-priced packages to include a range of useful technical indicators, including moving averages, a means of calculating and graphing movements relative to an index or other shares, and simple momentum indicators. These functions may be more than enough for the average investor to use, at least at the outset.

The more expensive the package, the more indicators will be present. Charting highly complex indicators involving the performing of a series of, say, statistical regression calculations can take a moment or two, even on a relatively fast PC. More expensive packages tend to include indicators that permit the calculations used in more sophisticated methods of trading. These include the analysis of share price volatility, used in option trading, **Gann analysis**, channel analysis, option strategy calculations and profit/loss diagrams, **Fibonacci lines** and various other esoteric methods.

Gann, Fibonacci analysis: sophisticated systems of technical analysis found on more expensive investment software packages.

There are two important points to bear in mind here.

One is that as the complexity of the system increases, so does the need for reliable and comprehensive data, especially data covering daily price ranges and trading volume. In my own trading I have found volume data to be one of the more important yardsticks I use. Stocks lurching higher or lower on heavy volume are usually telling the investor a story that should not be ignored.

The other aspect to this is that the more complex the indicators and data used, the more time the investor needs to devote to their study to get the best out of them. Specialist training courses may be desirable, as well as a lot of extra reading. So each individual must make up his or her mind about whether the cost of this investment in time is worthwhile in terms of the eventual end results it produces in (hopefully) extra share trading profits.

A key element of using an investment software chart package is being able to manage the price data stored in it. For example, prices must be adjusted to take account of rights issues, scrip issues and other similar events. Most software systems have some sort of price editing function whereby, with a few keystrokes, a batch of prices can be changed, for instance, multiplying all the prices in a particular file and prior to a certain date by 0.5 to reflect a one-for-one scrip issue, and so on.

It is difficult to advise on which chart package is best, other than to say that the user-friendliness of most DOS packages means that there is little reason to be put off using them because they do not come in Windows versions. As mentioned before, non-Windows packages tend to run faster, and that can be an advantage.

However, chart packages do cost money, and before splashing out on an expensive one, it is probably best to buy the cheapest one in the range first and get used to operating it, finding out what it can and cannot do. Most software suppliers offer easy upgrade paths that do not penalise the user who wants to try the 'entry-level' version first.

If you are contemplating trading exclusively on the back of a chart package, a more expensive system is probably needed. It cannot be stressed too much that dealing on charts can be a hazardous activity and is certainly time-consuming.

Running a dummy portfolio for a spell, making notional 'buys' and 'sells' and including the impact of the spread and dealing costs, is probably a good exercise to find out if the system you have devised works well and if you are up to the stresses and strains that trading brings with it.

USING INVESTMENT SOFTWARE SCANNING AND OPTIMISATION

Some middle and upper-end software packages include functions that make the task of finding out which stocks meet particular chart criteria less time-consuming.

The idea behind these is that the software can be programmed to search through the database in sequence, trying to identify stocks whose price histories match certain logical statements entered into the system. The entry of these criteria is not especially complex and, once entered, **scanning criteria** can be stored for future use.

scanning criteria: logical rules that can be programmed into an investment software package to find shares that correspond to key technical indicators.

For instance, one might want to store the following criteria:

● 20-day moving average crossing up through the 50-day moving average (a so-called 'golden cross').
● the same for the 30- and 90-day averages.
● all stocks with an RSI figure above 70 and falling, or below 30 and rising.
● stocks where the 15-day stochastic is over 90 or below 10.

These can be entered by inputting a series of 'equations'. In the case of the 'golden cross', for example, this would be:

1. today's 20-day MA is above the 50-day MA
2. yesterday's 20-day MA was equal to or below the 50-day MA

3. today's 20-day MA is greater than yesterday's 20-day MA

4. today's 50-day MA is greater than yesterday's 50-day MA

With a little logical thought and a bit of trial and error, composing these logical statements is not difficult. When a scan is run, the system will analyse the database of price histories and answer each question in turn for each stock, throwing up at the end of the period a shortlist of stocks whose price data, when analysed, met all the conditions.

The scanning process on, say, a database of 500 shares, for a calculation of this type will take only a minute or two in DOS on a 486 or Pentium PC. Each of the different scan criteria can be input in the same way and the results of each scan result compared. Stocks that meet more than one criterion—let's say, exhibit the 'golden cross' pattern and show a positive pattern on a couple of momentum indicators— can be subjected to more detailed further study.

Using software packages for **optimising** trading is somewhat more complex. It is based on the premise that taking, say, the 20- and 50-day moving average relationship as a rough guide, better trading results might have been achieved in the past by buying when the 24-day MA crossed the 55-day one but selling when the 19-day MA crossed the 48-day one. The 20/50 indicator approximates to this, but fine-tuning would have produced better results if it had been used regularly in the past.

The principle behind this is that for a particular share the computer will perform a series of repetitive calculations, examining the entire stored past history of shares to work out which different combination of buy and sell parameters would have produced the best overall trading results if they had been used to make buy and sell decisions in the past.

optimising: the process through which the definition of technical indicators can be fine-tuned to produce (based on past history) improved decision-making.

Inputting the appropriate decision rules in this case is somewhat more complex and the process of arriving at what seems to be the best set of indicators much more time-consuming. Even then, of course, there is no guarantee that the historical pattern will hold good in the future.

The other aspect of these systems is that they produce a table that shows when the trades would have been made, at what prices, how much would have been made in absolute and percentage terms, and how many gaining and losing trades there would have been following a particular precise trading pattern.

I know of examples where individuals have made substantial amounts finding particular shares that work well with decision rules of this sort, but technical analysts tend to keep details like this close to their chests, and of course you never hear about the (possibly more numerous) failures that placing one's trust in systems of this type might also generate.

It is vitally important too, when looking at the returns that such systems appear to produce, to feed in some estimate of the amount by which the returns might be depleted by the impact of the bid–offer spread and by dealing costs.

One should not dismiss systems of this type entirely, however. They are also getting easier to use. It is now possible to buy stockmarket trading software that both identifies cycles and determines optimised trading rules within a relatively simple format of 'point and click' in a Windows environment.

Software of this latter type is, however, relatively expensive and also relies on the investor making the correct selection of a limited number of stocks that are particularly susceptible to cyclical patterns of price activity. As noted earlier, the biggest cost of using systems of this nature is not the software, but the length of time the investor must work at picking the right stock.

A summary of the chart packages that include trading optimisers is given in the table at the end of this chapter.

DOWNLOADING DATA

Downloading share price data is a big subject in itself, and often casues more pain and grief for the investor than mastering the complexities of using the investment software that goes with it.

It is probably self-evident that the foundation of any investment software package is the ability to build up a stream of reliable daily price information that can be stored and retrieved as necessary.

In theory, of course, it is possibly to input such data manually from a newspaper share price page, but doing this day after day for even a limited number of shares will quickly become tedious, while building up a price history on a new share you may have become interested in is well nigh impossible, or at best very time-consuming.

There are successful investors who rely on the charts produced in publications like the *Hambro Company Guide* and the *Estimate Directory*, but having taken the decision to use investment software, finding an effective means of downloading a sizable volume of data on a daily basis is an important part of getting the best out of your chosen package.

Advances in technology are making this process easier and cheaper as time goes by, but buying data can be a sigificant cost. Generally, the better quality and more comprehensive the data, the more it will cost, but the better investment decisions you will be able to make.

The best data of all is known by the acronym **OHLCV**, which stands for Open, High, Low, Close and Volume. Getting data of this type enables a

OHLCV: open, high, low, close and volume. The five ingredients of price data needed to produce comprehensive technical analysis.

number of sophisticated chart formats (such as candlestick charts and US-style bar charts) to be drawn, while even if these are not employed, volume data alone is almost universally useful in making investment decisions. I never (repeat never) buy or sell a share without having a close look at the recent pattern of trading volume in it, and it is especially important when dealing in shares in smaller companies, for obvious reasons. Skimping on this aspect of data can be a false economy.

The data downloading services on offer have increased in number dramatically in recent years. Data is now available for download via teletext, direct from certain price display services, by modem pager, over the Internet, and by electronic mail. There are also services that supply data by weekly disk. Each of these methods has its advantages and disadvantages. Before examining each in turn, it is worth making the point that the ideal is probably to have a system that has the following characteristics:

- is reliable and maintenance-free
- covers the whole market
- is cheap, or free
- is either OHLCV, or at least gives trading volume figures
- enables the downloading of new price histories at minimal cost
- has an easy interface with a variety of software packages

Each of the main methods of acquiring data has disadvantages. But the disadvantages are fewer the more one is prepared to pay.

Teletext

The telextext services of BBC2 and Channel 4 contain comprehensive share price display pages updated several times daily. Taking the two services together, about 400 shares have prices updated seven times daily, while the Channel 4 service run by Teletext Limited also has the two Teletext 2000 pages, which contain closing prices for all listed shares on a daily basis, updated late in the evening.

Various software companies have interfaces that enable the easy downloading of prices and database maintenance of price files obtained using the Teletext 2000 service.

Using teletext to download price information necessitates fitting your PC with a teletext adaptor card. This is a standard PC expansion card with a socket attached to take the plug from a TV aerial. The user runs a spur off his or her TV aerial and plugs the cable into the back of the PC. This then enables telext pages to be displayed on the PC, and the data on them downloaded into a software package. Teletext adaptor cards currently cost in the region of £150 plus VAT.

The big advantage of using teletext is that it is free.

The drawbacks are, first, that you may not want to create price files for the whole market, but only download and save those that are interesting to you at a particular point in time, in addition, perhaps to the top 100 or 250 stocks.

The second problem is that although reliability has improved over the years, a teletext user is still at the mercy of TV reception, climatic conditions and the efficiency of the TV aerial used. In the days when I used teletext to update my software, I had to spend out not only on the expansion card but also in the end on a high performance aerial to improve the quality of the reception into the package and eliminate errors in the downloading procedure.

Teletext downloads also need to be done at a certain time each day, and arrangements need to be made to automate this procedure if the user is away for an extended period, although this is not an insurmountable problem.

Finally, and perhaps most importantly, a major drawback to teletext is that it does not give either OHLCV or even volume data.

Modem

Downloading data by modem overcomes a lot of these disadvantages. Various proprietary databases are available that offer data by modem. These contain OHLCV data with comprehensive coverage, enabling in some instances the more or less unrestricted downloading of back price histories, and avoiding the problems of poor reception, the difficulty of arranging updates while away on business or holiday, and so on.

The drawback to these services is one of cost. The more stocks included in the database, the greater the cost. This will eventually run into thousands of pounds if a service is taken that encompasses the whole market. There are, however, compromises available that lower the cost. For instance, Synergy Software offers a service that, for an annual subscription, bundles together the use of a software package with a modem-based data retrieval package that enables the user to have up to 400 or so price histories at any one time, and to download fresh ones at no extra charge.

This means that, as new shares become of interest, the price history can be downloaded quickly and easily, kept for a while and later discarded if necessary. The pricing for the service depends on the functionality of the software package chosen, with a mid-range package costing around £600 per annum.

The drawback of some of these services is that the user is locked into a particular service, and price data may not be easily transferable to other software packages.

Data display services

Price display systems like Market Eye and some satellite based services enable data to be downloaded into a range of investment software packages at no extra charge. Market Eye also offers a data download-only option.

I have already expressed some reservations about the cost and usefulness of real-time price data displays and the improvements or otherwise they may bring to one's trading, but if you are set on having a live price feed, then there will normally be no need to spend additional sums on downloading data for a chart package, provided, of course, you have ensured that the package chosen is compatible with the feed.

Data by disk

A few software suppliers have developed services by which a selected list of shares can be updated via a disk posted off to subscribers on a weekly or fortnightly basis. Services of this nature tend to be cheaper than on-line services, via modem or some other means of dial-up, but the user loses out to a degree on the timeliness of the information.

Nonetheless, for those interested only in longer-term trading opportunities services of this type are easy and cost-effective to use, the new disk being simply inserted into the computer each week and the updated price files copied across into the price files stored on the hard disk.

Internet-based services

The advent of the Internet has enabled services to be offered whereby price data can be downloaded daily from a remote computer simply by accessing the appropriate page. This topic is covered in much more detail in the next chapter, but it holds out the prospect of an era of lower-cost price information and other services as more investors get connected.

After something of a struggle with the Stock Exchange over access to its data, the Cambridge-based firm Electronic Share Information (ESI) was able to make available selected 'live' prices and end-of-day data comparable to that available via teletext for a subscription which at its cheapest runs at £5 per month. Although this appears expensive relative to the teletext service, it is probably worthwhile for many users because of the absence of any reliability problems and the easy availability of data from previous days in a computer 'archive'. The data is also in OHLCV form and downloadable in a form compatible with most software packages.

It is highly likely that more services of this nature will eventually be developed, and will bring down the cost of data closer to the relatively low prices charged in the USA for information of this type. The ESI service is also combined with a simple chart drawing facility and the ability to overlay one chart with any other.

Data by email

Related to this is the availability of price data by email. At the time of writing only one data provider was running a service of this nature, whereby data is provided on a weekly basis for around £125 per annum for a full range of market stocks and indices. This is somewhat similar to the 'data by disk' services, and suffers the same drawbacks. In addition, the user must either be linked to CompuServe or have an email account capable of taking messages from it.

Services using disk, email or the Internet typically provide the raw data in ASCII or CSV (comma separated value) format, which can then be imported into most proprietary software packages. It is as well to check with the data provider and the software publisher that transfers of this type are feasible before signing up for a service.

Last but not least, several brokers are contemplating launching, or have recently launched, on-line dealing and information services. At the time of writing it is not clear to what extent these will be able to offer low-cost data downloading facilities as opposed to simple live price display or quote-checking facilities.

The following section gives a summary of the different software packages available and their price points and functional capabilities. As noted before, it is well worth checking to see whether or not a demo disk is available for the software package that seems right for you. The actual functionality of the package can then be checked before you commit to buying or subscribing to it.

COST COMPARISONS AND FUNCTIONALITY

Comparing software products is a difficult exercise, but in broad terms you get what you pay for.

As I have mentioned previously, the more complex and more expensive systems are less suited to newcomers to the investment scene, and demand a lot of time and attention to extract the best value.

Table 7.5 shows a price band for each product, broadly corresponding to the entry-level, mid-range and advanced-level subdivision that most of the big software suppliers operate. There are a number of systems, however, where payment is on a subscription basis, normally bundled in with data provision. This has not been shown in the table.

Table 7.5 Software Costs and Functionality

Company name	Telephone	Contact	Product (w = Windows; d = Dos)	Price band <£100	£100–500	>£500	Port. Mgt.	Option model	Fundamentals	Teletext	Market Eye	Disk	Other formats
Alibro Software	0181 208 1067	A. Jewsbury	Marketbreaker 2000 (w)	•			•		•	•			•
Comcare CPAS	0161 902 0330	John Redgate	Candlestick Forecaster (d)	•			•		•				•
Dividend Assocs.	01264 737642	John Baker	PC Sharewatch (d)		•								
Dolphin Software	01702 545984	Ray Dolphin	Sharetracker (d)	•						•		•	•
Fairshares	01372 741969	Mike Long	Omega, Fairshares Prof (w)		•	•						•	•
Financial Software	0121 236 3180	B. Thomas	Predictor (d)	•								•	
Genie	01273 771865	Tom Williams	VSA (d,w)		•	•	•		•	•		•	
Indexia	01442 878015	J. duPlessis	Various (d)	•	•								•
Meridian	0181 309 5960	Andrew Lewis	Investor, Stockmarket 3 (d)	•	•								•
MESA (UK)	0181 303 7407	S Venovski	SUMMIT (w)	•									
Portfolio Control	0171 378 0657	C. Vintcent	PC, PC Plus, PC Prof (d)	•	•					•	•		•
Pricetrack	01275 472306	Nick Valentine	Pricetrack	•			•						
Qudos	0161 439 3926	B Millard	Microvest, Option Genius (d)	•	•			•	•	•	•		
Share Genius	0117 957948	Geoff Bacon	SG, SGOptions (d)	•					•		•	•	•
Synergy	01582 424282	M. Brookes	Various (w,d)	•	•		•			•		•	•
Trading Edge	0181 810 0607	J Anderson	Odyssey		•						•		•
Trendline	01707 644874	Bob Debnam	Metastock (w)			•		•		•	•		•
TTL	01277 353126	Jon Cloke	Invest, Insight, Supercharts (w)	•	•				•	•	•		•
Updata	0181 874 4747	David Linton	Shares, Invest, Profit (all w)	•	•					•	•		•
Winfolio	01204 385159	Steve Mann	Winfolio 2 (w)	•					•	•	•		•

In terms of what the products do—their 'functionality'—the general rule is that the more expensive the system, the more technical indicators it will have. However, even basic entry-level systems, particularly those produced by major suppliers such as Indexia, Synergy and Fairshares, have an adequate number of indicators for all but the most enthusiastic chartist.

In terms of additional facilities over and above these indicators (which are difficult to specify precisely in a table), the table shows the ability of the products to handle routine portfolio management tasks, such as CGT calculations, the recording of transactions and dealing costs, and the ability to keep a running cash account.

As readers may have deduced, I do not regard this as an essential component to a system. Many packages have the ability to export data into a spreadsheet or into an alternative personal finance monitoring system such as Quicken, thus obviating the need for an integrated portfolio management module. Other users, however, do find it easier if the facilities are all available in the same package. It's a matter of personal choice.

Comparatively few packages offer the opportunity to value options. In the main, these are additional modules that come at an extra cost to a basic package. Cheap (under £100) option pricing models are available as stand-alone packages. Market scanners and trading optimisers have not been separately identified but are generally a feature of the mid-range and particularly the upper-end software.

The incorporation of fundamental data is a feature of a number of packages, although generally this is not the main purpose behind an investor's purchase of such a program, and each of the products highlighted as offering this feature differs in the amount of data it can incorporate. In some it can be as basic as simply recording dividend yields and

PE ratios; in others the information is more sophisticated.

The Fairshares product, for example, is capable of including a variety of information, including profit and loss account and balance sheet data, details of directors' dealings, press comment and so on. This is available by subscription and comes to the user on disk. In many other systems, although the capacity to include fundamental data is part of the functionality of the system, it needs to be input manually, something of a disincentive to using it, especially for a database that includes as many as perhaps 400 or 500 shares.

Systems differ too in the different ways of downloading data that they support. Teletext download options are available for most budget-priced packages, but the data available through teletext is of less use in more sophisticated models, which require OHLCV data. Several budget packages also include a 'data by disk' service, which is one way that software supliers can gain a stream of revenue from a single purchase. These options, however, often represent a comparatively inexpensive way of getting the most out of the systems.

In the case of the mid-priced and upper-range packages, more data options are available. These include taking data from services such as Market Eye, satellite services, those using radio and pager technology, data by modem and electronic mail, and data from the Internet and World Wide Web. In general terms, the more sophisticated the package, the more flexible it will be in accepting data in different formats. Most allow the importing of data in ASCII format, however, and many US packages accept data in the format used by Metastock, one of the best-selling packages worldwide.

Several of the sophisticated systems do not use their own downloader, but expect that the user will use their package as an adjunct to another more generalised system, reading data held in its datafiles.

A rational strategy is for an investor to select a budget package from a supplier with a clearly defined 'ladder' of products through which a user can upgrade. The initial download option can either be via teletext or through another economical data source, for instance by email or through the Internet. As the user becomes more familiar, upgrading to a more sophisticated package can then be done at relatively low cost, and the option of more comprehensive data downloading can be explored.

IN BRIEF

- Investment software is increasingly used by private investors to keep track of their investments and to help make trading decisions.
- The investor has a choice between using a spreadsheet package in conjunction with a simple chart program, or buying a package that has both functions combined.
- Investment software is available in a range of prices, from under £100 to over £1000.
- Portfolio management modules contained in investment software packages enable users to record and analyse transactions, to keep track of their cash balances and investment profits and losses, and to produce valuations and Inland Revenue-acceptable capital gains tax schedules.
- Charting modules in investment software packages contain a variety of chart indicators. The more expensive the package, the more indicators it will usually contain.
- Mid-range and upper-priced packages often include software that enables the indicators to be fine-tuned to suit different shares, and which

enable the database to be scanned for shares that meet particular technical criteria.

- Downloading OHLCV data to investment software packages can represent a significant extra cost, but is usually worth it. Good quality data has the potential to improve investment decision making.

- The best strategy for the newcomer to investment software is to choose a basic package with a low-cost data download option, and then upgrade later if necessary. There is generally no penalty for upgrading.

- As the investor graduates to more complex packages, there is a hidden extra cost in terms of the extra time needed to learn about and get the best value from these packages.

CHAPTER 8

The On-Line Investor:
Shares and the Internet

The average private investor would need to be remarkably reclusive not to have heard of the Internet at some point over the past couple of years. 'Surfing the net' has become an overused buzzword. Newspapers are devoting increasing amounts of space to the subject on a regular basis.

Those connected to this international network of computers are still in something of a minority (the latest estimates suggest that there are several hundred thousand Internet users in the UK) but the numbers are growing rapidly and, among certain income groups, the percentage is much greater than average.

A recent estimate suggested, for example, that some 40% of *Financial Times* readers had Internet connections and, although many of these may have these link-ups at their place of work rather than at home, what the statistic shows is that many professionals and some private investors regard the Internet as an increasingly important resource to support their investing activities.

What this chapter aims to do is to give a brief outline of the Internet, how it has developed, how to get connected, and the resources it offers that can be used by investors either free of charge or at minimal cost.

I have already mentioned in the previous chapter that it is possible to obtain share price information and download investment software over the Internet, and even to deal in shares on-line, but there is rather more to it than that.

HOW THE INTERNET WORKS

The Internet is big. It is international in scope, but essentially a simple idea. It is nothing more than a group of computers linked together through modems and telephone lines. The computers that make up the Internet, however, take in two distinct groups.

On the one hand there are users, probably accessing the system from a standard home PC, and on the other there are larger-scale computers, often called **file-servers**. These provide the users with access to the files they contain. File-servers are often located either at commercial organisations, educational institutions or various arms of government and government-related organisations.

file-servers: computers holding information accessible by Internet users.

The networks and file-servers that make up the Internet have a number of functions. They store information and files that Internet users may be interested in. They allow electronic messages to pass from one Internet user's computer to any other user connected to the system (provided each person knows the other's electronic 'address'), and they allow users to connect to a remote computer and enter commands as if their computer keyboard were actually plugged into the computer at that site.

This means that information files, software programs and other information can be shared and transferred from one computer connected to the 'net' to any other.

One particularly interesting feature of the Internet is that nobody owns it or controls it.

It operates successfully because various organisations that make heavy use of it have been able and willing to invest in its infrastructure, and because the commercial organisations that are now also participating actively in it see the groups of people that use it as an attractive market in their own right.

The unregulated and freewheeling nature of the Internet can also be a force for good, in that it can bypass censorship and make information more readily available to closed societies. But it can also be misused, amongst others by pornographers, paedophiles and insider traders. And mirroring the concern over the potentially corrupting effects of certain aspects of the system is a concern on the part of investment regulators that the 'net' is capable of misuse by traders and investors sharing non-public information.

Ultimately, for the average private investor and for other legitimate users, the Internet is all about information. Although the Internet is big, as it has grown a number of useful facilities have developed which enable users easily to search for and pinpoint the information they require.

The Internet began as an arm of the US government connected with the defence establishment, but grew rapidly to encompass computer networks at universities and other institutions around the world, including some commercial organisations. The government-financed aspects of the Internet are proportionately much smaller now than they were, although Internet users may find that much of the information accessed through the Internet (especially, as it happens, on the investment scene) is heavily US-orientated.

This is already changing, with more and more UK- and European-based information and news becoming available. Investors will find a wealth of information from world economic news and background information on a whole range of markets, through to comprehensive price data from markets around the world, to free-to-download investment software and corporate information. Much of the information is either free or priced very competitively indeed.

GETTING CONNECTED

The essentials for getting connected to the Internet are a computer with a reasonable amount of free hard disk space, a modem and a telephone line.

The potential Internet user needs to open an account with an Internet service provider. There are a large number of service providers around, the important point being to choose one that enables you to dial into the service using a local telephone number. Most major providers have local-call 'points of presence' in major towns and cities around the country.

Table 8.1 shows a range of UK-based Internet providers with examples of their monthly charges and some other information.

Once the account is opened, the service provider should supply software enabling you to access the Internet easily and efficiently.

At this point there are a few worthwhile comments to be made. One is that it is important to remember that the speed with which downloading information (files, software etc.) can be accomplished is dependent not on the power of the computer you are using, but on the capacity of your modem.

The ideal compromise between speed and cost at the moment is a modem that runs at 28800 bps. As a rough guide this will enable connection to an Internet service provider's computer at, say, 19200 baud and permit the downloading of 100000 bytes of data in about a minute. Hence, a file that is

Table 8.1   UK Internet Service Providers

Company	Email address	Telephone	Monthly fee (£)
Atlas	info@atlas.co.uk	0171 312 0400	12.00
BBC	info@bbcnc.org.uk	0181 576 7799	12.00
Bogomip	info@mail.bogo.co.uk	0800 137536	12.00
Cityscape	sales@cityscape .co.uk	01223 566950	15.00
CIX	cixadmin@cix.compulink.co.uk	0181 296 9666	15.00*
Compuserve	70006.101@compuserve.com	0800 000200	6.50*
Delphi	ukservice@delphi.com	0171 757 7080	10.00
Demon	sales@demon.net	0181 371 1234	10.00
Easynet	admin@easynet.co.uk	0171 209 0990	9.90
Enterprise	support@enterprise.net	01624 677666	8.00
Global	info@globalnet.co.uk	0181 957 1008	10.00
Nethead	sales@nethead.co.uk	0171 207 1100	7.99
Netkonect	info@netkonect.net	0171 345 7777	10.00
Pavilion	info@pavilion.co.uk	01273 607072	12.55
PIPEX	sales@pipex.net	01223 25012	15.00
Star	info@star.co.uk	01285 647022	12.00
UK Online	sales@ulonline.co.uk	01749 333333	9.99
U-Net	hi@u-net.com	01925 633144	12.00
Zynet	zynet@zynet.net	01392 426160	10.00

* A certain number of free hours included

1.3 MB might take around 13 minutes to download from a remote computer.

The second point is that it is vital, in order to save on on-line charges, to make sure that your service provider supplies you with an 'off-line reader'. This is a piece of software—rather like an autopilot for your computer's routine on-line voyages—that enables you to perform various on-line functions, such as downloading information, particularly messages from newsgroups (see below), sending and receiving email, and so on, in the minimum time possible. The information can then be stored and read off-line at leisure.

A third facet of Internet connections that needs checking out thoroughly is to ensure, if you are

PPP/SLIP:
Internet connection that permits the downloading of graphics-based displays.

planning to use the World Wide Web (see below) extensively, that you have a direct Internet link (a so-called **PPP/SLIP** connection) via your service provider. This enables you to link your computer directly to the Internet and is flexible enough to enable you to use a graphics-based browser like Mosaic or Netscape to download both pictures and text.

Text-based software for browsing the web is available, but is less user-friendly. In particular, it does not permit the downloading of easy-to-read graphical information from World Wide Web pages. The cost of obtaining this extra facility is negligible, but not all service providers can offer it.

The cost of the whole exercise is less than you might think. Many service providers work on the basis of simple time-based charges for on-line usage, subject to a monthly minimum. Telephone charges come on top.

What does this add up to? In my own case, for regular but not unduly heavy usage, my charges average out at around £20 per month, but the figure has been as low as £9 and as high as £70.

It is, however, worth looking at an Internet connection the other way—in terms of what getting connected can save in other directions.

electronic mail:
email, a way of sending messages instantaneously to any other Internet address.

For example, the cost of electronic mail is negligible, with the connection time being a few seconds of local telephone time compared to perhaps 30 seconds or more per page for a fax, and 25p for a normal letter. **Electronic mail** (or email) can be used to send documents and files stored on your computer's hard disk, with the transmission time being just a few seconds and the costs just those of a local call, *irrespective of the destination*.

So much for the basics. Now let's explore the types of service that are available on the Internet, what use they are to investors, and how they can be accessed.

INTERNET RESOURCES

Newsgroups

One of the most interesting aspects of the Internet is the ability it offers users to canvas the views and make contact with a wide range of other individuals who also have 'net' connections. Newsgroups (sometimes called conferences or forums) offer the opportunity to request information, express opinions or contribute to a debate on virtually any topic.

Forums are run by individual service providers on a variety of topics, while there is also a whole raft of newsgroups run under the umbrella of **Usenet**, a US organisation. Access to all of these newsgroups is free although in some cases access is restricted and potential users may have to demonstrate that they have something to contribute.

Usenet: A US bulletin board network.

The newsgroup principle works as follows: the user logs on through a service provider to the newsgroups of his or her choice. The off-line reader will connect to the system periodically to download all of the messages 'posted' on what is really a giant electronic bulletin board. These can be read off-line and replies composed to some messages if thought appropriate.

Also, the user can post a message to the group, initiating discussion on a new topic. In effect, bulletin boards or newsgroups are simply a central point to which electronic mail can be posted for all other participants in the group to see. Users are then free to continue a discussion either by private email or in the public forum, as they wish.

The main investment-related newsgroups I have detected on the Usenet system are ones related to technical analysis, to individual stock recommendations, to general investment topics and one related to UK finance. The latter is really orientated towards personal finance topics, but is interesting nonetheless.

The other three newsgroups I have mentioned are heavily US-orientated and often contain rambling discussions on topics that may not much interest a non-US reader. Unlike the newsgroups operated by some of the UK service providers, Usenet groups are not 'moderated' (i.e. supervised) to prevent the discussions straying off-topic. But notwithstanding a lot of information that UK users may feel is worse than useless, there are occasional gems, including posts that highlight new sources of investment software, opinions on US matters that may be relevant to the UK investment scene, and so on.

Each service provider operates a different set of newsgroups for the community of users it services. In the case of the service provider I use, these include several groups on general investment topics, including the merits or otherwise of particular types of investment software and data providers, as well as occasional views on stocks.

I have found newsgroups an interesting source of information, but it is worth restricting the number you log on to quite strictly. Some groups have more than 100 'posts' per day, which can take some reading. There are systems available that enable posts on particular topics or from particular contributors to be filtered out prior to the updates being downloaded, but even so the daily routine of ploughing through newsgroup messages can become a chore.

On the plus side, I have communicated and had responses back from a number of fellow users on a variety of topics, and been able to access obscure sources of information by putting up an SOS message on a bulletin board. Newsgroups have allowed me to pick up some investment 'vibes' and investing ideas through keeping my eyes open when reading newsgroup posts. Hopefully others have gained insights from my contributions too.

Not surprisingly perhaps, Internet newsgroup users have particularly strong views on any form of on-line investor service and on technology stocks related to the Internet and the various industries servicing it. This can be useful if this is an investment area you find of interest, although some of the views expressed need to be taken with a pinch of salt. Internet newsgroups are particularly prone to people 'talking their book', i.e. recommending shares they already hold.

Just to give something of flavour, the posts I downloaded from the UK finance newsgroup today included the following 'headlines':

- Suggested Name for European Currency
- APR Question
- FT-SE100/FT30 Constituents
- Investment Data Services—Has anyone used their courses?
- Can I have a PEP with two different companies?
- UK Bond Rates On-Line Site

The World Wide Web

Non-Internet users and first-timers are often confused over the distinction between the Internet and the World Wide Web. The two are often taken to be synonymous, whereas in fact the web is simply a part, albeit perhaps the most high profile one, of the 'net'.

Whereas newsgroups permit interaction between single Internet users or groups of them, by and large the World Wide Web is a passive information resource. Web 'pages' are designed and launched and can be visited or (in the jargon) 'hit' by any connected Internet user. To get the best out of the web and its colour and graphics it is necessary to have a PPP/SLIP connection that enables colour graphics as well as text to be downloaded

web browser:
software enabling
the user to
navigate the
graphics-rich pages
of the World Wide
Web. The most
commonly used is
produced by
Netscape.

hypertext:
embedded links in
text contained on
web pages that
enable the user,
through a simple
mouse click, to
jump to another
area of the web.

quickly via a **web 'browser'** like Netscape or Mosaic.

The web is based around a concept known as **'hypertext'**, whereby clicking on a highlighted area will transfer another set of data from the host computer to your own. This enables web pages to have complex links both to data and text embedded in their own system and also to other relevant sites operated by different organisations. They thereby allow the user to explore wherever the mood dictates.

As an example, a Stock Exchange site might have various pages highlighting new issues, trading volume and index statistics, biographies of exchange officials and articles of interest on relevant subjects, each accessed by clicking on an icon at the original 'home page'. But it will also have hypertext links to other exchanges, leading companies, other investment-related sites, regulators and so on. Each link is accessible through a simple point and click, and the transfer of data is normally accomplished within a few seconds.

There are already a large number of stock market related web pages available. The following sections of this chapter mainly deal with web pages related to different aspects of the investment process, and the information that can be gleaned from them.

The web is growing exponentially at the moment, and keeping track of new web pages that may be of interest can be something of a problem. One solution to this is the existence of so-called 'search engines' which, by working on search criteria carefully specified by the user, can quickly present a user with a list of web addresses that appear to be relevant to the subject matter being investigated. Some of these may turn out to be red herrings, but then again others may contain links to other sites that turn out to be of relevance.

Table 8.2 Web Sites: General Jumping-Off Points

Site	URL	Brief description
Wall Street Direct	http://www.wsdinc.com/	Variety of net resources, including software (US orientated)
Lenape Investment Co.	http://www.voicenet.com/rsauers	Comprehensive list of investment-related Internet resources
Banks and Finance	http://www.qualisteam.com/	Links to banks and finance sites worldwide (some menus in French)
Investorama	http://www.investorama.com/	Good general site with a variety of links
Internet Sleuth	http://www.intbc.com/sleuth/index.html	Direct link to search engines on a variety of topics

In some of my journalistic work, I have, for example, successfully researched background information for a variety of topics, from software for charities, to money laundering, risk management and the economic background to Romania, simply by keying in a few search criteria and spending a little time exploring the resulting web sites.

The real beauty of the system is that a lot of the information is free of charge. As with some of the newsgroups, US content predominates in many areas, but the system is gradually being filled out with content from other non-US sources. When a suitable page of information is found that a user wants to retain, the page can be saved with a 'bookmark' that allows easy revisiting of the page in future. Alternatively, the user can email the information contained in a page to his or her own electronic address and view it off-line in the normal way, or print it out.

As well as bookmarks, it is also possible to build up a list of broad jumping-off points that contain a large number of links to other sites related to the same subject. Bookmarking sites like this means that a vast range of other sites is only a couple of mouse clicks away. Some of these are shown in Table 8.2.

Prices and data

One of the more interesting features of the Internet and the web is the opportunity they offer private investors to access data that has hitherto been largely the preserve of the professional investor, and moreover to do so at relatively low cost. There are a number of web services that charge, but the charges are often surprisingly modest.

Free sites are sometimes subsidised by advertising, since the connected community represents a target socio-economic group that advertisers find attractive. Registering for free services is sometimes used as a teaser to get the user hooked on the information being supplied, prior to charges being introduced at a later date.

At the same time there is little doubt that one of the side effects of the Internet has been to open private investors' eyes to the information that is available in other markets (notably the USA) at relatively low cost, and therefore begin a process of exerting downward pressure on information charges in the domestic market concerned.

This is a particular bone of contention in the UK, where the Stock Exchange has in the past exerted a rather baleful influence over data suppliers and their charges to end users. The market's monopoly of information has recently been challenged by the advent of competing exchanges such as Tradepoint (essentially a professionals' market but one wedded to the idea that data costs should be kept down), and also by the initiative mounted by Electronic Share Information (ESI). ESI launched the first Internet-based share dealing service and also offers what is arguably the cheapest service for downloading comprehensive price data for use in a spreadsheet or chart package.

Fundamental data on potential investments is obtainable, but sometimes only at a price, although again often a surprisingly modest one. Subscribers to the *Hambro Company Guide,* for instance, can gain access to the publisher's World Wide Web page and download the latest updated information on the companies contained in the Guide. The service may also be extended (with the cooperation of the companies concerned) to include more comprehensive data, including brokers' earnings estimates and annual reports.

In the USA it is possible to access corporate filings with the Securities and Exchange Commission (the US stock market regulator) free via its searchable web pages. At present no such free service exists in the UK, but on-line company searches are available at a price (which may eventually come down).

Another site, an adjunct to a personal finance newspaper, offers brief statistical comparisons and a searchable index of data on all UK unit and investment trusts, courtesy of trade associations and publishers of the relevant statistics. Although gaining further more detailed information may cost extra, the site offers a useful facility for narrowing investment choices in this particular area.

One highly positive aspect of all the developments like this is that the opening up of information which the professionals previously largely had to themselves removes the mystique from the investment process and, without too much exaggeration, opens up the possibility of true shareholder democracy, where all shareholders and potential shareholders have equal (or at least nearly equal) access to relevant information about various investments and market matters at the same time.

On-line dealing

In the USA, investing is part of daily life for millions of people, even down to the fact that many stockbrokers have a retail presence on high streets across America. In this environment too, the idea of clients dealing by PC or by some other automated means is commonplace.

One of the aspects of share investment in the UK that has arguably put off many potential private investors over the years has been the concern people have about being embarrassed talking to a broker. Will the broker have time to spend on their order? Will he be patronising and snooty? Will he be too busy? Will the investor feel embarrassed about betraying ignorance about the ins and outs of the market?

In fairness to the private client broking community, many of these worries are just old psychological hang-ups that may once have represented real problems. Now they no longer square much with reality, at least when it comes to dealing with execution-only brokers, who by and large are approachable and businesslike.

There are, however, those who find conversing with dealers a needless hassle, and who would be happy to do their share trading over a PC link rather than via a telephone conversation.

Services offering this facility have begun to appear. Password-protected, the user logs into the service, types in the details of the share trade required, and confirms the order. It is then passed to the broker. The trade is executed and the details confirmed electronically to the client.

At the time of writing the main alternatives available for dealing in this way are share trading over the Internet through the ESI system mentioned previously, and on the other hand inputting trades via private networks set up by individual brokers and other organisations.

ESI is in partnership with the execution-only broker ShareLink in its endeavour. Through the ESI web page, the registered user can pass through the ShareLink trading gateway, access live quotes on shares he or she is interested in dealing in, type in order details and, once the trade is executed, have the contract details confirmed by email within the hour. The user is required to open a ShareLink 'Marketmaster' account before this service can be used. This links the customer's trading account with a high interest bank account, simplifying settlement procedures.

Other services include Infotrade, set up by Apricot Computers and bankrolled by Mitsubishi. This service offers a bundled service of share information and dealing via ShareLink (again), City Deal

Services, and other execution-only broker. The basic slug of information to start off the service is supplied on CD-ROM and thereafter updated by modem. The information supplied includes fundamental information on a wide range of companies, chart drawing facilities and so on. The launch version of the service offered only rudimentary data of this type, but enhancements have been promised and the dealing interface appears particularly easy to use.

Other brokers, notably Fidelity, are thought likely to offer on-line trading services in due course, probably via a private dial-up network rather than over the Internet. In Fidelity's case the service is likely to include access to systems used by dealers, the ability to enter orders and have instantaneous confirmation that the order has been done, and the ability to combine an on-line facility with discounted commission rates.

This may be preferable to the previously introduced services, which are not particularly cheap in commission terms and do not by and large offer on-line order confirmation at the time the trade is placed. However, on-line dealing services are evolving all the time, and generalisations of this type are therefore risky.

There is, however, no doubt that on-line trading is popular in the US and will probably become so here. One of the leading retail brokers in the US now reckons to receive 35% of its order intake by means (such as PC links) that require no human intervention. It is easy to see the same system catching on in this country.

Software

One of the advantages, and cost saving elements, of the Internet is the ability it offers to transfer software programs from a remote computer to another

Internet user's PC. There are several sites, almost all in the USA, where investment software is available and able to be downloaded free of charge.

In the past this software has been in a **shareware** form. That is to say, the programs are fully working versions that can be used perfectly well by the person downloading the software, but need to be registered to gain the full user support, including manuals, access to later versions and so on.

More recently, however, some software sites appear to be changing this policy. A number of software sites on the World Wide Web, for example, enable software to be downloaded, but only either in a demo version, in a version that self-destructs after a restricted number of uses, or in a version that is 'crippled' in some way so that the user is obliged to purchase the fully working version if he or she likes the look of the package.

There are two basic ways of downloading investment software, or indeed any software, over the Internet. One is via World Wide Web sites. Here, if software is available for downloading, clicking on the appropriate underlined and highlighted phrase or icon will initiate a download and prompt the user to specify a directory into which the downloaded software is to be placed.

It is a good idea to have already created an empty directory before contemplating a download. When the download is completed, clicking on the .exe file among those downloaded will normally initiate the setup sequence and create a new directory in which the program can reside. Once this is accomplished, the files in the 'download' directory can be deleted.

The other means of downloading is through what is known as **FTP**, or file transfer protocol. Internet service providers differ in the programs they offer for accomplishing this task but at its most basic, the user will need to have some working

shareware: *free software that can be downloaded from the Internet for evaluation. If found useful, the user is under a moral obligation to buy the full version.*

FTP: *file transfer protocol, the means by which a file or files can be transferred from a remote computer to the user's own.*

familiarity with UNIX program commands. These are not difficult to master. The advantage of FTP over downloading from a web page is that it enables the user to browse through a much bigger list of directories and files, downloading the ones that appear to be of interest.

The process goes something like this: from a normal Internet protocol prompt (normally signalled as IP> or sometimes just a percentage sign thus %, the user will connect to the site, probably by typing the command ftp <sitename>.

Accessing, for example, the file-server at the UK's popular Imperial College site the user would type (from an IP> prompt) ftp ftp.sunsite. doc.ic.ac.uk. Once connected the user is asked for a user name. The convention here is to type in the word anonymous, guest or ftp. The user will then be asked for a password. Here, for a so-called 'anonymous' login, the user would type in his or her full email address.

Once accepted, from the system prompt, the UNIX commands ls (list) and cd <directory name> (change directory) can be used to root around for the desired file.

Directories are recognisable in UNIX by a string of characters on the left-hand side of the screen beginning with the letter 'd'; those that do not are files. Files normally have unintelligible code names (towards the right-hand side of the screen), but do have the file size in bytes displayed in the preceding column, so the user must be reasonably sure of the code name for the file and/or its approximate size before embarking on the exercise. Once the file has been identified, typing get <filename.file extension> will begin the file transfer. For those without a direct Internet connection the file will drop into the user's IP file at his service provider's host computer, from where it must be downloaded to the user's own terminal later.

Table 8.3   Web Sites: Software

Site	URL	Description
Bulletproof	http://www.bulletproof.com	The Edge trading software
Wall Street Software	http://www.fastlane.net/homepages/wallst	Various
Dollar	http://www.creative.net/dollar	Dollar technical analysis software
Elliott Wave	http://www.iinet.com.au/cewa	Elliott Wave Analysis
Data Broadcast	http://www.dbc.com	Various demos
Tierra	http://www.cyberspace.com/tierra	Various demos
Optionvue	http://www.optionvue.com	Option valuation software

All of this sounds rather cumbersome, but with a little practice it is quite easy. One other useful aspect of the Internet is that, because of its growth potential, many suppliers of software utilities make them available free in order to get them used. This means that, as well as investment software, a user may well find that a variety of other useful programs can be downloaded.

There is another aspect to the whole question of downloading software. This is that the availability of software over the Internet in effect internationalises the market for investment software. Like share price data sold by exchanges, software of this type is significantly cheaper in the USA, and this phenomenon is likely to exert downward pressure on prices of software originating elsewhere.

Examples of some software programs available over the Internet are given in Table 8.3, and readers who are connected are encouraged to experiment in downloading them. It goes without saying that downloaded files should be checked for viruses before being executed.

On-line publications and news

In a previous chapter I highlighted the need for investors to be on the look-out for information in newspapers and other publications. Some readers may, for example, have been shocked by the size of my regular weekly paper bill and concerned that this would make the cost of pursuing their investment activities prohibitive.

The Internet offers a way round this. Newspapers are increasingly publishing on-line as an adjunct to their news-stand product. Accessing these electronic papers can be a good way of making sure that the City pages of the leading quality papers can be read on a daily basis, at a fraction of the cost of buying the actual paper.

In the UK the *Daily Telegraph* has been the pioneer in this field with its site containing market reports and diary items as well as news stories and even cartoons. *The Times,* the *Financial Times* and *The Economist* also have sites, as does the *Guardian,* although the latter is more an extension of its weekly On-Line supplement. A number of overseas publications, including the *Wall Street Journal* and various investment newsletters, also have web pages. More often than not these tend to be accessible in an unexpurgated version only by payment of a subscription.

In these instances, the reader needs to make a judgement about whether the cost of the subscription is worth the charge involved. The rules given earlier regarding the paramount need to feel that you get something tangible from a publication on a regular basis and that it is always keenly read on the date of issue should be the guiding principle here.

Another recently introduced investment site, masterminded by IBM and using Reuters news feeds, takes the form of a news ticker that can be set to update periodically and through which, simply by clicking on a menu of news headlines, the full story can be accessed and read. The service, at the time of writing totally free to use, can be used to check on business developments and other news stories of investment interest, although it does not encompass detailed UK company news at this stage.

Table 8.4 gives details of various sites at which on-line newspapers and newsletters can be found and the reader is recommended to test them out, along with the IBM InfoMarket service described in the preceding paragraph.

Exchanges

An increasing number of financial markets around the world have sites on the World Wide Web offering

Table 8.4 Web Sites: News and Publications

Site	URL	Description
The Economist	http://www.economist.com	*The Economist*
Guardian On-Line	http://go2.guardian.co.uk	*Guardian's* On-Line supplement
The Times	http://www.the-times.co.uk	Electronic version of *The Times*
Electronic Telegraph	http://telegraph.co.uk	Electronic version of the *Daily Telegraph*
FT	http://www.ft.com	Electronic *Financial Times*
New York Times	http://nytimesfax.com	Selected stories from the *New York Times*
IBM News Ticker	http://www.infomkt.ibm.com/ticker.htm	Downloadable news ticker software (linked to Reuters feeds)
Bloomberg	http://www.bloomberg.com	Business news stories and stats
Knight Ridder Financial	http://www.krf.com	Ditto
San Jose Mercury	http://www.sjmercury.com	Silicon Valley news and views
Electronic Newsstand	http://www.enews.com	Links to various publications
Wall Street Journal	http://www.wsj.com/circ/	

Table 8.5   Web Sites: Exchanges, Government and Regulators

Site	URL	Description
AIM	http://www.worldserver.pipex.com/aim/index.htm	UK's AIM market: company details etc.
Securities & Exchange Commission	http://www.sec.gov	SC site including EDGAR: searchable database of US company filings
LIFFE	http://www.liffe.com	Comprehensive London futures exchange site
Chicago Board of Trade	http://www.cbot.com	US futures exchange site
Chicago Merc.	http://www.cme.com	US futures exchange site
MEFF	http://www.meff.es	Spanish futures market site
AMEX	http://www.amex.com	American Stock Exchange
Bolsa	http://www.bolsamadrid.es	Spanish stock exchange site
Swiss Stock Exchange	http://www.bourse.ch	Swiss markets
HM Treasury	http://www.hm-treasury.gov.uk	Treasury site
French Treasury	http://www.tresor.finances.fr/oat/	French treasury site (including bond data)
CFTC	http://www.clark.net/pub/cftc/home.html	US futures industry regulator

a variety of information about the exchange, trading statistics, share and option price data, and links to other sites of interest.

In the UK, for example, the AIM small company share market has a web site that offers details on all of the companies listed including recent press releases for each one, listing information, price charts and other data. This site can be found at the URL http://www.worldserver.pipex.com/aim/index.htm. The London International Financial Futures and Options Exchange (LIFFE) also has a site (URL http://www.liffe.com) which contains a substantial body of information about the exchange, its products and prices of the various instruments traded, normally on a time-delayed basis.

Investment exchanges in different territories are often a good source of information on the movement of local indices and leading stocks, providing a free source of information superior to that normally obtainable from newpapers or other sources. For investors who are interested in investing internationally, this is clearly a useful and valuable resource.

Table 8.5 gives examples of some of the exchanges displaying information of this type, and the addresses of their web pages.

Corporate information

The corporate sector as a whole in the UK has been somewhat ambivalent about the development of the Internet. An informal survey of the FT-SE 100 conducted in April 1995 revealed, for instance, that fewer than ten companies had an active Internet presence at that time, while only a further dozen or so had any plans to develop one in anything other than the long term.

The survey's questions were orientated towards the provision of information relevant to investors (i.e. press releases, annual reports and so on) and it is perhaps important to distinguish between this and the provision of consumer-orientated information.

Web pages aimed at customers and potential product users have become more prevalent in recent months, especially among companies keen to tap up-market consumers. Those with sites either active or planned include British Airways, Vodafone, Cable & Wireless, Guinness, Tesco and Sainsbury.

Many of these large organisations provide information of use to those seeking details about a company's product range, but fight shy of providing information that could be of use to investors. The ostensible reason for this is that the demand for investor information can supposedly be satisfied in other ways, without going to the additional expense of providing an investor relations presence on the World Wide Web.

The process may be a case of 'chicken and egg'. If enough investors ring in for press releases and annual reports then it will be worthwhile for the company to set up a web page or an automatic email list to cater for the demand for items of this nature. Conversely, publicising such a site costs money and clearly would only reach those investors who are connected. As it is, though, some of these investors feel intimidated about ringing to request items of this nature—a sentiment that would be avoided if the documents could be accessed on-line.

The prototype service that I would hope many 'footsie' companies might eventually adopt for private investors connected to the Internet would be a web page containing basic corporate information and a copy of the latest annual report. To this could also be added a system, similar to that currently operated by the Treasury, whereby any interested party can subscribe to an electronic mailing list,

Table 8.6 Web Sites: Corporate and Other Information

Site	URL	Description
Barclays Bank	http://www.barclays.co.uk	Barclays Bank stockbrokers and credit cards
Legal & General	http://www.Legal-and-General.co.uk/lg	Insurance company site with policy details
Sainsbury	http://www.j-sainsbury.co.uk	Sainsbury site, including press releases etc.
Tesco	http://www.tesco.co.uk	Includes annual report, news releases etc.
Hambro Company Guide	http://www.hemscott.co.uk/hemscott	Company information from the well-known guide
Interactive Investor	http://www.iii.co.uk	Information on unit and investment trusts, PEPs and other personal finance products
Apple	http://www.apple.com	Information on the computer company
Microsoft	http://www.microsoft.com	Information on the computer company
Intel	http://www.intel.com	Information on the computer company
Silicon Graphics	http://www.sgi.com	Information on the computer company
Hoovers Profiles	http://www.hoovers.com	Worldwide company profiles (subscription based)
European Union	http://www.cec.lu	Europa server for EU data

which ensures that press releases—in this instance relating to economic statistics and other matters—are sent simultaneously by electronic mail to all subscribers at the same time as they are released to the stock market. The service is free.

Were such a system to be adopted by the corporate sector, it might go most of the way towards eliminating the feeling that many private investors have that they are always somewhat behind the times when it comes to accessing financial information.

It may take time for such a concept to get off the ground in the absence of a legal requirement to provide such a service. With some minor effort on the part of authorities it could easily happen, for example by being written into Stock Exchange listing agreements.

Table 8.6 shows the types of service that some listed UK companies, and large US companies, provide, together with the appropriate URLs.

TO CONNECT OR NOT?

I believe strongly that the Internet and on-line information sources have a central role to play in making the market more accessible to the needs of ordinary investors in a way that the privatisation wave of the 1980s did not do.

Privatisations may have widened share ownership but they did not deepen it. They created many new shareholders, but most of these shareholders only held or hold a single share, and the success they may have achieved in this one instance has not yet been successfully broadened out into a wider interest in the market and a fostering of a regular investment habit.

This is a pity, but the advent of the Internet and on-line investment data and services can be a powerful force for democratising the market and opening it up to a much wider and computer-literate audience. Exchanges and data providers now seem generally to be recognising what can be accomplished and the next few years are likely to see a sharp increase in the services available in this area.

It should be stressed, however, that the availability of all this information does not eliminate the need for investors to make sound judgements about buying and selling shares, and about selecting good investments in the first place.

All the Internet and other on-line sources can do is deliver information more efficiently. What use the individual investor makes of this information is another matter entirely.

IN BRIEF

- Connecting to the Internet offers investors a relatively low cost way of tapping into more investment information.
- Internet newsgroups are interactive forums in which a variety of topics are discussed. There are several investment-related newsgroups.
- The World Wide Web offers information on a variety of topics related to investment, and the ability to search for information on investment topics and companies.
- There are a number of web sites that offer the ability to download share price data either free or at low cost.
- There are a number of web sites that offer the opportunity to download shareware or demo versions of investment software.
- Various newspapers, newsletters and investment publications have Internet sites. Using these can cut down on the costs of buying or subscribing to the conventional issues of the same publications.

- On-line trading is likely to increase in importance in the future.
- From the standpoint of the UK investor, the
  long-term importance of the Internet is that it
  will reduce the cost of investment software and
  data to the prices in the most competitive
  market worldwide (currently the USA).

More Advanced Techniques and Strategies

This chapter attempts to pull together some of things we have explored in the chapters on fundamental analysis, technical analysis and portfolio diversification, and give an insight into some of the more advanced analysis and trading techniques that can be used.

Broadly speaking, these fall into four categories:

- additional financial ratios that can be calculated from profit and loss account, cash flow and balance sheet numbers to help give a more in-depth picture of a company's financial position.
- how to spot creative accounting.
- using discounted cash flow techniques to value shares.
- additional ways in which share price information can be analysed in order to help time share purchases and sales more accurately.

Each of these sections should be regarded as a continuation of the material contained respectively in Chapters 3, 4 and 6. The relevant parts of these chapters should be read in their entirety before tackling this one.

MORE FINANCIAL RATIOS

In Chapter 3 we looked at how it was possible to examine company accounts and use the figures contained in them to calculate ratios that can reveal underlying strengths or weaknesses in performance.

To recap, the ratios we looked at were:

- Gross margin: percentage of gross profit to sales
- Operating margin: percentage of operating profit to sales
- Pre-tax margin: percentage of pre-tax profit to sales
- Interest cover: ratio of interest paid to pre-interest profit
- Current ratio: ratio of current assets to current liabilities
- Acid ratio: ratio of current assets less stocks to current liabilities
- Gearing: percentage of net debt to net assets
- Return on capital: percentage of pre-interest profit to capital employed
- Return on equity: percentage of pre-tax profit to net assets

These ratios remain the most important ones to calculate when first looking at a balance sheet, but there are some obvious omissions.

One gap that needs filling is to look at P&L account ratios that give a more detailed breakdown of a company's costs. A second is that none of the ratios mentioned previously is based on the company's cash flow statements, which can also be analysed in a number of different ways. And a third is to look in more detail at working capital (stocks, debtors and creditors), and at how productively or otherwise the company's assets, both capital and labour, are used.

Calculating all of these ratios might be thought to be time-consuming, but it can pay dividends in terms of the insight it gives into the financial condition of a company in whose shares an investor might be contemplating committing a chunk of hard-earned surplus cash. Not spending a little time investigating a situation in greater depth is foolish.

In any case, as indicated in a previous chapter, it is easy enough to program these ratios into a conventional computer spreadsheet file and calculate automatically by inputting some of the basic numbers. Doing this cuts down the time involved, makes the whole process less daunting, and allows the investor to focus on what the numbers actually mean.

I have illustrated this approach using an actual company, the JD Wetherspoon pub group. The financial ratios shown in the tables have been calculated by inputting numbers from the accounts into a pre-programmed Excel spreadsheet file. The template used calculates the ratios mentioned in the earlier chapter and those additional ones mentioned below.

Profit ratios

In the profit and loss account, the additional ratios not previously mentioned primarily relate to cost items pulled out before arriving at operating profits. For instance, by law companies must disclose in their accounts staff costs and numbers, and various items relating to directors' pay and shareholdings.

Expressing total *staff costs as a percentage of sales* is the most convenient way of measuring this item. To get the full value from it, however, one needs to compared the trend in staff costs to sales over a period of years to judge whether or not the company has its wage bill under control. Similarly, the total of staff costs and other operating charges (excluding depreciation), expressed as a percentage of sales, shows the extent to which the company has the costs under its direct influence under strict control.

Directors' pay can be a good indication of corporate management style. In almost every instance it should be taken as a positive factor if the directors have significant ongoing direct shareholdings in the business, ideally running into significant (say double figure) percentages of the share capital.

Direct shareholdings are preferable to share option holdings because the latter may simply have been granted as part of a pay and perks package, and do not represent the actual investment or retention of hard-earned personal cash in the business. A *sizable stake held by management* in this way means that the management team is highly likely to act in a way that maximises long-term shareholder value, since the board's own financial interests and those of the mass of shareholders coincide.

It should come as no surprise to anyone that management remuneration can be excessive. It is comparatively easy to work out whether management is giving value for money by taking the remuneration of the highest paid director (normally the chief executive) and/or the total for the board as a whole and expressing this as a percentage of either pre-tax profits or the market value of the company. Comparing a number of companies in the same sector in this way gives some idea as to whether managements are over- or under-rewarding themselves.

This is subject to the proviso that, in proportion, directors in small companies often appear to be paid more than those in larger ones, even though their salaries may be much more modest in absolute terms. But there is little excuse for management teams to be paid substantially in excess of the average for companies of a similar size in the same industry.

Table 9.1   Profit & Loss Account Items and Related Ratios

		Year to: 31st July		
	1992	1993	1994	1995
Turnover	21380	30800	46600	68536
Cost of sales	7773	10784	16835	37616
Gross profit	13607	20016	29765	30920
Staff costs	4226	5791	8372	12562
Depreciation	523	908	1422	2397
Other operating charges	3764	7241	11184	3729
Operating profit	5094	6076	8787	12232
Non-operating Items	–58	0	0	0
PBIT	5152	6076	8787	12232
Net interest paid	3074	1905	2310	2519
Pre-tax profit	2078	4171	6477	9713
Taxation	117	449	563	755
Profit after taxation	1961	3722	5914	8958
Minorities				
Preference				
Attributable profit	1961	3722	5914	8958
Extraordinary items				
Dividends	350	1546	2234	2927
Retained profits	1611	2176	3680	6031
Earnings per share	12.6	14.4	18.2	24.6
Dividend per share	2.38	5.4	6.6	8.0
Cover	5.29	2.67	2.76	3.08
Gross margin (%)	63.64	64.99	63.87	45.11
Operating margin (%)	23.83	19.73	18.86	17.85
Pre-tax margin (%)	9.72	13.54	13.90	14.17
Staff costs: sales (%)	19.77	18.80	17.97	18.33
Total op. charges: sales (%)	39.82	45.26	45.02	27.27
Tax charge (%)	5.63	10.76	8.69	7.77

The *tax charge* is simply the percentage that tax represents of pre-tax profits. This may be reduced by capital allowances if a company is investing heavily, but it is a good idea, if this is the case, to try to assess how likely it is to persist at this level. Good profits growth further up the P&L account can be eroded or even completely offset or reversed when it comes to earnings per share (a key driver of the share price) if the tax charge rises in the meantime.

Wetherspoon's profit and loss account figures and the associated ratios are shown in Table 9.1.

It is important that the figures are entered precisely and that the subtotals calculated automatically by the worksheet are cross-checked to make sure they agree with the accounts. In this table 14 lines have to be entered, with the remaining 13 calculated automatically.

In fact, this table illustrates some of the problems the diligent investor can come up against. In this case it can be seen that the figure for gross margin changes abruptly in 1995. This is not due to any underlying change in the business, but simply a change in the accounts in the way the figures are presented.

More pertinently, perhaps, it can be seen from the operating margin line that this figure has dropped steadily over the four-year period but that, thanks to the company's ability to raise extra funds from its shareholders, and thereby limit its interest charges, its pre-tax margin has risen. Looking further down the table, staff costs have remained relatively stable as a percentage of sales, but the operating charges percentage has been distorted as explained above.

Most interestingly, the company's tax charge has been substantially below the 30% plus norm, over the period. This is due to the heavy investment in fixed assets being made by the company, but the fact of a low tax charge always carries with it the possibility that at some future date it will rise and suppress growth in after-tax profit and earnings per share.

Cash flow ratios

Turning to the cash flow statement, this is often revealing enough in itself, without substantial further analysis. However, there are a number of ratios that can be calculated over and above a simple scan of the numbers and a look at the notes to the statement.

One of the main variables that can be picked out from the cash flow statement is the net amount a company has spent on new fixed assets. This can be compared with a number of other parameters.

First, depreciation: as was explained in Chapter 3, this is the amount set aside to replace fixed assets. It is normally calculated by dividing the cost of the assets by their expected life. By comparing depreciation to spending on fixed assets, it is possible to gauge the extent to which a company is investing for growth.

In some instances this approach does not work. In the case of a company spending on plant and machinery, the likelihood is that this spending will be modestly in excess of the amount set aside to replace earlier acquisitions of equipment. In the case of companies with assets that depreciate slowly, such as freehold property, a growing company is likely to spend many times its depreciation charge each year.

Fixed asset spending can also be compared with sales and with capital employed to see how consistent the spending is over a period of years. Another way of looking at the figures generated in a cash flow statement is to compare broad groups of 'spending' figures with the total for operating cash flow.

Cash outflows for most companies fall into three broad categories: those going to providers of capital (such as interest and dividend payments); those going to the government (tax); and those going to suppliers of new fixed assets and vendors of businesses acquired. Leaving aside tax, the other categories can be respectively grouped together as the net cash outflow for finance and the net cash outflow for investment. Both of these aggregates can be compared with the overall operating cash inflow.

Normally, the proportions of these ratios (represented in the table by NCO(I): Op CF and NCO(F): Op CF) will move around a little over time. It is, though, important to remember that, taking several years together, if the two ratios add up to more than 100% it means that the company is consistently spending more cash than is coming in. The inevitable result of this is that some form of additional permanent financing, most likely a rights issue, will eventually be required.

In the case of Wetherspoon, the numbers can be seen in Table 9.2.

Here again, it is important that the figures are input precisely, and that the plus and minus signs are also recorded. Accounting conventions dictate that in published accounts a negative figure (that is a loss, outflow or expense) is often represented by the figure concerned being bracketed.

Perhaps the most significant figure here is that fixed asset investment as a percentage of sales has remained remarkably consistent. The figure immediately below reflects Wetherspoon's orientation towards investing in property, which is normally held to depreciate very slowly. What the 1995 ratio shows in this instance, for example (a figure of 1569.46), is that the company last year spent on fixed assets a figure 15 times its provision for depreciation.

Fixed asset investment as a percentage of net capital employed, again comparatively stable over the period, may be a better guide to the group's pattern of investment.

The bottom two ratios in the table show the grouped figures for spending allocated to providers of finance (net cash outflow—finance, or NCO(F)), namely interest and dividends, and the similar figure for investment—namely spending on fixed

Table 9.2   Cash Flow Statement and Ratios

	1992	1993	1994	1995
		Year to: 31st July		
Cash inflow from op. activity	7142	7713	11028	19762
Interest received	15	299	86	55
Interest paid	−3472	−2667	−2370	−2803
Dividends received	0	0	0	0
Dividends paid	−265	−865	−1673	−2601
Net cash outflow (finance)	−3722	−3233	−3957	−5349
Tax paid	−122	−266	−460	−655
Purchase of fixed assets	−11700	−16364	−23217	−37620
Purchase of investments				
Purchase of subsidiaries				
Sale of fixed assets	2756	197	22	11
Net cash outflow (investing)	−8944	−16167	−23195	−37609
Net cash inflow pre-financing	−5646	−11953	−16584	−23851
Share issues	458	18297	22345	527
Loan repayments	5899	−3832	5449	18419
Change in cash/equivalents	711	2512	11210	−4905
Net capital employed	48222	66937	100614	127093
Depreciation	523	908	1422	2397
Sales	21380	30800	46600	68536
Fixed asset inv.: sales (%)	54.72	53.13	49.82	54.89
Fixed asset inv.: dep'n (%)	2237.09	1802.20	1632.70	1569.46
Fixed asset inv.: NCE (%)	24.26	24.45	23.08	29.60
NCO(I): NCE (%)	18.55	24.15	23.05	29.59
NCO(F): Op CF (%)	52.11	41.92	35.88	27.07
NCO(I): Op CF (%)	125.23	209.61	210.33	190.31

assets, investments and acquisitions. These have been expressed as a percentage of operating cash flow. In each of the last three years, commitments in these two areas, taken together, have averaged well over double the figure for operating cash flow, painting a picture of the company as an overwhelmingly cash-hungry business—at least at its current stage of development.

This is actually the flip-side of the low tax rate seen in the profit and loss account. If the company were to spend more within its means, then capital allowances to set against tax would be lower, and the tax charge would rise, depressing after-tax profits.

Balance sheet ratios

In the balance sheet, the more advanced ratios that can be calculated relate to the productivity of assets and employees and the efficiency of utilisation of working capital.

Calculating the amount of *sales and profit produced per pound of assets employed* is a relatively simple concept. Comparing these figures over time should ideally yield a steady upward trend.

The same is true of the figures for *sales and profit per employee*. These are straightforward calculations that are intuitively easy to grasp.

Working capital ratios take a little more explanation. The concept behind these is that it is important that undue amounts of cash are not tied up in stocks, since this costs money to finance, and similarly that amounts owing to suppliers are paid in a controlled way and not unduly quickly, while debtors (amounts owed to the company) are collected as quickly as possible. It is also important that these amounts bear a reasonably consistent relationship to each other.

working capital: the balance of the value of a company's stocks and debtors, minus the money it owes to short-term creditors.

The normal way of looking at this is to express these 'current account' items as a proportion of the sales item they represent, and then present the ratio by calculating the number of days it represents. In a simple example, stock turning over four times per year would (by definition) turn over once every 90 days.

For instance, if our company Universal Widgets has £100 m of turnover, cost of sales of £80 m, stocks of £33 m, debtors of £20 m and creditors of £15 m, the way that the various working capital ratios would be calculated would be as follows:

- *Stock days*: £100 m of sales divided by £33 m of stocks is equivalent to stock turnover of three times per year and stock days of 365/3 or 122 days. It is something of a moot point whether stock days should be calculated on sales or on cost of sales.
- *Creditor days*: Because creditors normally represent money owed to suppliers making up the total cost of the finished product—before profit margins are added on and the goods sold—creditor days are normally calculated on 'cost of sales' rather than the turnover figure. In this instance, creditor days would be creditors of £15 m divided into cost of sales of £80 m (i.e. collected 5.3 times annually), making creditor days equivalent to 365/5.3, or 69 days.
- *Debtor days*: Here the same principle is applied except that, because debtors normally represent payments outstanding from customers for finished goods sold at the market price, the debtors' figure is divided into sales. This gives, in this instance, £20 m divided into £100 m of sales, implying debtors collected on average five times per year, or every 73 days.

Looked at in a slightly different way, in this example the company is turning over its stock on average every 122 days, paying its bills to suppliers on the basis of around 69 days' credit and granting its customers an average 73 days' credit.

The ideal might be to collect from customers rather more rapidly than suppliers are paid, but the real point about working out ratios like this is that the trend should be monitored for any significant changes. Problems could be indicated, for instance,

Table 9.3   Summary of Balance Sheet Items and Ratios (£000s)

	Year ended 31st July			
	1992	1993	1994	1995
Tangible fixed assets	53095	71736	96547	133196
Investments	0	0	0	0
Stocks	302	485	604	885
Trade debtors	0	0	0	0
Other debtors	1600	1276	1546	2720
Cash	70	2519	15838	8824
Total current assets	1972	4280	17988	12429
Short-term borrowing	1828	1539	3690	1411
Trade creditors	3322	4209	4670	8343
Other creditors	1695	3331	5561	8778
Total current liabilities	6845	9079	13921	18532
Net current assets	−4873	−4799	4067	−6103
Net capital employed	48222	66937	100614	127093
Medium/LT borrowing	27910	22825	28242	46833
Other LT creditors	0	0	0	1021
Provisions	0	0	0	0
Net assets	20312	44112	72372	79239
No. of employees	571	766	838	1286
Sales	21380	30800	46600	68536
Cost of sales	7773	10784	16835	37616
PBIT	5152	6076	8787	12232
Pre-tax profit	2078	4171	6477	9713
Current ratio	0.29	0.47	1.29	0.67
Acid ratio	0.24	0.42	1.25	0.62
Debt: capital employed (%)	61.67	36.40	31.74	37.96
Net debt: equity (%)	146.06	49.52	22.24	49.75
Interest cover (X)	1.68	3.19	3.80	4.86
Stock/cost of sales (days)	14	16	13	9
Trade debtor days	0	0	0	0
Stock: total assets (%)	1	1	1	1
Trade creditor days	156	142	101	81
Sales: fixed assets (%)	40	43	48	51
Sales: total assets (%)	39	41	41	47
Sales/employee (£000)	37.44	40.21	55.61	53.29
PBT/employee (£000)	3.64	5.45	7.73	7.55
Return on capital (%)	10.68	9.08	8.73	9.62
Return on equity (%)	10.23	9.46	8.95	12.26

if the rate of stock turnover falls (i.e. stocks are kept for longer), if debtors are collected more slowly (debtor days lengthen) or if creditors demand payment more quickly (creditor days shorten).

In calculating figures of this nature the norm is to take only short-term debtors and creditors, and also to work from so-called trade debtors and creditors, ignoring, for instance, national insurance and social security payments, VAT and other debtors/creditors that represent statutory obligations and have unvarying payment periods.

As Table 9.3 shows, the nature of a particular business can have a major impact on these figures. In the case of Wetherspoon, the pub group's customers naturally pay cash over the bar so debtor days are nil, and creditors (brewers and other suppliers) are paid comparatively slowly, although the payment period has been falling. Stock turns over every couple of weeks, although here again this speed of turnover has apparently been distorted by the change in the basis of presenting cost of sales in the accounts.

It should be evident from these tables that using the balance sheet, profit and loss account and cash flow numbers in this way can give considerable insight into the financial characteristics of any business and, accordingly, into the likely worth of the company from an investment standpoint.

More generally, however, accounts numbers can and have been manipulated in various ways (although not, it must be stressed, in the above examples). The next section looks at how to spot if company accounts have been massaged to show a more favourable picture.

HOW TO SPOT CREATIVE ACCOUNTING

It is probably understandable (although it still shocks some investors) that company finance directors want to show their companies in the best light possible and that some seek to do this by choosing accounting policies that are designed to show a smooth upward trend in profits and to flatter the balance sheet.

Company year-ends are often chosen, for example, to be at the time when a company has the maximum amount of liquidity in its balance sheet. In the case of a seasonal business dependent on Christmas, for example, the year-end might be March 31st, when all of the cash from Christmas sales has been collected. For the remainder of the year, such a business may be a heavy cash user, and the balance sheet needs to be interpreted with this fact in mind.

However, creative accounting usually means something more than this.

The last few years have seen the demise of a number of companies (Maxwell Communications and Polly Peck being the obvious examples) where seemingly healthy companies with a clean bill of health from their auditors suddenly went into terminal decline. The end-result of these scandals has been reform of accounting policies in the UK, so that massaging of profits through the use of creative accounting is now much less easy than it once was.

The best book on this subject is *Accounting for Growth*, by Terry Smith, an analyst whose career at a leading broker ended abruptly because of the criticisms of one of the company's corporate clients in this book. The book is essential reading for all would-be investors.

Smith highlights a number of ways in which accounts can be camouflaged. These include the following:

- acquisition accounting
- differing use of extraordinary and exceptional items

- use of 'off-balance sheet' finance
- contingent liabilities
- capitalising costs (especially interest)
- brand accounting
- changes in depreciation policy
- use of unconventional quasi-equity instruments
- pension fund accounting
- currency mismatching

Some of these practices have been (or soon will be) effectively outlawed in UK company accounts. For instance, acquisition accounting, which has been subject to flagrant abuse, is likely soon to be a thing of the past.

Acquisition accounting

Under acquisition accounting the acquiring company has the opportunity to write down the value of the assets being acquired to a supposed fair value and to add in certain other expected future costs. These adjustments are taken off balance sheet reserves, thereby eliminating their potential impact on future profits (although not, of course, on cash flow). The example cited in Smith's book is worthy of repetition.

Coloroll, a home furnishings company, took over Crowther, a carpet business, in 1988. The acquisition cost £213 m, but in the subsequent accounts, Coloroll wrote off £224 m relating to this acquisition, more than its original cost. The goodwill in the purchase amounted to only £145 m, a fair value write-off in Crowther chipped in a further £4 m, but an additional £75 m was written off, supposedly to cover adjustments to stocks and debtors, redundancies, relocation and other costs. The 'other' item was a suspiciously large £33 m. But the chickens came home to roost with a vengeance, and Coloroll went into receivership shortly afterwards.

Exceptionals versus extraordinaries

In the case of the second example of creative accounting techniques—the differing use of exceptional and extraordinary items—accounts are
presented in such a way that costs are taken 'below
the line', but exceptional profits included in such a
way as to benefit profits.

'Exceptional' items—the rule is that they are
taken above the pre-tax profit line—thus form part
of the headline profits announced by companies,
whereas 'extraordinary items', though still representing a call on company funds, are taken 'below
the line'. Taking something 'below the line' signifies
that it is brought into account after the company's
attributable profits (earnings for ordinary shareholders) are calculated. If so, these costs will be ignored by many investors.

The distinction between what is termed extraordinary and what exceptional is largely a semantic
one. If a logical case could be made for the distinction between them, it is that exceptional items relate
to costs (or more often profits) that are part of an
ongoing business, whereas the costs of closing
down an operation, or something that involves a
permanent diminution in the value of an asset, is
deemed extraordinary and taken out of account.

Cynics (of which there is no shortage in the
City) point out with some justification that the real
distinction is that special profits are invariably considered exceptional and one-off costs are always extraordinary, irrespective of how they arise.

The good news is that recent changes to the
shape of company accounts has meant that this distinction has been officially abolished and that all
charges of this type are now taken off the pre-tax
profit total. However, despite having spent many
years complaining about the bogus nature of these
items, analysts are still tending to add back some

of the adjustments to produce so-called 'normalised' profits.

It is really now up to the investor to try to make a judgement about which sources of profit (and costs) are ongoing items, and which are likely to be non-recurring. The alternative is to do as the accounting reformers wanted in making these changes. This is, in making judgements about shares, to rely less on the profit and loss account and more on cash flow statements, which have simultaneously also been made more transparent.

Off-balance sheet finance

The use of off-balance sheet finance has also been considerably restricted in recent changes to accounting guidelines. This term is used where an expensive project, typically a development property or the financing of work-in-progress likely to take a long time to come to maturity, is placed in a joint venture company that is less than 50% owned but where the true 'owner' has an option to reacquire the assets at some future date. This is done because it means the assets (or more importantly their related borrowings) need not be included in the group balance sheet.

As well as property companies financing major developments, scotch whisky companies in the past financed stocks in this way, by creating partly owned joint ventures with banks, which held their maturing stock for a period of time with loans backed against them. The increase in the value of the stocks as they matured more than covered the effect of rolling up interest payments in the joint venture.

The preceding examples of creative accounting are now well on the way to being eradicated in the UK, but others are alive and well. In particular, examples of adjusting depreciation policies, brand accounting and capitalising interest can all be commonly found.

Changing depreciation rates

In the case of depreciation policies, if assets are written off less conservatively than before (say, over five years rather than three) then profits will be boosted by the reduction in the charge for depreciation. Applying a change of this type to an asset worth £100 m previously depreciated over three years and now depreciated over five years would benefit profits to the tune of £13.3 m. The old annual depreciation charge of £33.3 m (£100 m divided by three) is replaced by one of £20 m (£100 m divided by five).

This is actually less pernicious than it might sound, since the depreciation charge is itself a book entry and the change therefore has no effect on cash flows: it simply makes profits look better.

Incorporating brand values

Brand accounting is used by consumer products companies in particular to ascribe a value to the brands contained in their balance sheets. In a conservative company these would be considered intangible assets and have no value from an accounting standpoint.

Incorporating brand values increases net assets and reduces gearing. A legitimate way of valuing brands, if they have been acquired, is to say that their value is represented by the excess of the acquisition price over and above the tangible assets acquired at the same time—in other words, as a residual. In the case of internally-developed brands, some companies have used more exotic and subjective means of assessing their value.

Neither approach is satisfactory. In the first instance, of an acquired brand, the residual value of the brand may simply have arisen because the company overpaid when it acquired the brand owner. More often than not, the second approach involves applying some assumed, and subjective, market multiple to the cash flows generated by the brand.

Generally speaking, companies that use brand accounting do so for a reason. It is often to bolster their balance sheets, and generally to make investors think more highly of them. But brand values need to be taken with a pinch of salt. It is also a moot point whether or not they should be depreciated. Depreciating brand assets would rob companies of much of the benefit of incorporating the values in their balance sheet, since the effect of depreciation would be to suppress profits.

The argument against depreciating brand values is that companies that own brands spend heavily in advertising and marketing, and therefore that it is unfair to insist on another charge for depreciation.

Yet the fact is that some brands do lose their appeal irrespective of the sums spent promoting them, while others face problems from counterfeiting and legal challenges over their ownership.

The point is, when encountering companies that use brand accounting, not necessarily to avoid them but to pay some attention to the company's financial position excluding the value of its brand name assets.

Capitalising costs

Capitalising costs (most commonly interest payments) is common in the property industry. Here, interest accruing on financing long-term developments is not charged to the profit and loss account, but rolled up in the eventual value of the asset being created. If all goes well the charge is lost in the developer's profit margin. Short-term profits are boosted as a result, at the expense of some capital profit when the asset is eventually sold.

The problem with this approach arises when property values decline in the meantime, making the cost of the development, including this rolled-up interest, exceed its market value. This amounts to negative equity on a huge scale, and is normally likely to involve the developer in substantial write-offs.

It is also worth remembering that, while profits are benefited by this policy, in cash flow terms the interest still has to be paid to the lender at the appointed time.

Other methods

The effects of other forms of creative accounting, involving quasi-equity issues and adjustments to pension fund contributions, are being eliminated by accounting reformers. Currency mismatches— borrowing at low rates in hard currencies and selling in high-inflation soft currency areas and charging the resulting exchange adjustment to reserves (the problem that eventually sunk Polly Peck), are less common, but need watching.

Generally speaking, investors should beware, or at least be sure they understand the implications of any P&L account or balance sheet items that include the phrases: 'creation (release) of provisions'; contributions holiday; deferred income; deferred liabilities; earn-out arrangements; contingent liabilities (where such contingencies are large in the context of the balance sheet) and so on.

Investors can rest assured that while accounting reformers are much more diligent than they used to be at eliminating these practices, some companies display great inventiveness in dreaming up new methods of showing their accounts in the best possible light.

As I have stressed at several points in this book, cash flow is generally at least as important as profitability when it comes to assessing the real worth of an investment. Along with sales figures, flows of cash are much more difficult for the accountants to fudge, and methods that use these figures to value shares are worthy of more attention than they sometimes get.

There are established techniques using cash flow numbers that can be used to pinpoint the true value of a company, or at least corroborate a calculation of its worth arrived at by other means. The next section reviews these techniques in brief.

USING DISCOUNTED CASH FLOW MODELS AND RELATED TECHNIQUES

Discounted cash flow (DCF) is a long-established technique originally developed for use by companies appraising capital investment projects.

It works like this. The cost of a particular piece on machinery or a new factory is measured against the expected cash flow that the investment is expected to generated over its useful life.

Cash flow in each succeeding year is progressively adjusted downwards by a fixed percentage amount (i.e. discounted) to reflect the fact that uncertainty and the possibilities of future inflation mean that a fixed amount of cash expected to accrue at some point in the future is worth less to an investor than the same amount expected to be received today. So the current value to the investor of cash four years out is worth less than the same amount received in three years' time, which is worth less than the same amut received in two years' time and so on.

How to work out precisely what discount should be applied to these future flows of cash can vary. Often the discount rate is the **risk-free rate of return**, that is to say the yield on long-term or undated government bonds. In some models this figure is adjusted to allow for differences in the levels of risk in different shares. The more volatile or risky a share, the higher the discount factor applied to its future cash flow.

> **risk-free rate of return:** the yield on undated government stock. Normally used as the benchmark for discounting back future flows of cash.

Nowadays discounted cash flow models can be obtained that work as add-ins to Excel or other industry-standard spreadsheet programs. These normally entail simply plugging in basic historic P&L and cash flow data and making predictions as to cash flow growth on a year-by-year basis for, say, five years forward and thereafter applying a constant growth rate out into the far distant future. Entering the appropriate discount factor will produce a per share value, which can then be compared with the current share price.

Clearly this technique involves a considerable degree of subjectivity in assessing future rates of growth, but it has the merit that it is projecting forward from cash flow figures rather than, as analysts normally do, from a set of profit figures that, as the preceding section shows, need not be telling the whole story.

In addition, using market yields as a discount factor has a greater degree of objectivity than projecting forward from assumptions about likely individual price–earnings ratios and dividend yields. It is also useful in comparing valuations across companies in a relatively stable sector (brewing, food retailing, stores) where similar underlying growth rates can be reasonably confidently assumed.

The beauty of these models is that they can be constantly updated and the assumptions refined when, for example, new accounts are issued, bond yields and therefore discount factors change, and other new information comes to light.

Historical

Historical	1987	1988	1989	1990	1991	1992	1993	1994	1995
Earnings							734	750	1078
Depreciation							287	382	377
Other cash							181	–	4
Other non-cash							(457)	(554)	(344)
New capital investments							44	11	192
Free cash flow							701	567	923
Earnings growth								–19.1%	62.8%
Operating cash flow							990	1180	1604
Shareholders' equity							3943	4598	3623
New equity							3209	(95)	(2053)
Debt							11406	9076	9029
Total capital							15349	13674	12652
Return on equity								14.4%	20.1%
Return on total capital								3.7%	6.8%

Projected

Projected	1996	1997	1998	1999	2000	2001	2002	2003	2004	2005
Prior year cash flow	923	951	979	1009	1039	1070	1102	1135	1169	1204
Increase %	3.0%	3.0%	3.0%	3.0%	3.0%	3.0%	3.0%	3.0%	3.0%	3.0%
Cash flow	951	979	1009	1039	1070	1102	1135	1169	1204	1240
Discounted cash flow	872	824	779	736	695	657	621	587	554	524

	1996	1997
Sum of discounted cash flows		6850
10-year per share cash flow	£ 1.32	
Residual value		
Cash flow in year 10	1240	
Second stage growth rate	2%	
Cash flow in year 11	951	
Capitalisation	7%	
Company value at end of year 10		13581
Present value of future cash flow		10267
Shares (in thousands)	5173	

Table 9.4   Analysis Based on The Warren Buffet Way

There is also no doubt in my mind that they are often used by companies contemplating acquisitions, to determine the appropriate level for a take-over bid.

I once produced a piece of research on the smaller companies in a particular sector, looking at their valuations on this basis, only to find less than a year later that two of the group of fifteen had been on the receiving end of bids that equated almost exactly to their DCF valuation. Valuations done by this method—provided the assumptions made are realistic—should not be ignored.

As an example of the DCF method at work, Table 9.4 shows a cash flow model filled in on the basis of the latest annual accounts data for Hanson plc, the Anglo-US conglomerate.

The spreadsheet used here is one based on the principles outlined in Robert Hagstrom's book, *The Warren Buffett Way*. The spreadsheet format was devised by US investment guru Bob Costa and is downloadable from his World Wide Web site at the Internet address http://www.investorweb.com/.

It is only necessary to fill in historic figures for as many years as are available. The figures that are required to be entered are those in italic in the table, namely, the components of the free cash flow calculation, the operating cash flow figure, the figure for shareholders' equity and for debt and the projected rates of increases in cash flow for the ten forward years and for the second-stage phase of growth.

These figures can be tailored to take into account assumptions about the timing of growth or decline that is specific to the company, or that might be produced by the impact of the economic cycle. The total number of shares issued also needs to be entered, as does the appropriate discount rate and the current year-end date. All other items are calculated by the model.

In the case of this example, the model produces a notional value for Hanson very close to the current share price (pre-demerger), factoring in modest growth assumptions for future years.

Using DCF models is a good way of getting a handle on whether a particular share represents good value or not, although for obvious reasons it is not as good for use with shares that do are particularly cyclical, for recovery situations, or for those that do not have a particularly predictable pattern of sales growth.

Another interesting and relatively newly developed technique is perhaps best described as **enterprise value analysis**. This has been developed for, among other uses, comparing companies in similar industries but in different countries. It uses figures that are cash flow and sales-based, rather than profit numbers, which are more subject to international differences in accounting policies.

It also irons out differences in gearing ratios between companies in arriving at a comparative value, and also deals with the impact on the figure of partially owned subsidiaries and associates. The only adjustment that needs factoring in separately is if differing countries have wildly and consistently different corporate tax rates, since this will affect market valuations.

At its simplest the technique uses three basic measures: sales, earnings before depreciation interest and tax, and 'free' operating cash flow. These are compared with the so-called 'enterprise value'. This is the company's market capitalisation (i.e. its shares outstanding multiplied by the share price), plus debt, minus the value of any peripheral assets.

Operating 'free' cash flow is normally defined as earnings before depreciation, interest and tax minus a 'maintenance' level of capital spending and (strictly speaking) a figure to represent the effect of inflation on net working capital.

enterprise value analysis: a technique for valuing companies based on sales and cash flow parameters.

In the example above, Hanson would have an enterprise value/sales multiple of 1.99, an enterprise value to EBDIT of 10.5 and an EV/operating free cash flow multiple of 12.3. For most companies an educated guess needs to be made about the level of **maintenance capital expenditure**.

ADVANCED SHARE PRICE ANALYSIS TECHNIQUES

In Chapter 4 we covered a number of the most basic technical indicators that will be found on many entry-level and mid-priced technical analysis software packages. The ones described below are normally found only on the more expensive packages and provide additional insight into share price movements.

For reasons of space, only a handful of these indicators are mentioned below, simply to give a flavour of the variety of calculations that can be performed. They are split into those that relate to the market as a whole and those that are normally used with individual shares.

Readers are strongly advised to consult the manual that accompanies their technical analysis software package and more specialised literature on the subject if they intend to use these indicators for trading purposes.

Market-based indicators

In some technical analysis programs, and indeed often in newspapers and TV commentaries on the stock market, mention is made of the **advance/decline line**. This is a widely-used measure of the overall condition of the market and is calculated by taking the difference between the numbers of rising stocks each day and the number falling. The daily surplus or deficit is then added to or subtracted from a cumulative total and drawn on the chart.

maintenance capital expenditure: the level of capital spending needed to keep a company's productive assets in good order. Often deducted to arrive at 'free cash flow'.

advance/ decline line: a technical indicator measuring the accumulation of shares that rise versus those that fall on successive days.

Like many technical indicators, the real significance of this measure is when there is divergence between its movement and that of the market as a whole. If the market is strong, but the advance/decline line is falling, this means that the continuing rise in the market is suspect. Likewise, if the market falls but the advance decline line is rising, the underlying tone of the market is better than the index movement is suggesting.

breadth indicator: the advance/decline line expressed as a percentage of the total number of shares traded.

A variant of this concept is the **breadth indicator**. This takes the difference between advances and declines and divides it by the total number of issues traded. Study of past market peaks and troughs suggests that a buying climax (i.e. the top of a bull market) is reached when advances represent more than 70% of all issues traded.

Another advance/decline indicator often used by technical analysts is the McClellan oscillator. This plots the difference between the weighted 19-day moving average and a weighted 39-day moving average of advances less declines. Peaks and troughs are often reached before market turning points, typically when the oscillator is deep in overbought or oversold territory.

Coppock indicator: a long-term moving average designed to provide broad buy signals for the market.

Lastly, many investors (including a number of private investors) swear by the **Coppock indicator** as a reliable measure of signalling the beginnings of bull markets. The indicator is normally calculated as a weighted 10-month moving total of a share price or index, and the calculations involve working out a monthly average for, say, the FT-SE 100 index, and then calculating the percentage change over the same average 12 months previously. These percentages are then weighted in a 10-period moving average to create the chart. A buy signal is indicated when the chart rebounds from a low point. The indicator is held to be an unreliable generator of sell signals.

Figure 9.1 shows the current position of the Coppock indicator for the FT-SE 100 index.

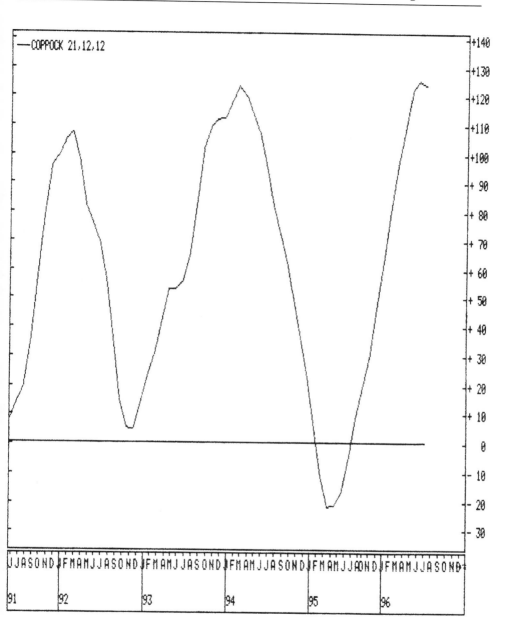

Figure 9.1   Coppock Indicator for FT-SE 100 Index. © **Synergy Software**

Share-based indicators

There are also a number of other indicators that can be used to analyse the progress or otherwise of individual share prices. Many of these give the lie to the suggestion that technical analysis is simply about spotting abstruse patterns on share price charts. In fact, many technical indicators apply proven and well-respected statistical techniques.

It is possible, for instance, to perform regression analysis on a time series of a particular share price. Used as a technical indicator, the theory would be to sell when the price moved down through the moving regression line, and to buy when it moved up through it.

In practice, however, regression lines give something of a feel for when a share price has departed from its normal trend about as much as it is going to, and bold traders can act accordingly, especially if the possibility of a profitable reversal is confirmed by other indicators.

volatility: the percentage amount up or down by which a share might be expected to move over a fixed time period. Sometimes expressed as the difference between a share's 12-month high and low points expressed as a percentage of the current share price.

Another interesting indicator is the **volatility** calculation. This measures the amplitude of swings in a share price around its long-term trend line and again uses standard statistical techniques. It is self-evident that volatility may vary over time, with shares having both quiet periods and those where activity is frenetic and movements in them significant. The chart of the volatility of a share price over successive periods of, say, 20 days or 90 days can be graphed by many technical analysis programs and is particularly useful in the traded options market.

When buying traded options, for example, the idea is to purchase an option when the underlying share is at some sort of support or resistance level but also when volatility is low.

As an example, Figure 9.2 shows the moving total of the 90-day volatility of Hanson plc.

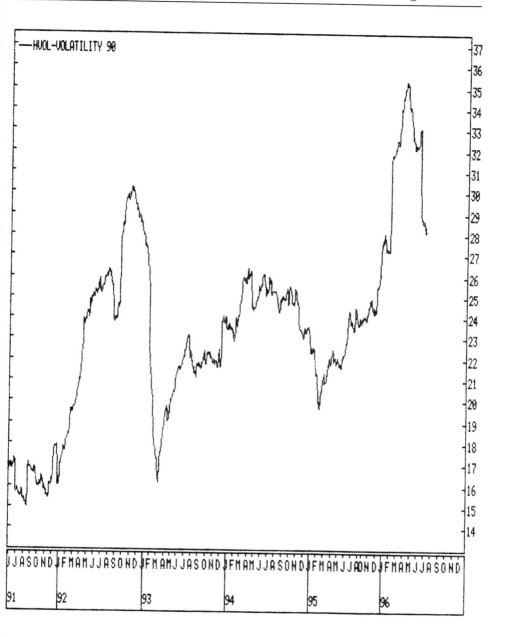

Figure 9.2   Moving total of 90-day volatility of Hanson plc. © Synergy
Software

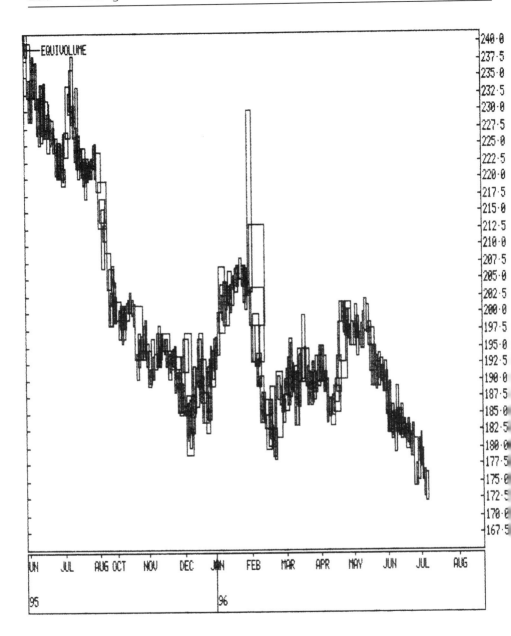

Figure 9.3   Hanson plc. © **Synergy Software**

As volatility increases, so the price of the option should rise, while—with luck—if the volatility rises because of a sharp move in the appropriate direction, the option buyer will also make money as a result of the increased intrinsic value of the option. This subject was introduced briefly in Chapter 6. To reiterate, it is very important indeed to read up on the subject of option trading before any deals are contemplated.

I mentioned earlier that trends in the trading volume in a particular share can be a good guide to the movement in a share price. Upward or downward moves that occur on high volume are usually more significant than those that do not.

Several indicators have been developed that look at volume in more detail. An example is a technique called '**equivolume**'. This attempts to draw a chart that combines the directional movement of a share with the volume of shares traded. Each day's trading is shown as a rectangle, with the vertical dimensions representing the day's trading range and the width of the bar proportional to the volume of shares traded (Figure 9.3).

Another method is called **on-balance volume** (or OBV) and was devised by the US stockmarket guru Joe Granville. The idea behind this is that, starting from zero, the current day's volume is plotted as either a plus or a minus depending on whether or not the shares closed higher or lower. If one day is followed by a second in which the shares rose, the volume is added to that seen in the first day. If there is a decline on the third day, the volume is deducted from the total of the previous two days, and so on.

As with other indicators, traders often watch for a divergence between the price chart and this indicator of volume. Another variant known as 'money flow' weights the volume of shares traded with the average share price for the day and aggregates the pluses and minuses arrived at over

equivolume: *a method of chart drawing designed to show the movement in a share price and volume traded in the same chart 'bar'.*

on-balance volume: *a chart of the cumulative volume on 'up' days minus the volume on 'down' days.*

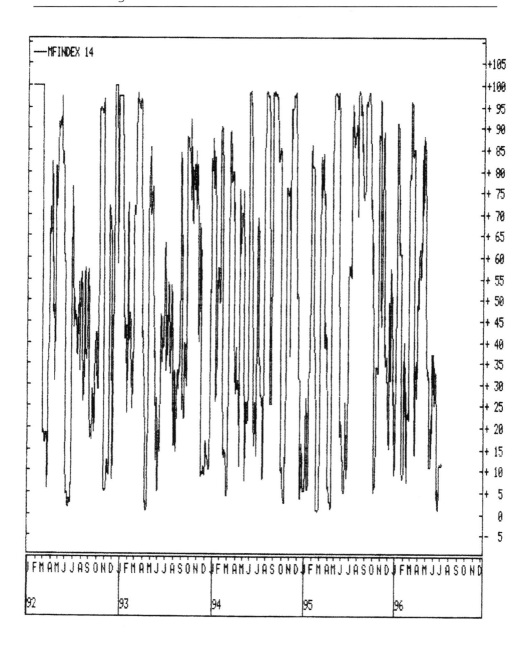

Figure 9.4   Burn Stewart Distillers. © Synergy Software

(normally) a 14-day period. The figures are then adjusted to arrive at an oscillator which fluctuates between zero and 100 (Figure 9.4).

The indicators described above, combined with those mentioned in Chapter 4, represent only a fraction of the various ways in which it is possible to analyse share price movements. There is an extensive library of material on charting and technical analysis, and the manuals of most chart packages also contain descriptions of how indicators are constructed.

I cannot stress too strongly my view that charts and fundamental analysis should be used together when assessing shares. Put simply, technical analysis can throw up interesting opportunities for further study, and also help with timing purchases and sales, but fundamental research is also vital in selecting portfolio constituents. Being painstaking over both aspects of the process narrows down the risks of losing money and increases the chance of making it.

IN BRIEF

- There are a number of additional financial ratios that can be derived from company annual reports.
- Profit and loss ratios break down the cost side of the equation in greater detail, cash flow ratios look in particular how cash is spent, and balance sheet ratios look at sales and asset productivity and working capital.
- Company accounts are frequently massaged to put a better gloss on the figures, although the more flagrant examples have now been outlawed by regulators.
- Favourite creative accounting techniques include altering depreciation rates, bringing

brands into the balance sheet, and capitalising interest and other costs.

- Discounted cash flow analysis is a powerful additional technique for valuing shares, and can easily be used in conjunction with other valuation methods.
- The same can be said for enterprise value analysis.
- Additional technical indicators include those relating to broad market advances and declines, to market momentum over time, to the volatility of individual shares, and to the analysis of trading volume.

CHAPTER 10

Dealing Diary: 1986–1996

By the time this book is published I will have marked the tenth anniversary of starting to trade in the stock market on my own account.

Although since 1970 my work has always involved the stock market, the pressures of bringing up a young family were such that, in common with many investors, I had to wait until chance provided me with enough capital to satisfy these demands and yet have enough left over to feel comfortable dealing in the stock market.

My stroke of luck was as follows: I worked and was a shareholder in a major City broking firm from the early 1980s up to 1987. This was the time that the run-up to the City's 'Big Bang' meant that firms of this type, hitherto very traditional, were opened up to outside influences and outside capital. In stages the firm I worked for became first an affiliate and then a subsidiary of an American bank between 1982 and 1986, retaining management autonomy until after the 1987 stock market crash.

The result of this influx of capital meant that I was able both to sell a proportion of the shares I owned in an employee share incentive scheme, and exercise share options granted a couple of years previously, pay off assorted debts, and still have a significant amount left over to invest in the stock market.

I allocated £28000 to begin my stock market trading career, but the lessons I have learnt in my dealings over the years are applicable whatever the amount available to be invested.

In the rest of this chapter, I give a brief outline of my stock market deals since then. I promise the reader that none of these details are exaggerated in any way, although I have omitted some of the more tedious details to move the story along.

At this stage I should also mention some of the restrictions under which I worked in the City. As an analyst specialising in a particular sector, I was barred—by my firm's dealing rules—from trading in shares in the industry I analysed and knew most about. Many of the early deals were the result of conversations with colleagues about companies in other industries that I thought looked interesting.

There is no doubt that having this specialist advice to call upon informally helped considerably, although it is important to stress that at no time did I act on anything that could remotely be considered inside information.

But it must be recognised that those working in the market have often had in the past an innate knowedge and information advantage over the rest of the investment community. In the last chapter to this book I will explain why I believe this may no longer be quite as important as it once was.

The other advantage a stock market employee has is favourable commission rates charged for staff dealing, although it is possible to make over much of this, especially in the light of the subsequent development of execution-only services for the small investor.

As a staff member my orders in the market took second place to those of clients, and, like any other investor, I also had to cope with the impact of the bid–offer spread.

I have divided the narrative into a number of distinct phases. In each case I describe the deals I did and support this with some statistical information. At the end of the chapter I demonstrate how to measure this trading record against some of the more normal benchmarks, and draw some lessons from it.

PHASE 1: JULY 1986–JANUARY 1988

For those who were not involved in the stock market at the time, it is almost impossible to describe the final phases of the 1981–1987 bull market in shares in London. This was the era of the Unlisted Securities Market (USM), dubbed the 'millionaire machine' by some in the City. Over the period between the USM being set up in 1980 and the peak of the market in July 1987, some 600 companies raised a total of £1800 m on the USM.

For much of the 1980s the bull market was a fairly sedate affair. In 1986, however, it began to assume the character of the 1920s. The events of 1986 and 1987 are probably the sort that only happen once or twice in a lifetime and one might count oneself as fortunate both to participate and to escape more or less intact.

My first deal resulted in a loss of £500 or so. On the recommendation of a colleague I bought some shares in Commercial Union. I made the mistake of averaging down, buying 500 shares at 319p and then a further 500 at 307p. Never, ever average down. I eventually sold the 1000 shares at 267p in November 1986 and resolved to be careful about the advice I took from then on.

In July and August 1986 I gradually invested most of the rest of my starting capital of £28 000. I picked a broad range of stocks, some of which are now no longer with us or exist in a different form. The list included the textile group Illingworth Morris, at that time a management turnaround story, the acquisitive paper and packaging group

Bunzl, the stores group Sears Holdings, Hanson (then called Hanson Trust), the motor distributor T Cowie (quickly sold for a small profit, missing out on a much larger rise later on), SAC International, a small USM company involved in specialist engineering consultancy, and Mount Charlotte Hotels, subsequently taken over by the Australian entrepreneur Ron Brearley.

The years 1986 and 1987 were periods of intense corporate activity. The firm I worked for was involved in an advisory capacity in a number of the major bids occurring at that time. These included in my own case, for instance, the Hanson bid for Imperial Group and the subsequent sale of Courage to Elders IXL, the defence of The Distillers Company against the bid from Argyll Group and subsequent (and ultimately controversial) 'white knight' merger with Guinness, and the Elders IXL bid for the food and brewing group then known as Allied-Lyons (now Allied Domecq).

There were also some other involvements, such as a steady flow of corporate work for Scottish & Newcastle, and work for corporate clients among the ranks of smaller brewing and distilling companies.

The result of all this activity was that for much of 1986 and the early part of 1987 I was so engrossed in my job that I was unable to pay much attention to my own financial affairs and the state of my investments. This had the fortunate result that I did not deal over-frequently, and hence was able to enjoy the fruits of the rise in the market over this period.

buy–hold strategy: investing by simply buying and holding a share for a lengthy period.

Readers will note from Table 10.1, which shows the results of this first phase, that the annualised gain of 68% recorded in this period was essentially the result of a simple **'buy and hold' strategy**. I dealt in only 16 stocks over that 18-month period. It can also be seen that, although there were gains across the board, the lion's share of the increase (in

Table 10.1 Phase One: 30th June 1986 to 31st December 1988

Five best trades			Five worst trades		
Stock	Profit/loss	Held for (months)	Stock	Profit/loss	Held for (months)
Control Securities	12182	7	Inoco	−1622	3
Hanson	8225	14	Hawker Siddeley	−1581	3
SAC International	6783	14	Control Securities	−835	22
Clyde Petroleum	2963	4	TN	−644	2
Bunzl	2239	12	CU	−520	3
Total gain in period	35891		Total loss in period	−5202	
Net investment income	−7215		No. of stocks traded	16	
Annualised total return in period (%)		68%	Starting capital		£25000
No. of winning trades		11	No. of losing trades		5
Average time held (months)		11	Average time held (months)		3
FT-SE 100 index at start of period		1649.8	Risk-free bond yield at start of period		8.8%

fact £26000 of a total net gain of around £30000 came from just three of the stocks.

Note also that the period covered by the table takes in the period running up to and in the immediate aftermath of the October 1987 stock market crash.

My best success in this period came from a share known then as Control Securities (now called Ascot Holdings). This was at that time a small property company based in Wales, effectively little more than a shell. But it became the vehicle for the ambitious Ugandan Asian Virani family. Led by Nazmu Virani, the family injected some property interests into the business and turned the company into a glamour stock by means of frenetic property trading.

A colleague of mine had met Nazmu Virani shortly after this process began and became very excited about the prospects for the company. I decided to put some of my own money into the shares and bought a total of 15000 shares at an average price of 19p a share, eventually selling the holding at 101p in September 1987.

I sold the bulk of my stock market investments in early September 1987 in order to buy a holiday home-cum-investment property. I jokingly referred to it as my 'bear market bolthole', without really realising that this was precisely what it would become.

The timing of this move, I will readily admit, was part luck and part judgement. It was related both to the unease I and a number of colleagues felt about the market, and the excesses of the bull phase that had by then just about run its course.

In my personal life there had been some traumas too. I was becoming increasingly dissatisfied with life in the City in the post 'Big Bang' era, and at sharp odds with certain of my colleagues over the direction of the market and some other issues. There was some writing on the wall in both respects. I decided to take some evasive action.

My father had died very suddenly in February 1987 and a few months later it seemed a good idea to invest some of my stock market gains in a small holiday property close to where my mother lived, just south of the Lake District. Over the summer of 1987 we found a suitable property and agreed a price.

People are often astonished when I tell them that completion on this property deal was fixed for 13th October 1987—six days before the 1987 market crash. The purchase price, £42 500, necessitated me selling a substantial proportion of my then stock market holdings in early September.

My unease over the course of the market was compounded by the chronic state of the settlement system at the time. As I attempted to wrest a cheque out of the system to send to my solicitor, trips to the back office began to resemble nothing so much as a journey into a world peopled by characters out of a Kafka novel or a Breughel painting, with mountains of paper and a system that was clearly overloaded. Something had to give.

I was out of the country on a business trip to the USA when the hurricane and the stock market crash struck. My escape from the stock market was tinged by the fact that I still had some investments that had not been sold. Contrary to the views of colleagues who felt that the setback was a temporary one, my own reading suggested that even if the stock market's leaders recovered, the smaller company sector (in which I had had some good gains) would take some time to get back to normal.

Two particular holdings caused me pain. They were Hawker Siddeley, an engineering company since taken over by BTR, and Inoco, then a small shell company being used as a vehicle by one-time 1960s and 1970s entrepreneur David Rowland. I cut my losses in both companies after the crash, taking a loss amounting in total to about £3000.

I still had some affection for Control Securities, having made so much money out of the shares in the recent past. I bought back 15 000 shares at a price of around 45p, but their performance was never quite the same again and I ended up selling this holding for a small loss two years later.

Control has since undergone a 100-for-one consolidation of its share price, and the shares in their old form now stand at the equvalent of 3p.

My temper was subsequently improved by a colleague's inspired recommendation of Clyde Petroleum, a small oil exploration and production stock. I bought a total of 10 000 shares at an average price of about 110p, subsequently selling the shares in April 1988 at a price of 145p. Even in the depths of the psychological depression after the crash there was still money to be made, and recouping some of the earlier losses gave me some cause for optimism.

There was, of course, a reckoning from this phase of the market. Although I had gains that amounted to about £30 000 made from my starting capital of £28 000, as a high-earning City individual at that time, I was subject to a hefty marginal tax rate. This had two consequences.

First, there was a stored-up tax bill from the gain I had made exercising my share options and selling employee scheme shares, and also from my stock market gains. With better and earlier advice, the tax aspect of this might have been planned to better effect. That was my own fault. The result was that I was faced with a later bill for £11 000 capital gains tax.

On the plus side, my surplus funds had been invested in a high interest earning account and there was a total of some £4800 in interest income, and dividends on the shares I had held over the period to offset (at least in my own mind) against this.

The 18-month period produced a gross gain of just in excess of 100% on my starting capital of £28 000, swelling to about £35 800 on a total return basis after including gross dividend and interest income. I also had a capital injection, from the sale of my incentive scheme shares, in the second half of 1987. This amounted to £32 000, structured as described in the next section. The effect was to bring the total invested capital at the start of the second phase in my dealings to £60 000.

This set me up well for the next phase in my career, although gains have never been quite as easy to come by again, for reasons I will explain.

PHASE 2: JANUARY 1988–SEPTEMBER 1992

In January 1988 I decided to leave the City and become a freelance writer. A severance package agreed with the firm I worked for took care of buying a car to replace the company one I had to give back, and also took care of the accumulated tax bill run up on exercising my share options.

The two payments almost exactly cancelled each other out and I was left with a clean sheet and the opportunity to sell my remaining shares, by then converted into tax-efficient **floating-rate notes**, over a period of six years. With the high interest rates of the time, the quarterly interest payments produced more than enough to pay school fees and other essentials while my progress into the self-employed world began.

In Table 10.1 I have shown the capital injection coming in October 1987, the date of the takeover, although in fact I kept most of it in the form of loan notes, cashing them in only gradually. The capital was gradually drawn down over a period of four

floating-rate note: a fixed income security, often received as a result of a takeover, where the interest paid fluctuates in line with short-term interest rates and which is redeemable at any time at the holder's option.

Table 10.2 Phase Two: 1st January 1988 to 31st July 1992

Five best trades			Five worst trades		
Stock	Profit/loss	Held for (months)	Stock	Profit/loss	Held for (months)
BAT	5649	19	BP	-1486	2
Lloyds Bank	1751	21	Aran Energy	-1092	4
Hanson	1424	8	Devenish	-970	9
Allied-Lyons	1345	21	Slough Estates	-764	16
Marks & Spencer	1176	21	ICI	-202	7
Total gain in period	11756		Total loss in period	-4514	
Net investment income	6268		No. of stocks traded		11
Annualised total return in period (%)		4.90%	Starting capital	£60000	
No. of winning trades		6	No. of losing trades		6
Average time held (months)		18	Average time held (months)		5.5
FT-SE 100 Index at start of period		1712.7	Risk-free bond yield at start of period		9.4%

or five years, and thereby produced a regular flow of lubrication for my stock market trading activities.

Phase two began with a bang but as a whole was relatively inactive. It would be a mistake perhaps to describe this phase as an extended bear market, but certainly there were phases of it that were distinctly uncomfortable, notably the time around the second anniversary of the crash and immediately prior to sterling's exit from the ERM in September 1992.

I have to confess that I found it hard to adjust at first to no longer being at the centre of the market action. I found out quite quickly the degree to which private investors at that time were at a substantial disadvantage compared to City professionals.

So there are some examples in this phase of how taking one's eye off the ball, even for a few days, can result in big losses. The deals in this period are shown in Table 10.2.

For the whole of this period, now I had no further staff dealing facilities, I moved my broking account to Charles Stanley, where a former colleague from a previous broking firm I had worked for handled my deals on a part-advice, part execution-only basis. In the period of almost four years between January 1988 and September 1992, I did only 11 trades, concentrating on building up my own business. In the 1988/89 period there were two outstandingly successful deals and a number of less inspiring ones.

For a long spell in my broking career I had followed the tobacco sector and knew that BAT Industries had been a cheap stock for many years. I ended up buying 2000 shares at around the 420p mark (105p in the current form). The shares were sold at the time of the Goldsmith bid for a profit of £5600. The profit would have been larger had I taken my broker's advice to sell at a profit of around £8000. Yet again I also took a substantial profit on Hanson shares, buying around 5000 shares at 160p and selling at 200p. A similar small turn in Ladbroke added to the gains.

I learnt, however, to beware of stocks for which I had had a previous professional attachment. I had advised the JA Devenish pub group in the later stages of my City career and thought highly of the management. But an attempt to capitalise on this experience ended in failure, proving that a detached view is essential to trade shares successfully.

The next burst of dealing in this phase was between 1990 and 1992. By October 1990 I felt that the market was set for another rise and picked a selection of early-cycle blue chips (Marks & Spencer, Allied-Lyons and Lloyds Bank). A foray in the property sector via Slough Estates resulted in heavy losses, as did a later venture into BP ahead of the ERM debacle. In the case of BP, had I only held my nerve and continued to hold the stock, the profits would have been substantial. As it was I ended up with a £700 loss on Slough and a £1500 drop on BP, the latter in the aftermath of a profit warning.

I closed out the trio of blue chips in July 1992 and what in hindsight proved to be reasonable timing, not perhaps getting the best of prices, but missing the later downward spiral in August and early September.

The result of this phase was a total gain just short of £12000 offset by losses of about £4500. Numerically, gains and losses were more or less even, but the policy of cutting losses early and running profits once again proved its worth. This is displayed to even better effect in phase three. My overall gains over the period were also boosted by substantial interest income from the loan notes and modest income from renting out the holiday property investment.

PHASE 3: SEPTEMBER 1992–DECEMBER 1995

I can freely admit that I missed the opportunity to buy into the market at the depths of the ERM crisis, although I remember graphically the point at which the market turned. The deals in this period are shown in Table 10.3.

Part-way through the period I changed brokers, moving to the execution-only specialist Fidelity Brokerage in early 1993, mainly in order to save on dealing charges. In the period between October 1992 and the end of 1995 I did 33 separate trades, recording total gains of £16 500 and accumulated losses of £8400. In this phase, the gains and losses were again numerically more or less equal, but the policy of cutting losses early, although it appears sometimes to result in missed opportunities, undoubtedly pays off as the years roll by.

There is another aspect to this, of course, which is not selling too early, something I have difficulty in doing, as I have explained earlier in this book. The prime example of this occurred in this phase of trading, with a company now called Northern Leisure, but at that time known as Whitegate Leisure.

Whitegate was a company that had been set up by a former executive from First Leisure to develop interests in discotheques and bowling, but had expanded too fast in the run-up to the 1991 recession and ran into severe problems. It was a chance meeting with the management that brought this company to my attention, in the immediate aftermath of the ERM debacle.

The company had an awful balance sheet, but interest rates were coming down and the signs were that the new management team had a firm grip on the business. I bought 25 000 shares at 9p. Over a period of less than six months the shares rose to the 30s and I sold out in two stages for a total gain of

Table 10.3 Phase Three: September 1992 to December 1995

Five best trades

Stock	Profit/loss	Held for (months)
Northern Leisure	4101	8
Eldridge Pope	2432	10
Yates Brothers	2115	6
Regent Inns	1487	7
ACT	977	6
Total gain in period	16476	
Net investment income	3714	
Annualised total return in period (%)	6.03%	
No. of winning trades	16	
Average time held (months)	7	
FT-SE 100 index at start of period	2553	

Five worst trades

Stock	Profit/loss	Held for (months)
Harmony Prop	-1233	2
Pentos	-1022	2
Dixons	-831	4
Menzies	-789	3
Wace	-716	1
Total loss in period	-8422	
No. of stocks traded	33	
Starting capital	£60000	
No. of losing trades	17	
Average time held (months)	2	
Risk-free bond yield at start of period	9%	

more than £4000—more than doubling my money. The sting in the tail is that the shares now stand at over 100p.

Other major successes during this period were in Eldridge Pope, a small West Country brewing group where I also noticed a new management team moving in. This produced a gain of some £2400. There was also another £700 turn in Ladbroke, a £600 gain in Invergordon on the widely-rumoured bid, and quick trades in Bulmer and Greenalls Group. Later on, I racked up a £1500 gain in the Regent Inns pub group following its flotation, a £2000 gain in the Yates Brothers pub group following its flotation and a near £1000 gain in the Burn Stewart whisky company.

Interspersed among these successes, many of which arose as a result of the fact that this was an industry in the process of great change and one I had followed closely for almost 20 years, were an almost exactly equal number of small losses.

The worst catastrophes were selling too early in Wace, the printing group that subsequently tripled from the price at which I sold at a small loss, a £700 loss in Simon Engineering, a £1000 loss on Pentos, a company that looked attractive but which eventually went into receivership, a £1200 loss in Harmony Property, an £800 loss in Dixons, and a similar-sized one in John Menzies as the high street boom failed to materialise. Again, had I held on to Dixons all might have been well. I sold at 179p: the shares are now over 500p.

Over this period too, the property investment had been on permanent let and produced a regular gross income of £4000–5000 a year to add to the stock market gains.

To complete this section on trading, this long-term property investment is now in the process of being sold and expected to produce proceeds in the region of £62500, a gain of some £20000, or just under a 50% increase over the eight-year period of our ownership. This gain is made more respectable when the income component is taken into account.

Throughout this dealing diary, dividends, deposit interest and property income have been stated after tax. On the gains side it is worth noting that with the exception of the aftermath of the crash, only in one year was the gains tax threshold breached, and then only slightly, reinforcing the comment made earlier in this book that the real advantage of the PEP concession is in enabling dividend income to be reinvested on a tax-free basis.

The next section looks at the performance of my trading against various benchmarks.

PERFORMANCE MEASUREMENT

In measuring how my investment performance measured up to the indices and the professionals, I have tried to adopt a consistent method of measurement throughout.

Stock market gains over a period of just under ten years have amounted to £65 000 and losses to £18 138. Total investment income in the form of shares and deposit interest was £6916.

There were a total of sixty stock market trades (i.e. matched buys and sells, 120 separate deals in all) of which 33 showed a gain and 27 were losses of varying size. But, and here is the most important message for the would-be stock market trader, the average gain over the period was some £2000 and the average loss just under £700.

These figures and various others are summarised in Table 10.4. The total gain on the property investment (which was acquired partly out of the gains made in the 1986–87 period and did not represent an additional injection of capital) has been some £34 000 on an initial investment of £42 500. Taxed rental income, after allowing for letting

Table 10.4   Overall Performance 30th June 1986 to 31st December 1995

Total stock market gains	65622	Property cost	42500
Total net investment income	6916	Property gain	20000
Total stock market losses	18138	Rent (net)	10529
Winning trades	33	Property gain (compound % pa)	7.80%
Losing trades	27	Total gain	137485
Average gain	2000	Total income	17445
Average loss	671	Total return (compound % pa)	14.50%
Compound gain on managed pension fund (% pa)	12.80%	(gross dividend income reinvested)	

	from 30.6.86	from 31.12.87
Total return on FTSE index	12.00%	11.80%
Total return on risk-free money	8.81%	9.44%

expenses and maintenance, has been in the region of £14000, making the total return some 82%, or a compound 7.8% per annum over a period of just over eight years.

Total gains in both property and stock market over the period of just short of ten years have amounted to some £137500 to which can be added around £17500 of taxed dividend and property income. This gives a return of 258% over the period, a compound rate of return of 14.5% after tax.

I am happy with this performance. One is always conscious that had certain profitable trades been held for longer, or if some losses had been cut more quickly, the performance might have been improved. Over the period from September 1988, when my accumulated pension contributions were transferred from my former employer's scheme and invested in a unit-linked policy, the gain achieved by the professional managers (bearing in mind this is tax-exempt fund reinvesting gross dividend income) has been an annual 12.8% compound to date.

On broader benchmarks, and on a comparable basis over the same period, the total return on the FT-SE 100 index has been a compound 12% per annum from June 1986 and 11.8% from December 1987. Investing in riskless government securities over the same periods would have given compound gross returns of 8.8% and 9.4% respectively.

LESSONS FOR FIRST-TIME INVESTORS

This trading record demonstrates a number of important lessons for both first-time and experienced private investors. I have listed these below (in no particular order).

- It is obvious that company selection and trading discipline is as important an influence as the overall trend of the market over a long time span. Smaller companies will tend to do better in more buoyant markets, provided the right ones are picked, but even in dull markets there will be some good performers. But paying attention to the economic climate is important.

- The paramount need in the stock market is to cut losses early. I believe it can be demonstrated very graphically from the figures in the tables above just how important this is. One of my faults as a trader is that I occasionally, as it were, 'fall in love' with individual stocks, and become blind to their shortcomings in different phases of the market cycle.

- Equally, one should stress that patience and the ability to resist the tempation to sell too early is vitally important. In my own case, I believe a little more patience might have produced better returns, but I am hamstrung by my personality and comparatively modest background. The novelty of being able to take a substantial profit of £1000 or so, quickly made, often proves too tempting.

- What the tables also show is that diversification is good. In this case, apart from the initial bull market flurry in shares, I have held a mix of assets over the years including floating rate notes, investment property and its associated rental income, and, in the case of my pension contributions, a professionally-managed fund able to reinvest dividend income on a gross basis.

- Overall, however, it is clear that over this period my own efforts resulted in a significant outperformance, both over the professionally managed portion of the fund, and over the likely return over the period for a fund that tracked the index. Some of this may have been luck, and it would be a brave person who risked his retirement nest egg on his own abilities to manage money better than the professionals, and I must stress that I did deliberately choose not to go that route.

But equally, taking control of one's own destiny, and maintaining reasonable liquidity does have its advantages. Good performance can be achieved by following good disciplines.

• Another clear lesson is that it pays both to be diligent in research, but also to use knowledge gained in the course of one's job to make judgements about particular investments. I do not mean by this the gaining of inside information, but simply keeping one's eyes open and investing where one's instincts lead, provided that at the same time proper risk control and loss-cutting principles are followed.

The point here is to make these ideas the starting point for further research, rather than leaping in blind. Particularly in phase three of the narrative it served me well, for instance, to invest in pub groups and discotheque companies at a time when I had gleaned a lot of background knowledge about the industry environment in which they were operating.

• Part of the rigorous discipline of trading is also sticking to a strict trading unit. In my own case, I began investing in units of around £3000 and have gradually raised this to around £5000. In the latter case I attempted, not always successfully, to limit losses to between £500 and £600 on a 'no questions asked' basis.

Careful scrutiny of the charts can produce examples where there is a strong resistance point underpinning the price with a stop-loss point below it. In dealing in options I have normally confined the position to between a fifth and a quarter of this trading unit, and generally bought long-dated, deep in-the-money calls at a point where technical analysis of the share price indicated strong support.

- My experience gives me mixed feelings about using charts for selecting stocks to trade, except in the case of the options market, where the gearing involved can produce big moves and where losses can be limited. In the case of equity investment, my experience has been that a chart may prove good at setting risk control parameters, and picking a buying range.

  Timing purchases and sales precisely using charts has only worked well for me on two specific occasions. Using moving averages has been particularly poor, but using charts of volatility in the options market has worked well. On the one occasion I used directors' dealings as a buy signal, the experiment was an abject failure.

WHERE THE MONEY WENT

My present investments comprise accumulated pension contributions of £170000, the investment property on which contracts have been exchanged at a price of £62500, stock exchange investments of £28000 (all in smaller companies), and £1500 in a high interest account. This means that my total funds invested or available for investment are just over £90000 compared to my starting capital of £60000 and total gains over the preceding eight or nine years of some £155000.

Where has that difference of £125000 gone?

The following list itemises some of the major expenditure:

Regular replacement of two family cars:	£29000
Business set-up/office equipment:	£43000
Musical instruments:	£10000
School fees etc.:	£21000
Holidays:	£18000

I am very relaxed about this expenditure. I have two children who have progressed from pre-secondary school age to further education during this period, one of whom was privately educated. Both are musicians. My assets include two two-year old cars, not admittedly of the luxury variety, and I and my wife have a shared passion for travelling, which we have been able to indulge to the full, the more so since I have been self-employed over this period, and therefore not tied to the rapacious demands of a City employer.

The travel has included two visits to America en famille and one to Canada, two holidays in France, and two in Scotland. My wife and I have travelled on our own to Italy, the Middle East, Amsterdam, and America on two occasions, and have other trips planned further afield.

This brings me to an important overall point about investment. This is that as an activity it is there, if conducted properly on either a large or a small scale, to produce funds that can be used for spending on the pleasurable things in life, as well as being set aside for a dignified old age.

It is as well to keep this in mind, rather than to pursue it as an activity purely as an end in itself. Spending the money is a pleasure, and even after the money has been spent, you can still keep score.

IN BRIEF

- The chapter summarises the results of ten years of trading as a private investor.
- The results demonstrate that it is possible for the small investor to beat the professionals, but that rigorous discipline needs to be observed.
- The income component and investment in alternative forms of investment (bonds, property) should not be ignored.
- Sticking to a rigid trading 'unit' is important.

- The results of cutting losses early is highly beneficial.
- My own fault as a trader is selling profitable investments too early. This is something to guard against.
- Above all, investment should be stimulating and fun. There is nothing wrong with spending your investment gains on other interests. The objective of investment is to produce gains that can provide you with more choices.

Afterword

I am only too well aware that some of the subject matter of this book is complicated. I hope, however, that I have approached it in a way that minimises the complexity and makes grasping the concepts accessible to the reader.

Investment can, after all, be an entertaining and immensely rewarding activity. Mastery of all the finer points is not necessary to be able to enjoy the game.

We should all, I believe, consider investing in shares.

The City bears its share of the blame for conferring a mystique on share buying that is not warranted. It has done this for its own reasons. But they are reasons that are now out of tune with the times and they have, in any event, largely been overtaken by events. The reasons lie in the form of technology that has resulted in cheaper dealing costs for small investors, while making information more readily accessible to individuals.

But this process has some way to go. And old habits die hard.

Recently, for example, the Stock Exchange changed its rules and cut small investors out of the process that had guaranteed them at least some rep-resentation in the new issue market. New issues have very often been the way investors have gained their first insights in and exposure to the market, and to cut them out of the loop in favour of already-dominant institutional investors is, in my view, a retrograde and short-sighted step.

Price data, a basic raw material that investors should use when making decisions about buying and selling, is also an expensive item in this coun-try, thanks in part to the fees levied by the Ex-change. It is certainly substantially more expensive than in the US.

But here again technology is working in favour of the little person. Internet-based services are offer-ing high quality data at substantially lower prices than has hitherto been the case, and the cost can only come down further.

Similarly, the presence of downloadable soft-ware at sites on the World Wide Web at low prices which reflect US software economics must exert downward pressure on the cost of these items too. Most exciting of all are the prospects that the Inter-net opens up for the speedier dissemination of cor-porate information to all interested investors, and not just to a few favoured institutions and brokers.

These changes are taking shape at a time when any sensible person must be reassessing the way in which he or she thinks about personal finances.

In particular, the idea of buying property with borrowed money has perhaps deservedly been shown up for the risky strategy it is in an era of low inflation.

Although the home-owning habit is deeply in-grained in the British psyche (less so in the Conti-nental one), I suspect that in future there may be a greater tendency to view the decision on whether to rent or mortgage with a greater degree of care and sophistication, and for alternative strategies to be

formulated that have do-it-yourself share investment at their core.

Of course, there are risks here. I am finishing
this book at a time when the stock market is looking
increasingly overvalued and when, paradoxically,
the housing market is showing signs of revival. It
may pay to postpone the switch.

There will be a setback in share markets in the
course of the next year or so. This does not invali-
date the case for investing in shares. Rather, it illustrates what I hope has been a strong message of this
book, that would-be investors need to be patient,
independent and strong-minded, but above all need
to be ready for the opportunities that a sustained
market setback will provide.

Further Reading

GENERAL

Adam Smith, *The Money Game*, Vantage
Charles Vintcent, *Be Your Own Stockbroker*, FT Pitman
Jim Rogers, *Investment Biker*, Wiley
Peter Lynch, *Beating the Street*, Simon & Schuster
                One Up on Wall Street, Simon & Schuster
Gene Marcial, *Secrets of the Street*, McGraw-Hill
Maggie Drummond, *The Investors Handbook*, Rushmere Wynne
Neil Stapley, *A Private Investors Guide to the Stockmarket*, Rushmere Wynne
George Soros, *Soros on Soros*, Wiley
                The Alchemy of Finance, Wiley

HISTORY/MARKET PSYCHOLOGY

Fred Schwed, *Where are the Customers' Yachts?*, Wiley
Charles Kindleberger, *Manias, Panics and Crashes*, Macmillan
Edwin Lefevre, *Reminiscences of a Stockmarket Operator*, Wiley
Charles Mackay, *Extraordinary Popular Delusions and the Madness of Crowds*, Harmony

FUNDAMENTALS

Graham Dodd, *Security Analysis*, McGraw-Hill
Jim Slater, *Investment Made Easy*, Orion
        The Zulu Principle, Orion
Terry Smith, *Accounting for Growth*, Century

TECHNICAL ANALYSIS

Brian Millard, *Profitable Charting*, Qudos
David Charters, *Charters on Charting*, Rushmere
   Wynne
John Murphy, *Technical Analysis of the Futures Markets*, NY Institute of Finance
David Linton, *Profit from you PC*, Rushmere Wynne
Brown/Bentley, *Cyberinvesting*, Wiley

TRADED OPTIONS

Geoffrey Chamberlain, *Trading in Options*, Throgmorton Press
Peter Temple, *Traded Options: A Private Investor's Guide*, Rushmere Wynne
Michael Thomsett, *Getting Started in Options*, Wiley

PEPS

Jim Slater, *PEP Up Your Wealth*, Orion

TRADING DISCIPLINES

Jack Schwager, *Market Wizards*, Harper
        The New Market Wizards, Harper
Alan Reubenfeld, *The SuperTraders*, Irwin
Simon Cawkwell, *Profit of the Plunge*, Rushmere Wynne

Glossary

advance/decline line a technical indicator measuring the accumulation of shares that rise versus those that fall on successive days.

annual report a statutory document that any public company must produce each year, containing its audited accounts and certain other information.

APCIMS the Association of Private Client Investment Managers, a trade association for private client brokers (tel. 0171 247 7000).

ASCII standard format through which data collected in one computer system can be translated for use in another.

beta factor a measure of the sensitivity of a particular share price to a given percentage movement in the market.

bid (offer) price the price at which a market-maker will buy stock from (sell stock to) a broker. The offer is the price at which the client can buy shares and the bid the price at which he can sell.

bid–offer spread the gap between the current buying price and the (lower) selling price for the same share. A factor when working out the effective cost of trading a share.

breadth indicator the advance/decline line expressed as a percentage of the total number of shares traded.

buy–hold strategy investing by simply buying and holding a share for a lengthy period.

buy signal a strong indication from a price chart that will prompt the investor to research closely the 'fundamentals' of a company.

call (put) option a contract that gives the holder the right but not the obligation to buy (sell) a parcel of shares at a fixed price for a specific period of time.

client agreement form a form which establishes the contractual relationship between a broker and a new client.

closed-end fund a collective investment with a fixed number of shares in issue and a strictly limited pool of money to invest.

Coppock indicator a long-term moving average designed to provide broad buy signals for the market.

CREST the computerised settlement system for UK equities introduced in July 1996.

dealing unit the normal amount of money an investor will allocate to invest in any one share.

depreciation a notional amount set aside each year to cover the cost of replacing fixed assets.

'discounting' the process by which the market anticipates events and adjusts the price of a share accordingly.

earnings multiple the ratio of the share price to a company's earnings per share (also called price–earnings ratio).

electronic mail email, a way of sending messages instantaneously to any other Internet address.

enterprise value analysis a technique for valuing companies based on sales and cash flow parameters.

equivolume a method of chart drawing designed to show the movement in a share price and volume traded in the same chart 'bar'.

execution-only stockbroking that comprises only a dealing service, without any sort of advice.

file-servers computers holding information accessible by Internet users.

Financial Services Act the 1986 legislation that governs the conduct of City brokers, fund managers and personal investment advisers.

floating-rate note a fixed income security, often received as a result of a takeover, where the interest paid fluctuates in line with short-term interest rates and which is redeemable at any time at the holder's option.

free capital the amount an investor has available to invest after all other commitments and contingencies have been provided for.

FTP file transfer protocol, the means by which a file or files can be transferred from a remote computer to the user's own.

Gann, Fibonacci analysis sophisticated systems of technical analysis found on more expensive investment software packages.

gearing the percentage that total borrowings (minus cash) represent of a company's net assets.

gilts fixed income securities guaranteed by the British Government.

'golden cross' the point at which a shorter-term moving average moves above a longer-term one, when both have recently resumed an upward trend.

herd instinct the tendency of investors all to act in a similar way at the same time, in response to an external stimulus.

hypertext embedded links in text contained on web pages that enable the user, through a simple mouse click, to jump to another area of the web.

indexation table a table of values showing indexation factors to be used when calculating capital gains tax liabilities.

intangible assets non-physical assets (such as brand names, customer lists and staff) whose value to the business is hard to calculate.

integrated securities houses investment banks which combine stockbroking, market-making and corporate finance advisory activity, as well as trading on their own account.

investment software computer programs designed to facilitate the monitoring of shares, share prices and share dealings.

limited liability the basis on which public companies are founded, that an investor cannot lose more than his original investment.

liquidity the ease with which investments can be bought and sold.

maintenance capital expenditure the level of capital spending needed to keep a company's productive assets in good order. Often deducted to arrive at 'free cash flow'.

market cycle the collective name for the stock market's successive phases of 'bull' (rising) and 'bear' (falling) markets.

Market Eye a well-known real-time share price display system used by active private investors.

module a segment of an investment software program with a specific function, such as managing transaction data or drawing share price charts.

neckline the level in a 'head and shoulders' share price formation which, if breached, may result in a substantial price movement.

net asset value the underlying value of a company's capital and reserves worked out on a per share basis.

nominee service the service by which shares owned by an investor are registered in the broker's name, to ease administration.

OHLCV open, high, low, close and volume. The five ingredients of price data needed to produce comprehensive technical analysis.

on-balance volume a chart of the cumulative volume on 'up' days minus the volume on 'down' days.

optimising the process through which the definition of technical indicators can be fine-tuned to produce (based on past history) improved decision making.

order-driven markets a method of share trading by which buying and selling orders are automatically matched by computer.

order-takers telesales staff employed by some brokers to act as intermediaries between clients and the dealers who execute their orders.

PEG factor a share valuation yardstick that compares a company's price–earnings ratio to its expected earnings growth.

PEP personal equity plan, a tax-efficient way of holding shares.

portfolio the collective name for an individual's holdings of shares in more than one company.

portfolio valuation service provided by a broker to bring the client up to date with the current value of his portfolio of shares.

PPP/SLIP Internet connection that permits the downloading of graphics-based displays.

price-sensitive information information which, when made public, is likely to have a material impact on a company's share price.

profit-warning a public statement from a company to inform investors that profits will be below earlier expectations.

redemption yield the notional yield on a fixed-income security were it to be held until maturity, comprising the annual percentage income to be received as well as the capital gain or loss that will accrue from the current price to the redemption price.

regional broker a small broker based in the regions but with, nonetheless, an electronic link to the market.

reserves a notional balance sheet item represented by the company's assets and/or accumulated retained profits.

retained profits profits after deducting all other prior charges, such as interest, tax and dividends.

return on capital the percentage that pre-interest profits represent of capital employed (total assets minus current liabilities).

reversal a long-term change in the direction of a share price.

risk-free rate of return the yield on undated government stock. Normally used as the benchmark for discounting back future flows of cash.

scanning criteria logical rules that can be programmed into an investment software package to find shares that correspond to key technical indicators.

share a stake in a company, representing entitlement to the assets that remain after all creditors and lenders have been paid.

shareware free software that can be downloaded from the Internet for evaluation. If found useful, the user is under a moral obligation to buy the full version.

stop-loss a discipline by which shares are automatically sold if they fall by more than a certain absolute or percentage amount.

support and resistance price levels at which, based on past investor behaviour, buying or selling, respectively, is likely to intensify.

trading volume the aggregate number of shares dealt in (either bought or sold) on any one trading day.

trend channel the path formed between two parallel lines joining successive share price highs and lows.

trigger effect the use of smoothing techniques to produce a line which, when intersecting with the raw variable, will give 'buy' and 'sell' indications.

Usenet A US bulletin board network.

volatility the percentage amount up or down by which a share might be expected to move over a fixed time period. Sometimes expressed as the difference between a share's 12-month high and low points expressed as a percentage of the current share price.

web browser software enabling the user to navigate the graphics-rich pages of the World Wide Web. The most commonly used is produced by Netscape.

working capital the balance of the value of a company's stocks and debtors, minus the money it owes to short-term creditors.

yield gap the relationship between the price of long-term government securities and the average dividend yield on ordinary shares.

Index

Other titles of interest...

WILEY

An exciting new series from one of the UK's leading investment experts...

Millard on...Traded Options
2nd Edition
Brian Millard

Millard on...Traded Options has been written for private investors, career starters with City investment houses, as well as finance and business students.

- Explains how to make profits whether the market rises, falls or remains static.
- Moves the reader from simple to advanced strategies which minimise risk.

0471 96780 7 1996 200pp Pbk

Millard on...Channel Analysis
2nd Edition
Brian Millard

Millard on...Channel Analysis shows how certain share price cycles should behave in the near future, giving the investor a powerful prediction tool. Read this book and you'll find out how to:

- Scan a pool of shares for new opportunities
- Take advantage of short term upward trends
- Select the best-moving averages
- Discover the magic of the compounding effect
- Identify the start and end of an investment trend.

0471 96845 5 January 1997 200pp Pbk

Millard on...Stocks and Shares
4th Edition
Brian Millard

Dispelling many modern myths, Brian Millard points to a logical well-tried approach to avoiding many investment pitfalls. The diversity of decisions to be made when dealing stocks and shares can be bewildering: when to buy and sell; which shares to choose; which rumours to act on; which newspapers to believe. With *Millard on...Stocks and Shares* you'll learn how to minimise risks in the decision-making process by carefully timing your decision to fully exploit market trends.

0471 96658 4 March 1997 256pp Pbk

Millard on...Profitable Charting Techniques
2nd Edition
Brian Millard

With a set of simple but powerful buying indicators, this practical guide shows:

- How chart patterns can be easily interpreted
- How to increase profits by exploiting charts and indicators
- Step-by-step explanation of how to read messages from chart patterns
- Take advantage of channel analysis methods to predict imminent changes.

0471 96846 3 January 1997 200pp Pbk

Other titles of interest...

Getting Started in Futures
2nd Edition
Todd Lofton

Totally revised and updated, this second edition covers the full range of markets, from traditional commodities like grains and metals to the dramatic new markets of petroleum and financial futures. It tells you in plain simple terms how the markets work, and how you can use them to earn financial rewards while limiting your risk.

0471 57988 2   1993   286pp   Pbk

Getting Started in Stocks
2nd Edition
Alvin D. Hall

This revised and updated version of the best-selling book in the Getting Started series provides a practical guide for individual investors who are serious about understanding today's equities environment and investing profitably in stocks. From blue chips to penny stocks, this fact-filled start-up guide explains in plain English, what they are, how they work and, more importantly, how they can work for you.

0471 02572 0   1994   304pp   Pbk

Getting Started in Options
2nd Edition
Michael C. Thomsett

- Master all the terminology
- Buy and sell puts and calls
- Hedge and speculate like a seasoned investor
- Understand time values, striking price, and expiration and use them effectively

0471 57974 2   1993   252pp   Pbk

Getting Started in Mutual Funds
Alan Lavine

The author explains how mutual funds are structured and how to choose a dependable fund and/or fund manager. The book includes step-by-step advice for making and monitoring each investment, and uses over 35 graphs and charts to pinpoint the top performing funds. Special sections feature frequently asked questions about mutual fund investment, retirement planning, using mutual funds, and a working glossary.

0471 57694 8   1994   224pp   Pbk

Getting Started in Metals
Jeffrey Nichols

This is a complete guide to investing in metals, explaining how precious industrial and strategic metals are packaged, how they may be invested in, and how strong a role they play in the investor's portfolio. Illustrated with over 40 charts and graphs, plus important concepts highlighted in sidebars, special sections also feature a working glossary for metals investors, and a comprehensive listing of sources for information for metals investment.

0471 55557 9   1996   208pp   Pbk

WILEY

Other titles of interest...

WILEY

The Ernst & Young Tax Saver's Companion

Ernst & Young

Updated annually, this best selling tax guide provides easy to understand tips and techniques for both the individual and business user. Containing the very latest information and laws, the *Ernst & Young Tax Saver's Companion* will help you start saving money immediately, as well as plan for a comfortable future.

- Year-round tax planning advice
- Top money saving tips and techniques
- Tax return completion guide
- Index by lifecycle events
- Calender of key dates in the tax year
- The very latest, authoritative information
- Accessible, easy to use and understand - you can save money by putting plans into action immediately
- In short...your very own tax advisor

Praise for *The Ernst & Young Tax Saver's Companion 1996*:

"...written in an easy style...breast-pocket size, well - indexed and indefinably satisfying...by the time next year's edition comes round, my bet is that all copies will have been aggressively dog-eared, highlighted and generally plumbed for information." - Business Age

Pension Power
2nd Edition
Debbie Harrison

Pension Power shows how the pensions industry operates its pensions schemes; and how, with this understanding, you can better control and maximise your own or your company's financial health. It's primary aim is to deepen understanding, to dispel fear and to put the control of the fund firmly in the grasp of those who pay for it and those who undertake legal responsibility for its successful running.

- Written by the leading journalist in the field who regularly writes for the Financial Times and is editor of Trustee magazine.
- Includes new pensions acts and legislation and will also include the November 1996 budget implications

Contents:
Help is at hand ● When things go wrong ● State pensions ● Company schemes ● Topping up ● High earners ● Pension transfers ● Pensions & insolvency ● Personal pensions ● Partnerships ● Executive pension plans ● Schemes for small businesses ● Annuities ● Working abroad ● Retiring abroad ● Trust law & trustees ● Introduction to pension fund investment ● Investment managers & Investment choice ● Appointing & monitoring the investment manager ● Monitoring the performance of the fund ● Safe custody of assets

How To Fix Your Finances
A Guide to Personal Financial Planning
Stephen Lofthouse

How to Fix Your Finances guides the serious investor through the financial planning process. You are helped to assess your current financial health and plan your financial future. The book offers clear guidance as to when you need financial advice, and when you can skip it.

Amongst the many topics covered are:

- Managing your cash
- Cash-based investments versus shares
- Investment and unit trusts versus a personal portfolio
- PEPs, OEICS and TESSAs
- Whole-life insurance versus term insurance
- Repayment versus endowment mortgages
- Improving your pension entitlements
- Why you must have a will

Stephen Lofthouse has worked in the brokerage and fund management industries. He was a top rated investment strategist and a director at James Capel & Co. He was Executive Chairman of James Capel Fund Managers Ltd and James Capel Unit Trust Management Ltd, before retiring from the City in 1993. He is author of the successful *Equity Investment Management*.

0471 96702 5   1996   398pp   Paperback

John Wiley & Sons Ltd

**UK Office: Baffins Lane, Chichester, West Sussex, PO19 1UD, UK
Tel: +1243 779777   Fax: +1243 770677**

**USA Office: 605 Third Avenue, New York, NY 10158-0012, USA
Tel: +212 850 6000   Fax: +2152 850 6088**

**Singapore Office: 2 Clementi Loop #02-01, Jin Xing Distripark,
Singapore, 129809   Tel: +65 463 2400   Fax: +65 463 4605**

WILEY